EARLY LETTERS

OF

MARCUS DODS, D.D.

EARLY LETTERS

OF

MARCUS DODS, D.D.

(LATE PRINCIPAL OF NEW COLLEGE, EDINBURGH)

(1850-1864)

Selected and Edited by his Son

MARCUS DODS, M.A.

ADVOCATE

HODDER AND STOUGHTON
ST. PAUL'S HOUSE, WARWICK SQUARE
LONDON, E.C.   MCMX

PREFACE

IN its main aspect the following collection of letters is essentially the autobiography of a probationer of the Free Church of Scotland in the middle of last century. That it includes letters that in a sense do not come within that description, and particularly letters of the writer's more youthful age, is due partly to an idea that this volume may be followed by another containing letters of later date, and that the two may thus cover practically the whole of Principal Marcus Dods' life.

It was, no doubt, remarkable that one who afterwards obtained in full measure the recognition of his Church, should have to endure so long a probation. His contemporaries have spoken of his bearing, and especially of his industry, during the six years of waiting ; and his case has often been cited for the encouragement of others in like position. Only now, in these letters, is the first hint given that there was a more serious side to the picture, and that this may have been the real 'Sturm und Drang' period of his whole life. Speaking of the new light the letters shed upon that period, one of his oldest and most intimate friends has written as follows :—

' Even at that time he was the last man to parade or reveal his troubles. Among his fellows he was known as a tall dark and scholarly student, refined reserved and even shy in manner, courteous kindly and witty in conversation, but also calm cheerful and apparently unburdened— certainly the farthest of us all from egotism of any kind or degree. None of us knew what he felt within the " smooth shelving sides " of that pit into which young men on their way to high usefulness (in Egypt or elsewhere) are sometimes cast.'

Of the present disclosure of what his own reticence so carefully guarded, little need be said. Such revelations by survivors are sometimes justified by the circumstances of the case. The present publication was undertaken, not without deliberation, in the hope that it might perhaps serve a larger purpose than the mere gratification of a friendly interest or curiosity.

The editor welcomes this opportunity of recording his sincere gratitude to a number of his father's friends, to whom he has never applied in vain for counsel, and in particular to the Rev. Sir William Robertson Nicoll, who has given invaluable advice and help; to the Rev. Dr. W. M. Macgregor, to whose fine judgment he is also very greatly indebted; and to Mr. Andrew Marshall, who has ungrudgingly spent time and labour upon the preparation of the collection.

EDINBURGH, *November* 1910.

CONTENTS

INTRODUCTORY NOTE

THE writer of these letters was born on April 11th, 1834, at Belford, in Northumberland, and was the youngest child of his father, the Rev. Marcus Dods, minister of the Church of Scotland there. His mother was Sarah Palliser, a lady of Northumbrian birth. There were six other children in the Belford Manse, four daughters and two sons, — Anne Palliser, John, Thomas Palliser, Mary Frances, Marcia, and Andrea Thomson.

In 1838 Marcus Dods the elder died, and Mrs. Dods moved into Edinburgh, where she took boarders, mostly schoolboys, in order to support her family. In course of time Marcus the younger was sent to the Edinburgh Academy, where he was entered in Mr. Ferguson's class in 1843. He left the Academy in 1848, and was apprenticed in the same year to the National Bank of Scotland, at its head office in St. Andrew Square, Edinburgh (where he made the acquaintance of his friend and correspondent, J. C. Stewart). He was not, however, destined to be a bank manager, and after two years he gave up his situation with a view to reading for the ministry. He matriculated at the University of Edinburgh in the autumn of the same year, 1850, at the age of sixteen, and

A

took his M.A. degree in April 1854. In the summer of 1853 he went to Brucklay Castle, Mintlaw, Aberdeenshire, for two months as tutor to the boys of Captain Fordyce. During the following winter, 1853-54, the three oldest Fordyce boys boarded with their tutor's mother in order to continue their various studies in Edinburgh ; and the connection lasted through the summer of 1854, which the four students (the tutor was only twenty years old to his eldest pupils' eighteen) spent together in Paris. Entering New College, Edinburgh, in the autumn, he was, after completing the ordinary four years' course, licensed by the presbytery of Edinburgh as a preacher of the Free Church of Scotland on September 7th, 1858.

In 1844 Anne, the eldest of the family, was married to Charles Gibson, and about a year later settled with him at Foulden West Mains, in Berwickshire. In the summer of the same year Mary, the second daughter, went to Manchester as governess to the children of a Mr. Bannerman : the earliest of the letters were addressed to her there. In 1853 she came back to Edinburgh, and Marcia, the third daughter, went in her place, not to Manchester, but to Wootton Park, near Ashbourne, Derbyshire, whither Mr. Bannerman had removed.

In June 1847 Thomas Palliser, the second son, married Katharine Wilson, sister of John Wilson, tenant of Edington Mains, Berwickshire. After his marriage he lived first in Lincolnshire, then in Dingwall, and in 1855 he settled at Anick Grange, Hexham, as a farmer, though he eventually dropped this occupation in favour of land agency.

In the autumn of 1854, Mary, the second daughter, married the Rev. George Wilson, Free Church minister of Glenluce, Wigtownshire, and a brother of her own brother Tom's wife.

In 1855 Mrs. Dods left Edinburgh, and till her death in 1859 had her headquarters at Anick Grange, the home of her son Tom.

In November 1858 the writer of the letters went to Newcastle as Assistant to the Rev. P. L. Miller of John Knox's Church there. By May 1859 he was back again in Edinburgh, acting as Missionary in the Free High Church Mission. In March 1860 he was asked to become Assistant to the Rev. G. R. Davidson of Lady Glenorchy's Church, and he held this post until his return to Newcastle, in June 1862, to fill Mr. Miller's pulpit during his absence through ill-health. He remained in Newcastle till the beginning of the following year, which finds him again in Edinburgh, and again associated with the Free High Church, where he temporarily filled the vacancy caused by Dr. Rainy's election to a chair in New College. In October 1863 the Free High vacancy was filled, and the writer of the letters became

Assistant to the Rev. Dr. John Bruce of St. Andrew's Free Church, Edinburgh. The letter of 9th June 1864 tells of his acceptance of the call to Renfield Free Church, Glasgow, where he was ordained on 4th August of that year.

During these six years (save one month) of probationership he was, of course, preaching from time to time as a candidate in vacant churches. In an old diary of his own, parts of which are printed as an Appendix to this volume, he says, under date September 1863: 'I have now been licensed five years and have preached at the following vacancies: Dalkeith (twice); Irvine; Kennethmont; Old Aberdeen; Kirkcaldy; John Knox, Glasgow; Garvald; Birdhopecraig; Laygate, and St. John's, South Shields; St. George's, Liverpool; Cheltenham; Helensburgh; Roxburgh Place, and Greyfriars', Edinburgh; Bannockburn; Trinity, Aberdeen; South Leith; Dudhope, Dundee; Portobello; have also had to consider the propriety of going to Singapore, Sydney, Naples, and Bombay.'

It will obviate the multiplication of footnotes if something is said at this point by way of explanation of the names of friends which occur in the text.

The friendship with the Macphail family was of very early date, and of life-long duration. The eldest brother was the late Rev. Dr. James

Calder Macphail, of Aberdeen and afterwards of Pilrig; the 'Mr. John' of the third letter of the collection is the Rev. John Macphail, formerly of Skye and Benbecula; and the youngest (by many years) is the Rev. Dr. Simeon R. Macphail of Liverpool.

Also among the most intimate friends of the earliest period were the family of Mr. Hogue, a dentist who was well known in Edinburgh in his time. Their kindness and hospitality were especially appreciated when the breaking up of the Edinburgh home left the writer and his sister alone together in lodgings. The family are inclusively referred to in the letters as ' 65,' or ' Queen Street,' and individually by Christian names of a more or less abbreviated character.

Dr. William Jeffrey was a very close friend during his medical course at Edinburgh University. He soon afterwards settled in practice in Jedburgh, and is there to this day.

Of the writer's Newcastle friend, Mr. Peter Mouat, it is unnecessary to add anything to what the letters themselves say.

Of his contemporaries at Edinburgh University and at New College, the names of only a few occur in the following pages. The late Rev. Dr. John George Cunningham of St. Luke's United Free Church, Edinburgh; the Rev. Principal (Emeritus) Dykes, D.D., of Westminster College, Cambridge; and the late Rev. Professor

Laidlaw, D.D., of New College, Edinburgh, were
in the same year in their Divinity course; as also
were the Rev. R. Stothert and the Rev. Dr.
R. J. Sandeman.   The last named is now senior
minister of St. Andrew's United Free Church,
Edinburgh.   'Dick' Stothert went abroad as a
missionary, and the friendship was continued by
correspondence; but he died some years ago,
and the letters have not survived.   The Rev.
Principal (Emeritus) William Miller, D.D., of
the Madras Christian College; the Rev. Professor
John Gibb, D.D., of Westminster College, Cambridge; and Professor (Emeritus) William Knight,
LL.D., of St. Andrews University were his juniors
at New College by a couple of years.

There remain the names of Alexander Taylor
Innes, LL.D., Advocate, and the Rev. Alexander
Whyte, D.D., of St. George's United Free Church,
Edinburgh, who has now succeeded the writer
of the letters as Principal of New College—two
friends whose intimacy lasted without abatement
as long as life itself.

The following account of the early surroundings
of the writer of the letters is made up of extracts
from a narrative of his childhood written, for
other purposes, by his sister Marcia:—

'THE mists that gather so silently but so surely and so
swiftly over the past, lie thick over all my memory of
the Belford days.   But the incidents that emerge from

the mist are quite clear to me, though it seems rather
as if I were looking back into a dream, or into some
story-book read in years long past, and it is strange to
think that I was one of the group of children who played
in that sunny garden so long ago. But though I have
nothing but the meagre recollections of a child, yet
I think the sort of home into which we are born, and
the life lived there, must begin to colour and influence
our lives even before our own consciousness can take it
in, or memory go back on it.

' My very earliest recollection of [my brother Marcus]
is of standing in the middle of the night by a bedroom
fireside where a woman I did not know sat with a bundle
on her lap. My sister Mary was beside me, and we
were in our nightgowns. The woman told us that this
was a new little brother who had come to us, and I
think I felt pleased, but rather overawed, for he seemed
so very small and unlike the babies I had seen and
played with. I have no recollection of his baptism, but
I remember stopping with the nurse on our way home
to show him at different houses, though the only distinct memory is that of our milkwoman, whom we
knew, and who said he looked " real like a minister."
She and some of the others gave us bits of bread, eggs,
packets of salt, and perhaps other things I have forgotten. I think it was thought right to give the baby
something on his first visit. I also remember standing
round a box from Littlejohn's in Edinburgh, at the
unpacking of a cake, and the joy with which we fished
from among the paper shavings little sweet biscuits.
We had never seen anything like them before, and we
held the name of Littlejohn in great reverence from
that day.

' Another of my pictures is that of our father walking

up and down the room singing Marcus to sleep. We
were all sung to sleep in those days, and the person who
could have put a baby into its cradle *awake* would have
been thought an inhuman monster. I even remember
the air he sang. It was "The Soldier's Return "—
"When wild war's deadly blasts were blawn," etc.
And this reminds me to say that those old songs were
like native air to us—we did not know when we first
heard them any more than we knew when we learned
to speak or to walk. Our father's violin (but we just
called it his fiddle) was, I believe, a loan from some of
the people at Belford Hall, and really a good one. But
be this as it may, he was able by his playing to melt
us or make us dance. I do not think his playing went
beyond those simple airs of which he says in one of his
letters, speaking of the song "Happy's the Love that
meets return,"—"These old songs are Love's mother-
tongue."

'The house where we three younger children were
born was the last of a short row that ran at right angles
to the main street of the village, which was also the
great coaching-road between London and the North.
Our house had a large piece of ground attached, which
lay to the side away from the others, so that we were
quite shut in and secluded from every one else. On the
further side was a high brick wall with fruit trees, which
separated us from the garden of Belford Hall. Part of
the ground was on a higher level than the garden proper,
from which it was divided by sloping, grassy banks
intersected by footpaths. Here there were large trees
which played their part in many of our games.

'Indoors too we had many amusements, though very
few toys. It was a great delight to get possession of
the schoolroom on a Saturday afternoon, for there we

could not spoil anything. Our father had always boys
whom he taught along with our own, and there were
always a few who lived in the house, so that the schoolroom was furnished with long desks and forms. Two
long desks placed together made a splendid boat, so that
seafaring was a very popular occupation on those indoor
afternoons. We went innumerable voyages to every
port we knew of, but I do not remember of ever arriving
anywhere without suffering shipwreck and coming to
port on strange boats and rafts, or by swimming, our
baggage generally going through even more adventures
than ourselves, and being fished out of the sea with
much danger to life and limb. Little Marcus was no
doubt often shipwrecked along with us, and rescued
as our most precious possession. For I think he was
pretty early entrusted to our care, my sister Mary being
very nearly four years older than I, and very sedate.
Anne and the big brothers made a great pet of Marcus,
perhaps the more so as he followed three sisters.

'The dining-room was the general living-room of the
family, though of course the boys would be in the schoolroom or out of doors most of the day. Our father made
use of the lowest walk in the garden—at the opposite
end from " the green " where we played—for pacing up
and down in quarter-deck fashion. At these times we
understood he was *making a sermon*. In the house, too,
he would sometimes pace up and down in a similar way.
But in the evening we were all together, and though we
were not allowed to do anything noisy, each pursued his
or her occupation. And certainly we were sometimes
allowed to make a tent of chairs and plaids in the corner,
and play till our bedtime. It will help to carry us back
to the old time to remember that all our various avoca-
tions were carried on by the light of a pair of candles!

Paraffin lamps were yet in the far distance, and I think
a pair of candles would be considered sufficient—indeed
I am sure of it.   Our mother sat at the head of the table
with her sewing, and our father at his big desk placed on
the corner beside her.   Sometimes he would play a game
of draughts or backgammon with one of the boys, or it
may have sometimes been with a neighbour.   This is
the only game I remember to have seen him play, unless
hop, step, and jump can be called a game—for certainly
when he was in the garden they would sometimes
challenge him to a trial of skill, in which I think he was
always a long way ahead of them.   But he was not so
tall as either Tom or Marcus grew to be, though I don't
know what his exact height was.   John was the one
who had most of his athletic skill, being very good at
all sorts of leaping, vaulting, and similar exercises.   Our
mother's great recreation was her garden, and in many
a trouble in after days it seemed to help her to go out
and rake, and sow seeds, and lay out beds for new flowers.
At Belford there would be a man to attend to the potatoes
and vegetables, but the basket with garden gloves and
big clasp knife and other implements was never far
away.   We also had our little gardens, even Marcus, and
I remember some of the boys persuading him to plant a
hare's foot in the hope that a hare might grow out of
it to make him more hare soup !   The gardens shared
the fate of most children's gardens, being a favourite
pursuit for a few days, constantly dug and raked and
watered (especially watered), and then forgotten till
they were choked with weeds, or killed with drought.

' Of small illnesses I do not think we had many,
though we had the experience of accidents usual in
a family.   As it is rather characteristic, I may record
how the family, hearing Marcus fall from the top of the

stair to the bottom, and flying to the rescue, found him patting a doll which he carried, and saying, " Poor, poor, Dollie ! "

'Instead of the constant and even lavish supply of delightful books of all kinds for children which there is now, we poor children, who loved a story above all things, had only one stout volume of fairy tales. There were, in fact, no stories for children, or very, very few. *Anna Ross* we delighted in, and we also discovered a shop (I think it was a saddler's) where there were penny editions of the Waverley Novels! And on Saturday we would get leave to go into the street, and after great consultations outside the window we would fix on one whose name sounded attractive, and go home in triumph with our new treasure. I fear liberties must have been taken with the originals, for I recall our grief and in-dignation when on reading the real *Kenilworth*, we found poor Amy Robsart going down through the trap door instead of the villain Varney, over whose just and proper fate we had rejoiced, well satisfied that justice should overtake the evil-doer. We also hunted out the stories in *The Spectator* and *Rambler*, of which there were hand-some editions. Shakespeare was on the shelf above our heads, but we only knew the pictures at the begin-ning of each play. Especially we knew Mrs. Siddons as Lady Macbeth, for our mother had seen her in this character, and could never forget it, though none of us were ever allowed to go to a theatre while we were under her authority. Once on coming from Edinburgh our father brought as a present to Mother, Miss Sinclair's *Modern Accomplishments*, then just published. She delighted in a story as much as we did. Though it seems an absurd book for children to have read, we certainly did do so, and called our dolls after the two

rival heroines.   The only story I remember our father
telling us was the story of Daniel O'Rourke's Visit to the
Moon, and our mother sometimes told us the story of
Cinderella in the Scottish version of " Nippet feet and
clippet feet."

'We were very little outside our own precincts, and
were seldom in any house but our own.   But once a
year we made a series of visits under the guardianship
of our nurse, to farms that I suppose were a few miles
distant at the most.   If these visits were not in themselves exciting, they were great events to us, and we
came home proud and happy and with much to tell of
the far country in which we had been.

'But the great event of the year was the visit to
Crookham to see our father's cousin, the Rev. Thomas
Hall, who was minister there.   Our father and the big
boys walked, but our mother and we children went in what
we thought must be the most delightful of all methods
of travelling, in a long cart, with long sacks filled with
straw for seats for the big people, and plenty of straw
in the bottom of the cart for us to sit among.   In the
cart with us went jars and tubs and vessels of all sorts
and sizes for the containing of fruit.   For Mr. Hall, who
was a bachelor, had a garden full of fruit which he could
not use, and our mother not only needed quantities of
jam, but was also great in the making of currant and
gooseberry wine.   We children were supposed to help
the servants in gathering the fruit, while the older
members went walks to Flodden or Etal.   But it was
such a lovely place to play in that I think we were
leniently dealt with in the matter of picking.

'Of course visitors and visiting would not be by
any means as common as they are now.   Our father,
however, went sometimes to Edinburgh, and once I

remember our mother going. But her absences from home must have been few and brief, for her life, like our father's, must have been a very busy one. He had his preaching, teaching, and visiting his people, and writing for periodicals, chiefly *The Christian Instructor*, of which he became editor after Dr. Andrew Thomson's death in 1831. There was also his book on the Incarnation, which grew out of the controversy with Edward Irving. His writings must have added something to his income, for he had once laughingly promised his old friend Miss Maclagan that if he ever made £50 by his writing he would give her a silk dress, and he found himself obliged to fulfil this promise! Certainly it must have been necessary to supplement his income in some way, for his stipend never rose above £90 a year, and there were seven of us to feed and clothe and educate. The boarders, no doubt, enabled us to live in a pleasant house and garden, but judging from the management in after years, I think it is unlikely that there was any margin over for saving.

' Our father was held in high esteem by various ministers in Edinburgh—Dr. Chalmers, Dr. Andrew Thomson, Dr. Gordon, and also had for a friend Dr. Watson of Burntisland, author of a book of Family Prayers much used in its day, and the father of several well-known sons. The eldest of these, Dr. Charles Watson of Largs, was for a time a boarder at Belford, and never quite lost touch with the family. And afterwards, Marcus and he renewed the old friendship, which continued till Dr. Watson's death. I know, too, that among the clergy of the English Church in Northumberland our father was known and respected as a man of high character, ability, and learning. And also, what is better still, there have come from time to time testimonies from one and another, of good received by parents and other relatives through the influence and teaching of our father and mother.

'But I was only a child, and could see things only from a child's point of view, and no events of any importance had ever come within my view till the dark days of our father's last illness. In the year 1826, twelve years before his death, he had been brought to its very gates by an illness which in the vague way in which illness was spoken of long ago, was always called inflammation. From this illness he seems completely to have recovered ; and it is to this time he refers in a passage which I will transcribe here, since it is from a pamphlet on a subject long since out of date, namely the question of whether the Apocrypha should be printed with the Bible. He speaks of the Bible as " a book from which many have learned much more than I have done, but which few have had reason to regard with a more pertinacious grasp. Should my views," he continues, " of that book be erroneous, they have, at least, neither been rashly formed, nor lightly adopted on the authority of other men. If I maintain them warmly, it is because I have won my way to them painfully. My own experience abundantly proves the correctness of the maxim—*Nihil tam certum, quam quod ex dubio certum*—and it also abundantly testifies the power of the Bible to afford the most effectual supports in that hour when support is most urgently needed, and most difficult to be found. Few have passed so far into the domain of death, and been per-mitted to return. I have felt the breath leaving me that I expected not again to inhale. I have counted the dull heavy throb of my heart, as it grew fainter and fainter, fully anticipating at every pulsation that it

would heave but once more and for ever be still ! I
have gazed on the faces of those dearest to me, till my
eye grew dim in the blackness of death and I could no
longer see : I have listened to the soothing voice of
affection till my ear grew torpid in the apathy of death
and I could no longer hear ; and I have felt the icy
chillness of death shooting through my veins, arresting
the current of life in its course, till sensation itself forsook
me and I could no longer feel. And while thus placed
on the very line that separates time from eternity, what
was it that under a deep consciousness of guilt enabled
me to look forward in the momentary expectation of
finally passing that line, calm and tranquil as I am now ?
It was just that Bible of whose Divine inspiration I once
as foolishly maintained the low view that prevails as I
thank God I have now long and cordially renounced it.
I consider the opportunity afforded me of bringing it
to so severe a test as one of the richest blessings of my
life. And recalled as I have been to longer days, I wish
to consider every day lost which does not add to my
knowledge of its contents or deepen my experience of
its value. I am well aware that the trying hour will
return, and when it does, one of my most anxious wishes
will be satisfied, if the prolongation of my life be made
the means, however humble, of extending the knowledge
of the Bible, of maintaining its integrity, and preserving
its purity."

'I cannot tell when our father's last illness began,
nor do I know the details of the illness, but I know it
lasted for many months, over a year, I am quite sure.
But one Saturday afternoon I remember seeing him
sitting playing at draughts with some one (I can't remember with whom). He was in the easy-chair which
had been got for his use, and he half rose, and then

sank back again.   Then there was hurry and confusion,
and he was taken to bed, and it was on the following
Saturday he died.   I *think* I can remember the look
on his face when we were taken to his room and
lifted up to kiss him good-bye.   I cannot remember
about the funeral at all, so perhaps we were not allowed
to see much of it, though John and Tom would of course
be there.   But I do remember how on one of the days
before, Marcus was found to have opened the door of
the room where our father lay, and was found sitting
on the bed looking at him.   It is impressed on my mind
the more, no doubt, by my recalling so vividly my own
shrinking from that which I could not at all connect
with my father.   He died on 29th September 1838,
having been born on 7th December 1786, and married
on 6th May 1818.

   ' In transcribing our father's epitaph, which I feel
must find a place in this narrative, I cannot do better
than introduce it in the beautiful words which Dr. Taylor
Innes used of it at a later period, when he quoted it in
a review of the younger Marcus' first original work,
The Prayer that Teaches to Pray.   " More than once,"
he wrote, " it has happened to the scholarly tourist
among Northumbrian hills to be startled into an exclamation of delight by finding, among rude memorial
stones, an epitaph which has no equal (at least in our
own tongue), even under the majestic architectures of
Westminster and St. Paul's.   It is from the strong and
delicate pen of the late Dr. Maclagan of Aberdeen.   If
we quote it upon slight pretext, it is because we are
not sorry to spread the knowledge of an inscription
which competent judges have held to be among ' the
finest in the English language.' "   The inscription is
as follows :—

ERECTED BY
THE MEMBERS OF THE SCOTCH CHURCH BELFORD
IN MEMORY OF
THEIR BELOVED PASTOR

THE REV. MARCUS DODS

WHO DIED XXIX SEPTEMBER MDCCCXXXVIII
IN THE 52ND YEAR OF HIS AGE AND 28TH OF HIS MINISTRY
A MAN OF NOBLE POWERS
NOBLY USED
IN WHOM MEMORY AND JUDGMENT
VIGOUR AND GENTLENESS
GRAVITY AND WIT
EACH SINGLY EXCELLENT
WERE ALL HAPPILY COMBINED
AND EVER DEVOTED
WITH EQUAL PROMPTITUDE AND PERSEVERANCE
TO THE LABOURS OF CHRISTIAN GODLINESS
AND THE DEEDS OF HUMAN KINDNESS
THE DELIGHT OF HIS HOUSEHOLD
THE FATHER OF HIS FLOCK
THE HELPER OF THE POOR
HE CAPTIVATED HIS FRIENDS BY HIS CONVERSE
AND EDIFIED THE CHURCH
BY HIS LEARNED AND ELOQUENT PEN
THE EARTHLY PREFERMENT
WHICH HE DESERVED BUT DID NOT COVET
THE EARTH NEGLECTED TO BESTOW
BUT LIVING TO ADVANCE AND TO DEFEND
HE DIED IN FULL HOPE TO INHERIT
THE EVERLASTING KINGDOM
OF
CHRIST JESUS OUR LORD

' Looking back on this home of our childhood, the impression is of a life lived within narrow limits, but with a good deal of freedom within those limits. As I have said, we were seldom beyond our own bounds. But

B

though we were thus to a certain extent constantly under the eye of our mother, yet we carried on our own pursuits, and lived our own lives untrammelled by many restrictions. One thing for which I feel we had cause to be very thankful was that we were entirely at home with our parents, so that we were not tempted to do, out of their sight, anything we would not have done in their presence, or to pretend anything that was not true. The idea was early and unmistakably impressed on our minds, that *to be good* was the main thing in life ; that there was nothing else that could come into any comparison or competition with this ; that in fact nothing else mattered *greatly*. We knew that this was what our parents desired for us above all else, though I do not think there was much direct speaking about it, beyond a little explanation of our Sunday lessons, or an occasional word when we were saying our prayers.

' On Sunday morning we all learned our lessons for the day, the younger ones committing to memory Paraphrases as being easier than the Psalms, and also a simple catechism called, I think, *The Mother's Catechism*. The big boys learned Psalms and chapters of the Bible. Our mother always had a Sunday-school on Sunday afternoon in the schoolroom, and we went in too, though I think not always. But I can't think what we did besides, for we certainly neither played nor ran about in the garden, though Marcus' only recollection of his father was of walking with him in the garden on Sunday afternoon. Perhaps it is as well I have forgotten, for surely we must often have got into mischief with so few books as we had. There were two small periodicals, the *Child's Companion* for the younger ones, and another for the bigger ones of which I have forgotten the name. But both were so small that they could not occupy much time in reading. *Little Henry and His*

Bearer we almost knew by heart, and it was a great feast when some one lent us Mrs. Sherwood's *Tales Illustrative of the Church Catechism*. At a later date we had the loan of an odd volume of the *Fairchild Family*, and the evil doings of the children gave us considerable satisfaction. Even in these far-away days it seemed as if the whole setting was funny and old-fashioned, though it was none the less a great boon to us.

' After our father's death it was thought by our mother and the friends who advised her that as she was accustomed to the care of boys the best thing she could do would be to come to Edinburgh and take schoolboys as boarders. All her life she kept a little cotton bag, in which we, knowing she would now have to work for us, gathered our Saturday pennies and any stray coins (they would be but few) which came our way. We imagined our little hoard would go a long way towards paying for the much-talked-of journey to Edinburgh. Of the journey, though it was the first any of us had taken, I remember nothing, but that Marcus, putting his head out at the window of the coach, lost his cap, and so arrived in Edinburgh bareheaded!

' He was always a lovable child. It was a sweet, simple, *aefauld* nature that I think always won favour with every one. I mention this here because through all the chances and changes of this our mortal life, there was no change here, and to the eyes that had seen him from the beginning it was not even in the least obscured. The nature grew and strengthened and widened, and had its upheavals and its settlings, but the child heart was as plain in the man of seventy-five as in the dear wee boy that arrived hatless in Edinburgh so many years ago.

' After a period of anxiety and waiting, boys began to come, and the home in 24 Rutland Street, then undisturbed even by dreams of the Caledonian Railway, was filled with a busy company. After a few years a move was made to Ramsay Lodge, a pleasant, old-fashioned house standing in ground sloping steeply to the North from the level of the Castle Esplanade down to the Princes Street Gardens. From this almost country-looking dwelling Marcus and a group of school-fellows set forth, day by day, to descend the long hill which led to the Edinburgh Academy, their straps of books over their shoulder and the *clacken* in their hand, which, at that time at any rate, was quite as indispensable a part of the Academy boy's outfit as his books.

' On Sunday, morning and afternoon church was the rule. In the very early years the High Church, in which we sat, was one of the three which were hospitably housed under St. Giles' roof, and it was not unusual for us to hear the singing of our worshipping neighbours when we were at a totally different part of the service ! After the Disruption, we had a long time in the Music Hall until the Free High Church was built at the top of the Mound, a situation very convenient for Ramsay Lodge.

' After dinner we all sat round the fire, our mother in the middle, and Grip, the very obese mustard-coloured Dandie, occupying the hottest and most luxurious spot he could find. It was then our Psalms were learned and the Academy Bible lesson gone over, and after the Psalms came an apple or orange. We were also encouraged to write notes of the sermon, a business which we often found difficult, as we felt that our minister, Dr. Gordon, was apt to begin a sentence at the beginning of his sermon, and never come to a full stop till the end ! Afterwards, when we went to his class on a week-night in his own house, we found him full of instruction and delightful.

' Fast-days were very much like Sundays, only that we

were allowed to read " everyday " books, but not to play
any games, or be disturbing to older people in any way.
Letters were not written, and the piano was not so much
as thought of.

' It was before we moved to Ramsay Lodge that our
eldest sister Anne was married, in the year 1844, and
in the following year she and Mr. Gibson went to live
at Foulden West Mains, six miles from Berwick-on-
Tweed.   There for many years every holiday was
spent, and it would be almost impossible to overestimate
the influence those holidays had in the making of the boy
Marcus.   It was his first taste of the free, active, open-
air life of the country, and nothing he had ever enjoyed
could come up to it.   To be allowed to drive a cart
(whatever might be the nature of its contents !), or to
ride on the broad back of a cart-horse, when at " lowsin' "
time they went to the water,—these were sources of pride
with which perhaps few, if any, future triumphs could
compete.   Nor was the indoor life less stimulating.
Even the most casual visitor could hardly remain un-
acquainted with Mr. Gibson's favourite authors.   And
that he was emphatically one of those who read much,
but not many books, was of the less consequence to the
boy to whom the whole world of letters was as yet un-
trodden country.   Who could have helped loving Cowper
(especially in his Letters), or Johnson, or Macaulay, or
Carlyle, when read aloud by that true lover ?   Old Sam
seemed to live again for us, and the grand, rounded,
rolling periods of Macaulay were as a sweet morsel under
his tongue, while many an hour's mending and making
of little garments was brightened by the varying scenes
of the Waverley Novels set before us in lifelike vividness,
with all their humour and their pathos.   The affection
lavished on the young brother by the parents descended
to the next generation.   It was always a day of high

festival and excitement when uncle Marcus was expected. He was at once their playmate, their hero, and their slave, and many were the devices by which they sought (always in vain) to cheat their father of his company.

'In later years there were other homes for him to visit, when Tom and Mary were settled within comparatively easy distances of Edinburgh. Marcus and I, left solitary there, would indeed have felt stript and bare but for the knowledge that encompassed and upheld us on every side, of the love and welcome that waited for us in each of these homes. Every possible occasion was made use of for a visit, and fancy made many and many a flight in which bodies could not participate. In these youthful days it seemed to us as if these homes were like the solid foundations of the earth which cannot be removed. Now all are gone, but the love that made them is the most precious as well as the greatest among the things that abide.'

PART I
1850-1858

PART I

1850—1858

(Age 15-24)

UNIVERSITY AND NEW COLLEGE YEARS

To his sister Mary

I won't exactly say that I am blushing at present on my face, but in my heart I am, for being so long silent ; but I know you will excuse me, so I need say no more about it. Miss Janet Fairbairn changed her name to Mrs. Binnie yesterday afternoon at 3 o'clock, and set off to Stirling by the 4 o'clock train. She was reported to have been very shaky during the ceremony, which was a long address from Mr. Goold as to the respective duties of man and wife, etc. Miss Tod came down from Dingwall *to see the sight*, and left them all well ; but I think she has left her heart with your little namesake, who, she says, is the most delightful little bairn she ever saw, and so polite and well brought up, which makes a great difference in after life in this world. Mary can talk a little now.

I asked Mr. Martin if he could give or get me any writing in the evenings, but he does not seem to have heard of anything.

Perhaps you remember my little room at the head of the back stair : it is now the most snug place you ever saw ; the cupboards have been taken out, and a bed, chest of drawers, table and washstand put in, *and my gas has been put right*—do you remember ?

Mamma is in much better spirits now than she was a short time ago, and she is at present quite well notwithstanding the changing weather. She has not much trouble with the boys, since the ——s left, which is a great comfort to her.

My dear Mary, I hope you will give me a long letter of advice soon, for I feel more earnest about religion now than I have done formerly, and I think that your prayers (for I know I am in them) have been heard so far.

But I must stop, for it is past 12 o'clock, and with love I am . . .

To the Same

RAMSAY LODGE,
16th *March* 1850.

According to promise I now commence my letter, but am sorry to tell you it won't be so long as I intended, as I have had to write a letter for Mamma to Tom about an advertisement in the papers.

I think I will tell you about myself first. I have (to begin at the beginning) got up every morning this week at an average of quarter past six o'clock, which you must understand is very early for me, and I hope to be able to get up still earlier than this. The way this began was my friend Stewart despising himself for knowing so little : I told him I was *ditto*, so at the Institution one night about eleven o'clock (he had been up to tea and been home with Miss Millar), we set rules for each gaining a little more knowledge, which consisted in the following, viz., to get up at six o'clock and have time to read the Bible and relieve your mind to God, which I now find is a most important duty ; then a good long study before breakfast, which I think sharpens you up both in mind and body, and makes you cheerful for the day. I sometimes go out and have a run for a minute or two in the Gardens, which are in delightful proximity for that purpose—and we have had most splendid mornings here lately. I then get breakfast and go to the Bank in nice time, and get home about five or six o'clock, and do not study till half-past seven, when I read Homer till nine. I then take Hume till prayers, and always get to bed a little after eleven. I do Virgil and Euclid before breakfast. I make Saturday evening a holiday, and go to Hately's congregational singing-class on Wednesday evening. Enough of *the humble individual.*

To the Same

RAMSAY LODGE,
15th May 1850.

I hope you have not been longing *exceedingly* to hear from me ; the fact is, I was just going to write to you when you made such a fine apology for not writing me that I thought I might swallow my apology (which I was just going to commence my letter with) again, and keep my letter back a little.

I have been studying very hard at night, but for the last three mornings Mr. John [1] and I have been wonderfully lazy, and I had to plead cold in the nose to make up for it. I can, however, look back upon a good deal of Greek and Latin with triumph. What a great amount of pleasure and real happiness it gives to a person to see himself gaining daily more and more knowledge ; but as Charles said to me in one of his letters, and as I myself know, that is nothing without knowledge of God ; you

---

[1] Mr. John Macphail, who was one of Mrs. Dods' boarders.

look upon everything with a different eye, on prosperity
as God's blessing, on misfortune as a gentle rebuke or
to try your faith.   But even although you do not fix
your thoughts upon God in viewing anything, yet His
hand is so plainly seen in every object, that truly it
could only be a fool who says there is no God, and that
God is not a God abounding in goodness and long-
suffering mercy.   I think it is one of the most delightful
things possible to ponder over what this world is—why
it was made, how it fell, and how it was redeemed ; you
are completely carried away, and if God had not given
us His Word, the narrow and revengeful mind of man
could not easily believe that God would really receive
for His Son's joint-heirs in eternal life those creatures who
hate Him as their worst enemy, and continually rebel
against Him.   And it is scarcely possible to see how,
if a man were seriously to think over his state, and the
offer held out by God to him if he would turn from his
sins, he could possibly reject it.   It is really a wonderful
love, and how deserving of all that men can give.   For
the last month or two I have been in a state of surprise
at myself, when I think how long I rejected this offer ;
and even after I did seize it, how often I have sinned and
crucified Christ over again.   I wish you were here that
we might have a read, talk, and study together.   I think
I get on better at night by myself than with Mr. John
in the mornings, as I depend more upon my own resources.

I am reading Foster's *Essays* just now, having been
told to do so by Mr. John Millar,[1] who has given me a
great store of good advice.   I don't remember of ever
having read a book which pleased me so much as F.'s
Essays ; it is so exceedingly true, you go along with it
just as if it was your own writing.

When will you be here ?   I do wish you were here, but
this is a very long letter although it is in little compass.

[1] Classical tutor at New College.

I suppose they all here like you as well as ever, at least you must take it for granted, as they are all in bed. It is the *morning* of the 15th of May.

PS.—I never wrote a letter so fast in all my life. I never once stopped to think what to put down, or to read over to see if it was correct ; so you must exert your imaginative faculties (not that your faculties are merely imaginative, for I suppose the Hebrew and Latin will give that the lie) to fill up the blanks.

To his sister Marcia

RAMSAY LODGE,
28th September 1850.

MY DEAR PORTIA,—I love thee, love thee still ! ! I 'm reading Roman history just now, so don't be alarmed. I would have written you sooner, but two reasons prevented me : first, I had nothing original to tell you, and second, you never wrote me, so I had no questions to answer ; therefore, O most noble Portia, blame me not ! and now what am I to say to thee who fillest Crieff with thy praises, and the halls of Edinburgh ? I must give you an account of *self* when everything else fails ; self creeps or rather stalks in claiming a tribute. But to be brief, I am at present studying ten hours a day, so I calculate as how I 'll be able to hear you Æschylus, Homer, or anything you capricious may take a fancy to. I still go to ever kind Mr. Millar every Friday night and get polished. You 've no idea how deep I 'm getting, in fact it 's quite alarming lest I tumble in and drown myself some fine morning. Every day, however, I find that I 'm more stupid than I tho't I was. Oh, how I wish I had a year to grind up before coming out to College. But that cannot be, as to-day I gave in my application to be a candidate for a bursary—to Prof. MacDougall, who opened his door himself, saying there was nobody

at home. He asked me if I was the son of the late M.D.,
etc. I think this is enough about the humble individual.
And now about yourself. When will you be back,
Miss Marcia ? he said, for everybody is wearying to see
you, I can assure you, and no butter about it. I 've
a routine of questions to answer just now to whomsoever
I meet, and one of them is, ' When 's Marcia to be back ? '

You will get some jam when you come back, but as
for the apples and pears, they will all be done, and as
Anne would say, ' There hae been greater losses since
Sherriemuir.' Do you ever get any Greek read now ? I
can tell you what I think a most beautiful passage—Saul's
conversion in the Acts ; you should read it, and also,
' Your old men shall dream dreams,' etc. If you were
home I could show you some delightful bits, but perhaps
you know them all if you have been reading much.

To his brother-in-law, Rev. George Wilson

RAMSAY LODGE,
16th November 1850.

I don't exactly know what excuse to make for not
writing sooner in answer to your very kind notice of
arrival. It is now too late to ask if you 've recovered
the effects of your midnight voyage, or any other particulars of your route from this to Glenluce ; but I have
really been *very busy*, not to say that for every half-
hour since I saw you I 've had urgent employment, but
this combined with laziness has been the cause of your
not having received a letter from me ; and really I don't
think the one I 'm about to write will contain a very
great quantity of news.

I was, as I expected, unsuccessful in getting the *money
part* of the Bursary, but I have greatly enlarged my small
stock of knowledge. There were seventeen students trying

for it, and some of these so old I had no chance. I have
entered Pillans' and Dunbar's senior Latin and second
Greek, and I am to continue my mathematics at home
so as to be ready next year for Kelland's second class.
I will find the Greek very easy, I think ; we read at present
Xenophon and Homer, and in Latin, Curtius, Livy,
Horace, and we are to read Tacitus. Pillans is much
the nicest of the two, although Dunbar gets through much
more work than him. I have an hour between nine and
ten which I employ in writing or reading in the library,
and I feel quite confused among so many books ; and
when I leave I know I will regret not having made more
use of such an advantage for reading.

We here have had a grand week (last week) in the opening of the College ; [1] all the professors gave most splendid
lectures, which every person admired ; and Dr. Paterson's
speech (address rather), which I suppose you have seen,
was very much liked, being so very apt and like himself.
The classes are now in full force, and a new system begun,
each professor having two, instead of one class as formerly.

We have very few, only six, boarders, four little boys
(two of them Stirlings [2] whom I teach), and a medical
student, and Mr. John. The Stirlings are as like their
brother as can be in everything they do, even to scratching
their heads, which one of them does *the same* as Andrew.

To the Same

RAMSAY LODGE,
1st *February* 1851.

I didn't think there had been such a very ' awfu'
pause ' in our correspondence as two months, and I really,

[1] New College. At the opening of the new buildings the Inaugural
Address was delivered by the Rev. Dr. Nathaniel Paterson of Glasgow,
Moderator of the Free Church Assembly of that year.

[2] Of Muiravonside, near Linlithgow. The whole family of boys,
five in number, consecutively boarded with Mrs. Dods.

as well as yourself, have no apology to make.   I couldn't
ask you to write often (especially when Popery is so
strong and needs so many lectures to expose it), as you
must have a great deal of work.   I have been very busy
myself ; all my day is occupied, that is to say counting
a walk and reading books such as Alison, and Campbell's
Lives of the Chancellors.   I am reading Bogue's Essay just
now, and intended to read Gaussen's *Theopneustia* (which
you mention), and Chalmers on the same subject.   I
hope with my studies I shall be able to act upon your
advice, and always look for assistance from God.   I
have not yet made up my mind about becoming a member
of the Church : in your next letter could you mention
some book which would help me to prepare myself ?
Dick Stothert, my greatest friend at school, is likely to
be in Edinburgh next winter, and will attend Logic with
me and be with me, I suppose, all along.

I heard a capital lecture on Popery on Monday last
from Mr. Goold ; it was upon the infallibility claimed
by the Church.   Dr. Cumming of London is making a
stir here just now.   In fact he 's ' Cumming ' it strong !
Oh, horrid !   John used to call me effeminate looking,
but I 've got an answer for him now out of the mouth of
a Dutchman : ' No vunder, ven my Moder vas a voman.'
I know you 'll say that was just to fill up the letter,
and the truth is I am beginning to feel rather scarce of
anything to say.

To his sister Mary

RAMSAY LODGE,
10*th March* 1852.

Mamma and I are very much obliged for your two
letters.   I have very little time, I can assure you, to
write to anybody except John.   I don't know how it is,
but whenever I 've any time for writing, my letter goes

to Greenock (*to a place* is put in the accusative, which I think will solve your ' *Carthaginem*,' but as I have not a delectus, unless you quote the sentence, I don't know —that 's a rule, ' to a place is put in the accusative ') I think it is because I think (unconsciously) that he is solitary there, and also he writes to me *very often*. It is absurd me beginning *just now*, for I 've very little time *just now*, so you must excuse me till—I don't know when, for whenever this session is done I must begin to prepare for my M.A. examination, if I wish to pass.

If you would like to know what I am doing at present —Plane Trigonometry and Perspective, Cousin's Psychology, Sir William Hamilton's Notes, and I 'm nearly done with my friend Thucydides, and that 's all at present (except French and German), and I like all that I do, except Mathematics.

I read a chapter in the Septuagint every morning, and one in the Greek Testament in the evening. I wish I could read the Hebrew ; when you come you must teach me it. The sale here is to be on the 8th April, and Charles is coming to get a few things, I believe—perhaps Tom, not likely. I have been reading Papa's book again, and it does me more and more good every time I read it. I always get something which I had not before noticed, but I must soon get to the bottom of it.

Many thanks for your advice ; I find daily that without prayer everything else is nothing, even reading the Bible, and prayer itself I feel to be profitless unless with the Spirit's assistance to let me feel my wants and make them known unto Him who I feel is more ready to supply me with spiritual blessings than I am to ask them.

I am just thinking whether to take a Sunday-class just now, or whether I should not first instruct myself more, and perhaps next session take a class. I wish

C

you would tell me what you think.   I wish this were far, far longer.

To his sister Andrea

[? Summer of 1853]

I have just seen —— home, and she has behaved herself like a real good creature.   She, her brother and Nicolson [1] seem to form a beautiful conspiracy to make me happy and comfortable.   It's really most delightful to find even those whom you did not count your friends hardly, exerting themselves for you as a husband does for wife, one might say.   The fact is, —— to-night asked me point blank if I wished some work, so I explained that I didn't feel quite at ease, even though writing the essay—so she said that her brother had applied to the keeper of the funds of Advocates' Library to see if he could take me.   The treasurer or head librarian said that all his funds were out at present, but that one of the young fellows employed is going away next week, and he will likely take me in his place—it is from ten to four.   You will think that this exceeded even the high opinion you have formed of these honourable members of society, but this is not all; in case I should not get that, Dallas [2] had spoken to Nicolson about me, so that they have found a situation at Portobello which, if not filled up, they would recommend me to. Now truly isn't this serene, beautiful, noble, what you will ?   And of course all reflects on that great-minded, little-bodied, sweet, 'amiable, good-tempered' sister of . . .

[1] Mr. Alexander Nicolson, afterwards Sheriff-Substitute of Kirkcudbrightshire, and later of Renfrewshire at Greenock ; famous as a Gaelic scholar.

[2] Eneas Dallas, author of *Poetics*, and *The Gay Science*.

To J. C. Stewart

GLENLUCE,
5th July 1853.

MY DEAR GILES (I can't call you by any other name),—
Many thanks for your letter, the more so as you fulfilled
your promise, which—but oh! I won't be severe just
now. If you had little to say, I am much in the same
condition. I got here in rain, and I remain here in
rain. 'The rain it raineth every day.' You seem in bad
spirits, at least your letter was, and more particularly
your tea-party. Poor chap, how I pity you. I
wish you joy of all future teas for your noble behaviour
on that most trying occasion. I would almost have taken
toothache and had to leave. But if you 're in bad spirits,
I might be in ten times worse, but I 'm not. I 'm as
jolly as possible. The fact is, Germany is up the spout,
and consequently a damper is thrown over my hopes
for next summer in that quarter, but you need not
mention this as I don't know yet at all. Sir James Hay
wishes very much that I should stay at Dunragit during
summer, but I 'd rather be in the Advocates' Library.
I may get the Fordyces or somebody else to take. 'Never
say die.' 'If you don't succeed the first time, try, try, try
again.' Since coming here nothing particular has taken
place. I 've done some German and a little morals, and
walked a little, and talked a little, and read a little, and
slept a good deal, and smoked none at all.

Have you fallen in with the inexpressive she, who
was to send you into an unknown land? I think it
would do you a great deal of good. I 'd give up all
claims I have on anything in curls or braids, if it would
do you any good.

I hope you 'll go up and see them at No. 2. Mary will

be delighted to see you, and John and you would get on stunningly if you only knew each other. He 's dull, and I would feel greatly obliged, really, if instead of giving me the benefit of one of your hours you would step up and cheer him up a bit. You and he can talk of Shakspere as long as time will let, and although he does not laugh, don't think he wishes to get quit of you—in short, don't think him such a nasty fellow as he would wish you to suppose him. You both, however, think the world has used you ill, and this subject I would have you avoid, as it is certain to make you a cold, dry piece of timber. Think the best of everybody, old boy, and they will think and do the best for you, no fear. Throw a little tinder from yourself into the old world, and it will crackle and blaze and become quite jolly upon it. Every one gets hard knocks, no doubt, but the only plan is to duck, and then they either miss you altogether, or only inflict a very slight tap, a sort of admonitory thing to quell the boisterous within one. But, my dear Giles, I 'm sure we would put up with everything far more manfully, reasonably, and advantageously, if we only considered that this world and all its buffets is for no other end than that we may, by some trial of our strength in resisting the temptation to repine and so on, be made perfect for the full enjoying of God. It 's a beautiful system altogether, notwithstanding the Fall.

Please excuse the haste and vile writing of this letter, of which you will now be about tired, I suppose ; but don't be savage, but kind, and answer me immediately, which I am sure you would if you only knew how I like to hear from you. Remember me very kindly to your mother, and if sympathy has the power they say it has, you may assure yourself of the most warm love of . . .

To his sister Andrea

GLENLUCE,
19th July 1853.

Your letter, which came and ought to have been
answered a long time ago, is still fresh in my heart, where
it went straight and took possession. I don't remember
in the least what was in it, no more than I know the
component pleasures of a bathe, but there was an all-
overish sort of freshness about your last, which took
me and made me (difficult to believe !) like you better
than ever. I would *so* like to see you all ; one day at
West Mains would do more for me in the way of holidays
than a hundred anywhere else. Don't think this is a
mere statement of bosh, ' no, no, no,' I say it advisedly
and with reason. If you wish news from me, you 're
disappointed. I 've none to give, except that I had a
delicious letter from Giles yesterday, which I have read
and re-read, and at last committed to my pocket beside
yours and Charles's and Mary's, all choice productions,
as full of pleasure, each time I read them, as a new book.

Kiss Joe all over as she did my cake. I only wish I
had her (and it too, by the way), and I would perform
the arduous task in a brace of shakes.

I am not getting on particularly well with study here.
I don't like the half-work, half-play system, and would
give a half-dozen days of this sort of work for one jolly
good grind in the company of Messrs. Liddell & Scott.
Isn't Mary a stunner ? You 've no idea how she helps
me at home in the way of a little conversation and sich,
tho' I often wish for you again. I 've done a little more
than half of my essay, and Dick and I have had a little
tough correspondence on the subject. I doubt if this
is worth a penny, but I 've been rather in the dismals
all day, and hope you 'll excuse and soon write, and

make Charles and Anne (oh ! if she would, eh ?) write
to . . .

To his sister Marcia

' *Black clouds and silver linings.*'

ESSAY
On the Moral Faculty

2 SOUTH CHARLOTTE STREET,
13*th August* 1853.

MY DEAR DOBBIN,—This is not an Essay on the Moral
Faculty, but an answer to the letter which I did not
receive from you to-day.   Mamma and Mary, however,
each got one, and Mary says you have not got over your
dullness yet, poor Dob, and that you sit by yourself all
the evening.   I wish I was at Wootton some of these
evenings.   Perhaps I don't, but after all you will have
a jolly lot of time to yourself for the improvement in
Greek and other things which I have always prevented
you from doing.   There is no fear of your being dull in
the same room with any Greek book, far less with a
Greek Testament.   I have some hopes of you coming
home and reading and appreciating Homer.   Perhaps
such enjoyment would be rather too much to look
forward to.   But, really, do walk into it.   Have you a
grammar ?

You have now certainly lots of time for writing to me,
and if you don't—great long things 2d. each—you may
imagine, but no words of mine can express, the terrific
consequence.

We here are in a most exquisite state of poverty—
selling out, in short.   I got Thin to give me 5s. for the
Breeches Bible, which in my opinion, as books go, wasn't
worth 2½d., and I got 5s. from him for Dupin and Park-

hurst, two spoony books which I dare say you don't
know.

Giles and I have been walking as usual, and last night
I went down to help him with a thing for the Bank, for
which assistance he gave me a smoke, my tea, and a read
of Alexander Smith the new poet's verses. So you see
traffic is ris. Giles was very much riled that he did
not see you to bid you good-bye. He has a very great
idea of you ; and of course whenever he praises you up
I run you down, and so runs our talk. I think we
spoke about everything and everybody last night, and
walked round about and up and down and along
George Street and back again till we both thought
ourselves in for a rowing, so we parted.

I 'm very unsettled now that I 've got my Essay done.
The night after you went away Mary stitched it up, and
I wrote a note confessing myself the perpetrator, and laid
it in my desk till the time comes ; and now I 'm reading
up for the Fordyces, but very lazily, for what can one
do in a week ? Really what lots of delightful evenings
you will have when you get into the way of shutting your
door, and in winter your shutters, and feeling, ' Now
then, at it ! ' throwing your legs under the table, your
elbows upon it, and passing your fingers precipitately
through your hair. But, by the bye, these may not be
the preparations of a female student, so I 'd better not
commit myself rashly. At all events you seem to have
your wish in having time to study. And, oh ! delightful,
you 'll hear no gossip for a year !

Now, Dobbin, as it 's universally allowed that the
next best thing to conversation is epistolary correspondence, you must write screeds that will astonish
the postman and bring gain to the Revenues.

To his sisters Mary and Marcia

BOYS' SCHOOL ROOM, BRUCKLAY CASTLE,
MINTLAW, 29*th August* 1853.

Most beloved girls, *Arcades ambo*, in short, dear sisters mine, I know you will put a good construction both on what and how I write to you. I write to you both together because I could not write a long letter to each of you, you know, and besides I wish to tell you both all about this place, and that would be tiresome if done twice over. I need not tell you all about how I got here, but merely say that I was kindly received by two of my boys in the carriage at Mintlaw, six miles from this. On Thursday I was quite settled, hours marked out, and begun to lessons. We begin at 7.30 a.m., first reading a chapter of the Bible, then going fiercely into mathematics for an hour, then logic or Foster till breakfast at 9. At it again at 10, and then Greek till 12, when we go out to fish, shoot, walk, or ride—which last we have done to-day and enjoyed—dine at 5, lessons from 6 till 7.30. Then I come up here and sit by myself, but after a little generally one of my old boys comes in on pretence of doing a prop. or something. And so on we go pretty comfortably. And I need not tell you I am in good spirits, except, of course, when I begin to be soft, and lie out at the window, looking steadily towards the South till I think I see the kitten running over the slates at No. 2, and anon jumping in at Mamma's window. Such little interludes do sometimes come, and only add to the zest of being here helping a little.

PS.—I 've had dinner, and tell Mother I wore my dress-coat for the first time—perhaps the ' Jeemses ' did look a little at the cut of it, but what if they did ? I wish Mamma could get my two glasses of wine daily. I

think it would do her good, and what is the use of it to
a great hulk of a fellow like me ?

To J. C. Stewart

BRUCKLAY CASTLE,
MINTLAW, 5th *September* 1853.

Many, many thanks for your letter. I found it like a
sunbeam, or a pat of butter on my plate, this morning
at breakfast. I recognised your handwriting with *unspeakable* pleasure, which, notwithstanding your elaborate
and acceptable lecture on lucid style, it would be useless
to endeavour to explain. I will certainly let Tom know
of your hearty sympathy with him in this fearful affliction
by which he has been visited.[1] I had a very delightful
letter from him, showing that God has been pleased to
teach him that it is done by the loving hand of a Father.
He writes me that Sarah died seeing, as it were, with her
eyes her Redeemer stretching out His arms to receive
her, and entreating all around her to partake of her
happiness. It is most extraordinary to find the work
of the Spirit brought to such a perfection in a child of
three years old, and most lovely to see the death of a
child who has had no time to experience the misery of
the evil of this world, and who has merely been born
that she might pass into eternal joy. If parents could
only dissolve the earthly tie, how deep would be their
gratitude to Him who has done so good an action towards
them ; but how terrible it must be to see the little chairs
and beds empty, and the clothes, and books, and toys ;
they do indeed need a strong arm to uphold them, and
if they could not see beyond the dim horizon of this
earth, most certainly utter despair would follow.

I am glad to think you have been enjoying yourself

---

[1] He lost three children, all he then had, in one month from scarlet
fever.

at Aberlady : I wish you could come here on your way
North. I have only smelt tobacco once lately, and that
was the gamekeeper's to-day, when out shooting. I like
this place very much, but feel the responsibility very
much. The two eldest are seventeen, and at that age,
you know, are very open to influence ; of course,
my first aim must be to make them feel that they
have a work to do in this life, and that it is not mere
time for sleeping, reading and eating. I could do
nothing towards this in myself. Hourly I feel my entire
and utter weakness to improve to good the position in
which I am placed. But what a glorious thing prayer is.
I have no doubt as to being enabled to make the boys
work, but I 'm very much afraid of them taking after
my example. I begin with them by reading a chapter.
I would like prayers too, but am not sure that they would
derive the benefit which I would desire.

Enough of *ego*, I should think, but really what else
is there? for unless I repeat that *I* am enjoying myself,
I don't know what to say. My thoughts since I came
here have been, like my legs, taking advantage of the
country to stray a little, and to write or talk nonsense
wittingly I begin to think not only a fault, but a sin.

Don't believe me to be the blockhead this dry letter
betokens, but your far more willing than able and always
loving correspondent . . .

To his brother-in-law, Charles Gibson

BRUCKLAY CASTLE,
13th September 1853.

It is pouring rain to-day, and very cold. I have just
been warming myself to keep my hand from shaking by
playing at dumb-bells with a couple of lexicons—rather
heavy matter, I can assure you. ' To what base uses

may we come, Horatio,'—tho' I don't see after all why they should despise strengthening the body because they are made for the mind.

There is nothing we don't do here for amusement, from playing chess to eating gooseberries. Fencing is a favourite thing for wet days, but one of the foils is smashed, so ' there 's an end on 't,' or rather there 's no end on 't, and there 's just the rub.

I make the boys here read a letter of Foster's Essays *per diem*, and write out their sentiments : one of them does it well. I delight greatly in teaching these two boys ; they are very eager to know, and intelligent, and are constantly posing me with questions about what we read. I feel the responsibility tremendous, especially regarding their religious training.

Remember me, and I will be over and above happy and remain at my duty : that duty 's a capital solace.

To J. C. Stewart

BRUCKLAY CASTLE,
MINTLAW, 21*st September* 1853.

I flew at your letter when it came, but as you don't say a thing about how you feel regarding matters in general, I expect another immediately on receipt of this. I wish you would not fill your letter with a set of hum-bugging tourists, but say something about yourself, as it 's the only way I at present possess of learning anything concerning you. Of course I didn't mind a bit what you said about my style, you might have compared it to a banker's letter, or aught else under the sun ; for remember I go to Aytoun's next year, and then if I 'm hopeless——

I am of late taking amazingly to teaching, and am even beginning to think my proper sphere to be that of the pedagogue — a leader of youth — a splendid idea, but how few (none) fulfil it. I can't conceive any finer position for a man in this life than to be surrounded by a swarm of young fellows, who may be of eminent service to their country, and who can by proper training live to the glory of their God.   Permit me to be a little enthusiastic here. I know the dark side too.   But I think the exception is the boy who knows that he has a belly, but as for a mind, far less a soul, such a thing could not penetrate the solid sensuality of his composition. Such can only be endured by the feeling of duty, which can conquer all things, and of course besides this there are times when in all business we feel fagged, and then we should make use of chess, tobacco, or any *innocent* thing which turns the thoughts from the entire barrenness of this world, when such thoughts would have a bad tendency.

Please excuse all brevity of expression or other misdemeanours throughout this letter ; if there is any you can't make out, believe me you don't lose much, but at the same time know that I cannot give you more in the present state of my literary labours. I could say lots to you if you were here, but meantime believe me . . .

To his sister Andrea

BRUCKLAY CASTLE,
MINTLAW, 27th *September* 1853.

Talking of pupils, you said you could hardly realise me a ' grave, learned preceptor.' Truly no ! nor could I. I am afraid if you did inhabit a bust on the top of the bookcase (which I wish you did), you would be in danger of reeling from your position by the riot of the occasional joke. The arguments in *Barbara* or *Bokardo* are in general of rather an insane order, and I shudder to think of Sir William's [1] eye if he saw them.

What erroneous views you seem to have of your own character, regretting that it is formed (of which I am very glad), and running yourself down like a clock. As for what you say about me, I have only mournfully to say, ' 'Tis distance lends enchantment to the view.' Were you as near me as you seem to be to yourself, you would shrink from the inspection, and sit down to cry for despair. And even on your own showing, you must be better than you say, for if you were so weak and all that sort of thing, of course you would either not have so many difficulties, or receive more strength to contend with them. As for your pupils,[2] I (and all sensible people) must feel them to be receiving rare advantages, and if Bobby does not become great in his country, Sarah great in her house, and Markie Lord Chancellor or principal of a college, it is not the fault of their present instructress. Really, Andie, don't suppose I mean butter—you know I 'm not in the habit (quite the contrary); but I say this because I think you take too low an opinion of yourself. This with most people is well, but with you I suspect it may be hurtful. Of course, no one with a rightly consti-tuted mind can ever be satisfied with his amount of pro-gress. I think satisfaction is an unhealthy sign, just as want of appetite in the body is the first symptom of disease. I would like to say such lots to you, but I dread rubbish and wasting your and my time, so I must tell you the news . . .

Marcia is, as you say, a queer creature, but a nice one. I 've not heard for a week or so from her. I heard from George Wilson at Dingwall. Tom fainted twice on the

---

[1] Sir William Hamilton, Professor of Logic and Metaphysics in Edin-burgh University.

[2] The children at Foulden West Mains.

quay at Inverness while waiting for him ; poor fellow, I suppose he is almost worn dead with his late suffering. I wish we could bear some of his burden for him.   I suppose you heard of Walter Stirling's illness and death. It is very difficult to imagine him dead now, and a few months ago so full of vigour and fun.   I hope and believe that with so good a mother so long at his bedside he may have been led through Christ to conquer death.   He was a nice, affectionate little fellow, and the family must feel it very much indeed.   I hope it may impress Frank, naturally so serious.   But you see, my dear Andie, that my paper is done, though my will is fresh as ever.

To his sister Marcia

BRUCKLAY CASTLE,
MINTLAW, *3rd October* 1853.

I received your note last week, and take the first opportunity of answering it.   Yours was quite as short as mine, but if I am able I will write longer this time. I am bound, indeed, to send as much as I can for a penny, as I have only 7d. left.   But as there are no calls for money here, except in stamps and church, I don't feel dreadfully alarmed.   I suppose you have been told by Mary that Captain Fordyce went into Edinburgh, saw Mamma (who was charmed with him), and made an arrangement about the boys.   They are each to have a little iron bed in the bedroom, and Mamma is to sleep in the dining-room, as used to was ; so at least I suppose.   I wish you were to be at home, it would make it all so comfortable ; but I suppose you are better where you are, and of course I will study better without you, for you know I never worked when you were anywhere near.   I 'll need to work hard and make the most of my time if I am to teach Hay, Lloyd, and the

Fordyces. Besides, the next will be my most difficult session. However, I am getting quite fat here, so some hard work will be requisite to keep me down.

How does your Greek come on ? I 'm doing Sophocles with them. Splendid. I would like to do it with you. Do work. I 'm sure it will be of use to you afterwards. What do you expect to be if you live ? I 'm thinking of turning pedagogue. It 's a splendid thing, and I don't think I could be a minister as I ought. I 've been thinking a great deal about this lately. I would have a widowed feeling if I was to be anything else but a minister, but I must see that this be not mere imagination.

To J. C. Stewart

BRUCKLAY CASTLE,
MINTLAW, 13th October 1853.

Many thanks for your letter, notwithstanding all the base excuses for its poverty which flow in so thick towards the end, and which I can only excuse on the plea of their honesty. What do you imagine I like about your letters ? Certainly not the composition, nor the thoughts embodied therein, nor scarcely the news : one great subject of relish is the handwriting ; I also love to see the signature, but the main thing is, of course, that it is *your* signature. Whether the letter may be what you call bad or good, it is yours all the same and equally acceptable ; your drafts here will, I hope, always be honoured. Of course I relish what you would call a good letter more than a short little scrap of commonplace, because the former would more vividly represent its author to my tardy imagination. You say, however, that it was written in a wretched state of body and mind, and if I did not pity you and give you my most hearty condolence, I would be unworthy of enjoying your more healthy moments. The more so, since at the present sitting I am outwardly and inwardly comfortable. Outwardly, I am alone at a table littered with books, Greek, Latin and mathematical, centred by a mellow-burning light—none of your hard gas, but the softest oil —the whole room an emblem of peace ; the stillness of solitude only disturbed by the flickering sound of the happy little fire. In body well, but tired with the day's enjoyment, my knees sufficiently galled by the saddle to keep me mindful of a pleasant forenoon's ride. But since enjoyment generally, I believe always, flows outward, I trace my present comfort of body to a corresponding state of mind, and however paradoxical it may sound, it is because I have lately been led to consider more strongly that everything beneath the sun is vanity, that I find a relish in everything surrounding me. Of course it is no more than a part of our Christian creed that God through Christ is the giver of every good and perfect gift ; yet I have never felt it more peculiarly the real fact than since I came here, partly from hearing of the deaths of five intimate friends.

I wish you had been more particular in your letter, especially about that love affair. I wish you would do the thing sensibly.

Write immediately, and excuse brevity,
All undue gravity or extra levity.

To his sister Marcia

BRUCKLAY CASTLE,
MINTLAW, 14th October 1853.

I was equally surprised and delighted to-day by receiving your golden letter. But if you only got your expenses, and had to buy stockings and tassels and every other ladies' knick-knack, are you not robbing yourself ? for I can subsist perfectly well on 6d. till I get home

(which is very soon now) : there are no bookshops here,
you know.   However, I feel exceedingly grateful for your
£, and still more so for your kind consideration.   I
went to the post for the letters to-day, as the boy is into
Aberdeen along with his mistress in the carriage, and as
my sole remaining boy and I were riding about we
thought we would go there.   I must say I cannot plead
guilty to your reiterated charge of being a bad correspondent.   It 's these blue sheets that deceive you.
There 's a fearful lot in them, more than five or six of
your scrunty little notepaper sheets.   As for Andie, you
know she 's my younger sister (at least as every person
thinks so, I 'm almost beginning to think so myself,
though she 's so far before me in conscientiousness), and
I send her great sheets of fraternal counsel, and she 's
such a conversable little creature, I can't help writing her
long letters.   No offence, ma'am, you 're very delightful
in your way too.

I wish I had been inside Isaac's [1] belt on Saturday.
Oh, how splendid England must be ; although I never
saw it I know quite well what it is like.   Great loamy
fields with fragrant hedges rustling with merry little
birds, and great clumps of magnificent trees ; they, I
think, are the tokens of England.   You seem to have
taken wonderfully to the riding : do you never fall off ?
I hope Mr. Isaac keeps a sharp look-out.   I would advise
you to try a hedge with a deep ditch and a broken fence ;
it 's a delightful sensation.

I 've read *Queechy* just now, and would like to have
a long talk with you about Carleton.   He 's better than
Mr. John, though they are just the same characters, and
so are Ellen and Sophie.   In short, I don't think Miss
Wetherell has many ideas, but what she has are good,
and she makes the most of them, and that is the right

---

[1] A groom at Wootton Park.

D

thing after all. I think people ought to advertise all
their good ideas, at least to their friends. What do you
say to begin? Perhaps you think the reciprocity would
be all on one side, but you know, if nothing struck me
I could get some from books. I 've got a collection of
Greek and Latin *deliciae* for the little red bookie. I
noticed to-day in the library here a copy of Papa's book,
which has come since I came. It 's interesting—at least
it shows that they take an interest in me. I hope and
pray that it may do them good. I 've had a sort of
holiday to-day, as Mr. Fordyce took James and Alick
into Aberdeen, and William and I have been hewing
down trees for exercise.

Don't let the Greek grammar hinder you from going
ahead with the Testament. I 'm copying out Sir Wm.
Hamilton's lectures to help on my boys, and enjoy the
logic exceedingly. I did not at all know what I was
getting when there.

You heartless creature never ask whether or not I 've
got a prize for my Essay—£35 too. I must begin and get
up a little anxiety about it now, for I should hear this
week or next. But I suppose little Dick will sweep
it off.

I wonder if Mamma would not go to Dingwall now;
I think it is really time she stopped working. I feel it
far more when away from her, picturing her sitting
wearied on the sofa hardly able to speak with headache.
But perhaps in her case there is to be no calm before the
sunset. And do you know, Marcia, I 've been thinking
that she has lived conscientiously a Christian. The more
I compare her life with her temptations and trials, I come
to the conclusion that she has received the presence of
the husband of the widow in answer to her prayers. It
would be very delightful if she could enjoy Tom's home
for a little, to see in him the reward of her exertion.

Tom, too, I think, would like this more than ever. But I see that it is just post- and tea-time.

PS.—Write immediately or I 'll be home. Do, like a nice creature.

To the Same

2 SOUTH CHARLOTTE STREET,
EDINBURGH, *November* 1853.

You 're a dear, delightful creature ; I love you exceedingly, and I wish I could write you a letter, but really I don't know what to say. I ate an onion to dinner, and have been half asleep ever since.

I don't know if I ever expressed my thanks to you for the £1 you sent me for the watch. I never heard of such a delicious conspiracy. Fancy any one having four such sisters. In novels you read of the hero's sweetheart (so to speak) being such and doing such. But four collected in behalf of me—oh ! it 's magnificent. Don't think this is blarney, for it 's before breakfast, and in expectation of doing Potter [1] afterwards, so I 've enough to keep down the safety-valve.

I wish you had been here (I don't mean that, you know, but still—) last week when —— and Miss Fergusson were at tea. It was delicious, and only needed you and Andie to put the copestone to a magnificent night. I had such a delightful walk home from Rutland Square with ——, all alone in the moonlight. I give myself very great credit for not proposing *ipso loco* (which in the vernacular is, on the spot), as Mr. —— would have done, and for not writing a letter next morning, as everybody else would have done. Then those darling ——s are always coming up, and are such jolly creatures, it does me good. They 're in a perpetual state of snigger, honest snigger, true mirth, no gammon, reality, not a falsehood.

----
[1] Potter's *Mechanics.*

I wish you saw the Fordyces, and heard Aytoun's lectures. I could give you long notes of both, but Mary is saying with ' reiterated vengeance,' ' Come AWAY.' [1]

I 've gone away, had my breakfast and a letter from Charles, the latter of which I enclose, not to aggravate you, but to help you to enjoy Christmas in the enjoyment of others. Really I would give up my holidays for you, but as it cannot be, we must be content. Remember, old woman, you 've been almost half your time away. Think of it. It appears no time at all.

Nothing of my essay, except one night I dreamt that I got a letter saying, ' It 's all very fine, but you only stand fourth.' I hope—earnestly too, as I 'm half afraid the reality will be wanting.

PS.—Potter oppresses me.

To his brother-in-law, Rev. George Wilson

2 CHARLOTTE STREET,
EDINBURGH, 14*th November* 1853.

Many thanks for your many letters; I have really been overwhelmed with them lately, and last not least, though shortest, with the news of your manse. I wish you many happy days in it and in your parish. I have a sort of idea, which I know cannot come true, that I would like to be at the flitting and laying out of the garden and sorting the books. I wish I could send you something for your manse, but at present finding it impossible I am left only to hopes.

As I know you take a tutorial interest in me, I will tell you what I do :—Get up and read Calvin, and write out in Latin what I read the previous morning. Breakfast, from 9 to 10.30 Potter's *Mechanics* (I write out the

---

[1] A quotation from the dominie at Foulden, Berwickshire.

propositions I read the day before), 11-12 Nat. Ph. at College, then come home and do more Nat. Ph., and then go to Mr. Millar's for Plato and Exegesis of G. Test. (*very fine*), and from 4 to 5 Aytoun. Then from 5 to 9 it is a case of rush home, bolt dinner, answer difficulties, and hear Aleck Fordyce and James Lloyd their lessons, etc., etc. Then I intend to reserve after prayers for writing Aytoun's essays.

I do not, as you might suppose, act as chaplain here, but Mamma still reads prayers. You remember asking me once or twice while with you to do so, and that being a beginning I was glad of, though something may have dropped from Miss —— to make you aware of my want, at that time at least, of expressing the prayers of others. Since then I hope I have had one or two steps in progress ; but I thought it best, the Fordyces being so near my own age (17 they are), that Mamma should continue for a time. I would like to hear from you about this, as you are the only one I have to ask about such things. I will feel greatly obliged if you will write soon.

I think Mamma will pass a sick but pleasant winter. She makes herself ill by standing in the kitchen all day.

Please pardon the brevity of this, as I have no time or news to prolong it ; but do write soon to . . .

To his sister Marcia

2 SOUTH CHARLOTTE STREET,
EDINBURGH, 9*th January* 1854.

I presume that your answer to my last letter has been lost in the snow ; at all events I have not yet received it. That you may not in future have any excuse on that score, know that this comes with such fervour of love as to thaw for itself a passage. I feel a whole Fire of London glowing within me, and well I may, for that is our Aytounian exercise for this week, and as I am to describe it as an eye-witness, I have been almost minded to set Auld Reekie in a blaze, and sit pen in hand on some convenient spot. Talking of snow, the Fordyces have not yet got back, owing, as you would say, to the inclemency of the weather, and we had no classes to-day, the Senatus being engaged in blowing up some young men who on Friday last were found smashing windows, professors' hats, students' noses, and other college property.

I need not tell you now about West Mains, as Mary told you last week. She and I agree capitally, except in the mornings, when she keeps up a battery *en échelon* (I think it is round a corner it means) upon me vainly endeavouring to snatch a little more of nature's sweet restorer.

I don't mean to hurt your feelings, but I'm reading Prometheus just now.

$$\text{`} \pi o \nu \tau \iota \omega \nu \ \tau \epsilon \ \kappa \upsilon \mu \acute{\alpha} \tau \omega \nu$$
$$\grave{\alpha} \nu \acute{\eta} \rho \iota \theta \mu o \nu \ \gamma \acute{\epsilon} \lambda \alpha \sigma \mu \alpha, \text{'} \text{ etc., etc.}$$

O you creature, I wish I could pour out upon you my pleasurable feelings in reading it. Poor, silly English words from a poor —— ——'s pen fall 'full many a fathom deep' below expressing it.

I'm to be examined in all Potter in a week or two, so don't be surprised if my shaking so communicates itself to all around as to cause something earthquakey, even so far away (alas !) as Wootton.

—— told Mary that Æneas was going to ask me to breakfast, but unfortunately I was out of town (on Saturday before Xmas). Fancy Æneas and Marcus over eggs and coffee !

If you wish to enter into sympathy with me just now, read the quarrel of Brutus and Cassius.

I could write you whole volumes of love, and long for the ancient cuff on the side of the head, ' the old familiar touch,' and you may believe me to remain your devotedly attached, ever thinking of you, tender-hearted-in-regard-to-your-griefs, rejoicing-in-your-happiness, alive-to-your-interest, and most affectionate brother . . .

To the Same

NATURAL PHILOSOPHY CLASSROOM,
Pouring rain, 28*th January*, half-past 2 [1854].

I came here at 11 o'clock to a vile examination in Potter, and as I have written all I can, and can't go away for the rain, I relieve my feelings by the sweetest of occupations.

If you wish a review of Smith's poems, I can't give it you. I just read his *Life Drama*, that which has wrought his fame. There are no doubt some very fine passages (short passages), but there is not a bit of originality in the plot, and many of the scenes are neither more nor less than abominably disgusting. He may turn out something good yet, and has an iron in the fire just now. But as for him ever being a Byron, or a Cowper, or a Scott, that 's nonsense. The great feature of his poem is rhapsody, and a favourite expression of his is ' Gods ! ' Now that is low, vile, and I think betokens a small mind. However, this may be owing to his want of good education, though don't suppose he is so low as you hear. He was a designer in a warehouse, and such generally stand up to the middle rank.

How different a book is Sir J. Stephen's *Essays in Ecclesiastical Biography*, which I have just been reading. He 's a good man, and really to compare his talent to that of Mr. A. Smith would be to compare incommensurable forces. There is such spirit about Stephen's *Essays*.

They are very well written indeed, and very informing. But no man is without his faults, and he does not believe in Eternal Damnation. Yet he believes in Eternal Bliss, *i.e.*, he believes that God is merciful, but he cannot believe that He is just.

I am at present reading one of the *cleverest* productions of the day, *Poetics*, by a fellow called Dallas. I think he must be a nice fellow, for he calls his sister asleep a flower. Judging from the style of the work, which is brim full and running over with images, I should imagine him an ardent *young* man, and from some passages, I hope he is a good man, and from others I see he is a reading man, and a man of some reminiscence withal. This of the man, and of the book what shall I say ? That the theory is correct, I think, but the practice is too little spoken of, and besides, if I remember right, you once read the book yourself.

I like Aytoun's lectures very much, and also his exercises, though I made a horrid stick of my Fire of London. There was a great deal of damp in the air at the time. Aytoun has been lecturing on the old English poets, one of whom ends his book with the following lines :—

> ' Thus ends the book of Maister Wace ;
> Whoe'er a better book can weave
> Hath thereunto my hearty leave.'

But I fear I 've given you nothing but letters in this letter, and very bad letters, for I know nothing about anything just now. It 's really dreadful at College being dipped into each of the sciences, not by a strong-handed wench like the mother of Achilles, who only needed a vestige of heel, but by an old fellow working for fees as our Alma Mater does, who only puts the point of your nose, the tip of your tongue, or perhaps half an eye, into Greek, then hurries you to Geometry, then to Algebra, Latin,

Hebrew, Electricity, Galvanism, Magnetism, Statics, Dynamics, Rhetoric, Sound, Heat, Belles Lettres, and half a hundred other things, all of which I have been hurled through during the last few days of my existence, and am expected to stand examinations on any or all of them before I can be recognised as a legal son, an M.A., of the old (dear old, after all) University. If I pass M.A. this spring I would like to go on the spree for a year, and do something at Greek or Hebrew, or anything that would be of use.

Believe me always your letter-expecting brother . . .

To the Same

2 SOUTH CHARLOTTE STREET,
EDINBURGH, 24th April 1854.

I think you might have written to a poor creature some time since : however——, I don't know where to begin. Andie is here, you know, sitting stitching Mary's sh-fts, and wishing she had got to *la dernière chemise d'amour*. She's inoculated with Westmainianisms, punning of all sorts, and such expressions as ' Did ever any living ? ' She speaks of people ' herding at her,' and of pieces of work being ' got on end.' I wish you were here just to complete the sororal trio. Perhaps it would be too much—your cuffs and Andie's nips and Mary's looks would perhaps have made such a tender person as I am succumb.

But I 've more good news. On Saturday last I was capped by the shaky old Principal, who placed on my head a dirty velvet cap of surprising size, and of no available use as a head-dress, seeing that it was as flat as a scone, and indeed not in appearance altogether differing from a good round burnt bannie. He also pronounced over me these words : ' Marce Dods, Magistrum in Artibus liberalibus ego te creo.' I and my fellows were clad in seedy gowns for the occasion, and the whole ceremony excited the ludicrous within me so forcibly that it was with the utmost exertion only I could keep my laughing from being audible. Of course the Principal said we had passed through our University career with unparalleled splendour, and then advised us to be good boys and reflect lustre on the glowing bosom of Alma Mater. (If we always wore the gowns we had on then, a halo would continually surround us, for nothing was left of them but *shine*). We then received the right hand of fellow-ship from the professors, a shaky yet sincere right hand of Lee himself, then a malicious little twitch from Kelland, as much as to say, I know a thing or two more than even you, though you are an M.A. of Edinburgh. (I wish you heard Philip Kelland on the theory of waves ; he knows the equation of every curve in the world, and has it at his finger ends, each of them being things like :—

$$y^2 = \frac{\delta\psi^2}{\delta \cdot 4h} - \sqrt{1 - f^{n-1}} \times \cos(\pi - (a + \theta)), \text{ etc., etc.}$$

Another accomplishment of his is to write on a space no larger than the point of a pin, ' Philip Kelland, Pro-fessor of Mathematics in the University of Edinburgh.' This is a favourite amusement among the present race of savants.) Then we got some more shakes, and last, two great hearty rugs and laughs from MacDougall and Aytoun, who seemed to have undergone the same stress on gravity as I had done. Andie thinks the point of a pin writing sounds rather like the Middle Age question : ' How many angels can stand firmly at one moment on the point of a pin ? ' But I can assure you it 's a good scientific truth.

I 've been rather busy this winter, what with the For-dyces and Lloyd and myself, and then *I could not get off*

going to the Philosoph. Inst. with ——. I must say
she is a nice creature, but so are they all, all honourable
women, Kippen, Lamb, etc., etc., etc.—. The Fordyces got some good prizes, and I got one from Aytoun,
and we all set off for Paris on Friday week. We are to
board either at Paris or Versailles (Geneva up the spout).
I am going to make a last effort to learn French. I have
just to teach them for four or five hours, then write some
of my Essay on Cowper and do some Hebrew, and then
I will speak, read, and act French. None of your tan-
talising gammon about coming round by Wootton. No
more of that if you love me. What a fearful scribble this
is. All about myself too, but pardon the egotism of
one whose title is A.M. I never thought of that view
of the matter before, and perhaps it is inauspicious for
one naturally—Ah !—φεῦ, φεῦ, φεῦ, φεῦ, φεῦ, αἰαῖ, αἰαῖ,
ὀτοτοτοτοτοῖ ! ὀτοτοτοτοτοῖ !

> ' Our sincerest laughter
> With some pain is fraught.'

Read and excuse all this nonsense and answer long
and luxuriously . . .

To the Same

2 SOUTH CHARLOTTE STREET,
EDINBURGH, 4*th May* 1854.

Andie and I sit down pen in hand to send you a scribble.
I am just on the wing and in momently expectation of
being summoned to saddle my nag. Yet I can't help
sending you a line to express my gratitude for the slippers,
which (gratitude) has been consuming me ever since I
received them. They 're ducks of things fit to wear at
a wedding, if people would only consult either comfort
or ornament, and not base fashion. It was exceedingly

good of you to think, not of me, for that 's your duty, but of the comfort of my toes. I had not received them before I wrote you last, or I would have thanked you then, of course, although you were so base as to accuse me of neglect and all the rest of it. If your deeds corresponded with your words you would be a disgrace to society. I never received such a collection of downright insolence from any person, even a female, as in your last letter. I wish you would change your style a little.

To satisfy the cravings of yourself and Mr. ——, with whom you seem (allow me to say) to be on very intimate terms, I may tell you that I had the profound honour of an interview with the hero. Æneas and Marcus discussed not the merits of Achilles or Hector, but of imaginative and imitative art, particularly poetry ; also the Philosophical Institution fell in our way, and the learned and judicious made some acute criticisms upon Mr. Blackie. It always makes me sad to see Dallas, for I 'm afraid he, along with other young men of that standing of talent, will come to grief. They write away brilliantly enough, but I 'm afraid there 's very little *real* matter in what they do, and a set like them, if they set to work in earnest, might influence the age.

If you have not read Bungener's *Priest, Infidel and Huguenot,* or his *Voltaire and his Times,* you ought. It 's no trouble to read his books, they are so capitally written.

I 've been collecting signatures to my diploma the last day or two, and walked fifteen miles up and down Edinburgh yesterday in that service. I 'll do the same for you when you 're A.M.

I made an appointment with Dick Stothert to meet him at half-past six this day week on the Boulevards, or some such place.

This was merely to thank you for the slippers.

To his Mother

HOTEL WINDSOR,
PARIS, *May* 1854.

I am just going to write you a sort of journal, and send it away every fortnight or three weeks ; you may send it to Andie, telling her to keep them for me, that I may refresh my memory when I come home. I think I will be able to send you our address before I put up this letter. Don't address 'Hotel Windsor,' for we leave to-day to go to lodgings.

But to begin. On Wednesday morning (the 10th) we left London at a quarter before six and reached Folkestone at 8.30. In the train there were two foreigners who were eating sausages and potted head almost all the way. I saw them on the steamer looking very ghastly. We got across to Boulogne in three hours, and on landing were shown into a room among a lot of grim-looking fellows, one of whom dived into my pocket ; but on my saying 'Cap' he pulled out his hand and said 'All right.' In a short time we left for Paris through the queerest country possible. It seems to have been planted with trees in long rows right across the country, and then little patches cut out and sown with grass. There were several most lovely spots of this kind, the grass growing so green in the shade, and little purling brooks running through to keep everything cool, and much need, for I'm grilled already, and this is only May ; the very thoughts of July make me brown. But the windows here all open like folding-doors, and stand open all day, so that one can live if one only stays at home. On our journey to Paris, I found that I knew as much French as some of my fellow-passengers, for we saw one rush into a refreshment room and shout out with the most correct pronunciation : 'Garçon, garçon.' The per-

sonal presence, however, of the desired garçon sent all
his French back into the railway carriage beside his
conversation book, and all he could get out in answer
to the garçon's 'Oui, Monsieur,' was 'Eh—ah—I say,
look here.' We heard him in the next division to ours
practising afterwards, that he might come better off
at the next station.

We got to the hotel here about 8 o'clock. But about
the custom-house, by the bye, it was a mere form with us.
A fellow just put in his hand by the side of one of my
portmanteau divisions, and didn't even look at the other.
Mrs. Fordyce's trunk was not opened at all. Almost all
the goods lying at stations on the line we came by had
'Fragile' and 'Haut' marked on them, showing the
pernicketiness of the trade of Paris. This is a very large
and full hotel, and French enough, although they wish
it to be English. To show you what a *height* the French
can carry foppery, I may tell you that though my room
is on the sixth story, yet I am provided with a large fixed
mirror, more than a yard square, and also have on the
chimney-piece an alabaster clock.

On Thursday morning (after a very comfortable sleep,
not a single flea, and a wash with soap, but in a very
small basin—especially after my ocean at home), I sallied
forth, as they were not ready for breakfast, and went
into the gardens of the Tuileries, which extend from
one side of the Palace down the Seine, and are planted
with very grand trees, which branch over delightful cool
walks. There are also some artificial ponds with fountains and swans, and the whole place being studded with
statues forms quite a Parisian scene. But, most luxurious of all, there are millions (I don't exaggerate) of chairs
piled up for the use of the public. I saw a lady, quite
respectable, unfortunately set her foot on the binding
of her dress, and I felt deeply moved for her, thinking

she would trollop away home, as any Edinburgh lady
would do in similar circumstances. My pity was quickly
changed into almost envy, when I saw her take down
two chairs, set her feet on one and herself on another,
tuck up her dress, haul out a housewife (which Andie
did not make for me), and commence repairs on the spot.

We got breakfast in the café, and after that Alick and
I strolled away up the Seine towards Notre Dame. It
was rather ominous that I should on my first stroll fall
into so dangerous a quarter as I did. There is a mile and
a half of bookstalls with the most tempting books—all
sorts, sizes and prices. But don't fear for me, for I
don't know enough French to beat down yet, tho' of this
more anon. There are great lots of schools of swimming
on the river, both for men and women, separate, of course ;
and great long houses full of tubs, bottomless, opening
into the Seine, where the washing of clothes goes on. We
went through the Louvre, where I first attacked a French-
man in his vernacular. We went in the afternoon to
the Champs Elysées, which are not so pleasant to my
taste as the gardens of the Tuileries : there is such a din
of carriages and people. The principal characteristic
of Paris seems to be unnecessary noise. You can't go
out one moment of the day but you meet a horrid
drummer leading about a lot of soldiers ; and the horses
have bells on their collars. Hundreds of shops have
written up on the window ' English spoken.' The res-
taurants with tables outside look very comfortable in
the evenings. They drink *vin ordinaire*, which is nothing
at all but something to drink ; no effect follows any
amount of it. Every one here smokes, and wears mous-
tache, and no whiskers. The men kiss, first one cheek,
then the other. The women are showy, and almost
all brush their hair back in the old style, but I 've not
offered either my 'and or 'eart to any of them yet, and

indeed have seen no very startling beauty. We all
dined at a restaurant in Palais Royal, where we had about
twelve different dishes, no frogs that I saw, but cocks'
combs and all sorts of queer-looking things. After
dinner we walked round the Palais Poyal, examining the
gorgeous shops with which it is surrounded. How
Andie would revel in the nick-nacks ! There is nothing
of the species natty which you could not get. We got
tea, or rather coffee, in the Palais Royal too—a large
square with a fountain playing, and a band playing too,
in the middle.

On Friday we just strolled about and saw what we
could. I went to the book quarter and got a Pascal's
Thoughts, just a perfect copy, for 15d., and it 's about
the only book I wish. But you can have no idea of the
splendid tomes that lie tempting the public. We dined
at the Poissonnerie Anglaise, and for dessert had a sight
of the Empress. We saw her again in the evening, and
again at the Palace to-day. She 's getting quite a
common sight now to us. She is very beautiful, just
like the pictures one sees of her. The Emperor may have
been there, but I always gaze so at her that I 've no time
to look for him.

On Saturday we flitted to lodgings, where we will stay
until Captain Fordyce gets a place for us. I have not
yet seen Monsieur Monod, but suppose we will call for
him next week some time. After flitting, we set off to
the Louvre, and walked through several miles of painting
by Rubens, Titian, Tintoret, Guido, Cuyp, and others,
through rooms full of things used by Napoleon and the
kings of France, amongst others the prayer-book of
Charlemagne with boards of carved ivory and diamonds.
Egyptian and Grecian and Italian antiquities all passed
before our gaze, or rather we passed on till we were
quite done, and till our necks were broken by the beauty

of the paintings on the roof.   This is Saturday afternoon
when I write, but as letters take just about twenty-six
hours from this to Edinburgh, I will keep it till Monday,
and let you know how I like Monod, and where to address
my letters to.

Monday.—We went to Monsieur Monod's church
yesterday, but did not hear him ; we heard a very good
sermon in French, of which I understood a little.   We
then walked home through crowds of fellows smoking
and laughing at sights, etc., etc.   They seem to use
Sunday here very much as we use Saturday.   The shops
are all open in the day, but shut a little earlier in the
evening than usual.   Carts and everything go about just
as on everydays.   But I don't think we suffer much
danger from this, for it is so fearful a contrast to Scotland
that the shock will scarcely be got over in the short time
we are here.   I am looking forward already to coming
home.   We began to study this morning.

To J. C. Stewart

CHEZ MADAME VALLONY,
1 RUE DE FLEURUS,
PARIS, 31st May 1854.

Here I am really in *la belle France* among real French
men, women, and poodles.   It's rather queer not to be
understood in our own delightful language ; not even
a dog deigns to acknowledge an *Anglais*.   ' Not a word
to throw at a dog ' is most decidedly my case.   I need
not tell you what you can get in a guide-book about the
Louvre, Tuileries, Versailles, Luxembourg, and all these
places.   There are miles of splendid picture-galleries,
almost all of them really good paintings.   But the thing
the Parisians should be most proud of is their gardens ;
these are delightful.   Tall trees are planted thick, and
beautiful fountains play all about : but beyond this I

E

think Paris is a muff of a place. The people are not in earnest about anything—at least in general. Then there is no business, it 's all for fun, they seem to think. The manners we have met with are certainly inferior by a great deal to our own ; they nearly lay their whole body on the dining-table, and the ladies in this house are certainly unworthy of the name. And how they eat, and drink *vin ordinaire*! At breakfast we get a great host of fried potatoes and two helpings of hot beef, and then a regular breakfast follows—eggs, coffee, and bread and butter, and *vin ordinaire*.

I have a good deal to do, too much indeed, but we get along comfortably enough. I stroll about in the day and see what is to be seen, but it is fearfully hot already, and the people solace you by saying the thermometer rises to 112 sometimes. We were at Versailles to-day, and it is quite different from anything we have ; there are about six miles of paintings, historical and others, and to all these places you gain entrance by showing your passport. In the park of Versailles the walks surpass description, and everything else.

It 's a fearful place this on Sundays, which are just exactly like our Saturdays—the people all go a-shopping or to see exhibitions, etc., which if not open on other days are yet sure to be open on Sundays. It is most disagreeable walking to church through lanes of punches and tumblers, and games at football, and everything you could think of. I have been in several Popish churches, on lawful days, please observe. I did not see one man going to confess, thought hosts of women were whispering away through little gratings — the padres behind. Some of the churches are very beautiful ; one near here has shells (real shells) for the holy water, about three feet long, and the pulpit is very pretty, being supported, lightly, by the stairs on either side in the form of an arch.

The ' Boolevards ' are rotten places, being a mere street with trees on either side—nothing like the trees in the gardens, and dreadfully dear shops all along. I don't know anything to tell you here that you would care about. Paris is to me a very sticky place, partly from not knowing the language and partly from its entire contrast to anything I care for. One thing I can tell you in the comfort line, which perhaps you already know, the railways here are most capitally got up and managed in everything. They are about one-third cheaper, I should think, and much more comfortable ; they start at the very moment. Then a circumstance belonging to the fine art department is that there are no pretty women here, or very few. They all dress their hair *à la Eugenie* ; she is very like the ordinary pictures of her. I 've seen her several times, as she goes to drive daily in the Champs Elysées and Bois de Boulogne, which are the parks here. I don't think (but am not certain) that I 've seen the Emperor. There is no shipping on the Seine, and only *one* or *two* steamboats, little wee things more for fun than for use, as everything else is.

I 've got a beginning to make to an essay on Cowper, but he 's a difficult fellow to treat, every one so much agreed about him. You don't care for him, don't you not ? I can't exactly understand that ; and if you would give me your reasons it would do me good. I 'm ashamed to send you this letter, but if you forgive and answer it, I will try and do better next time. Meanwhile this will give you the address of . . .

To his sister Marcia

CHEZ MADAME VALLONY,
1 RUE DE FLEURUS,
PARIS, 30*th June* 1854.

You are the most delightful of long-waisted, trailing-robed, glancing-eyed, white-armed (and all the other

Homeric adjectives) women.   All lesser loves, such as
that of which you accuse me, dwindle into utter invisi-
bility before the star of your delightful epistle.   I just
got it to-day, and gloated over it, and would have been
perfectly happy had it not been for the shade of gloom
over it, of which more anon.

But first of sublunary matters : I need not dwell on
the usual Galignani thing — Monday Louvre, Tuesday
Luxembourg, etc., etc.   Both of these are most superb,
bewilderingly so.   Miles of Rubens.   'Think of it, dis-
solute man.'   Père la Chaise, Tuileries, etc., etc., have all
gone down.   But you know, Dobbin, you can get this
in any guide-book or *Two Months in Paris by a Cockney*.
So I'll shortly tell you what I think of this ; and, first,
'It's very funny' (as a friend of ours would say) not
to be speaking French in fun, but to need to speak it,
and that to real French men and women, and all in *la
belle France*.   Only think that even when you have a
headache you must come out with your '*merci*' and
'*voulez-vous passer*,' and all that.   I suppose I will learn
some French, for here we are, and what can we do ?
I've already acquired some notion of how to beat down
an old bookman (though I have only to confess to a
Pascal's *Pensées* and a Fénelon).   Tell me, by the way,
as long as I remember, what you wish me to get for you,
and what I should get for Mary and Andie, and all the
little West Mainians . . .

All that you say about going home and being dull is
very true, and only another instance of the truth of the
old simile—this life a wilderness and we the pilgrims.
But there is nothing like hope for buoying human hearts,
and I can conceive one who has no hope beyond the edge
of the wilderness to be inconsolably dull, but in any other
circumstances it is pusillanimity.   And then you know,
Marsh, however bad a thing is, there is always some light

in it (moreover the great thing that helps me always is to keep actually near you the fact, ' this is a state of probation '), and we of all people have to be glad.   Look at Tom and John and Anne (what could be better than her household ?) and then Mary too, to all appearances going to be as happy as may be.   For Mamma, all I can hope is that she is prepared to receive her reward. Whenever I am away from home things are all invested with a sort of poetry, and with Mamma this expresses itself in admiration of how she has lived.

About books, if you wish to read a book worth spending time on, read Butler's *Analogy*.   It is worth ten dozen De Quinceys (pardon !) or any other published book for making you think and satisfying you.   It 's none of your half-way muddles, but begins at the beginning and goes clear through.   I quite agree with you in thinking it good to read a good many half and half books, along with the double stunners.   They are just the frog pies that give you a whet for the *poulet* to follow.

I 'm afraid this is a horrid prosy letter, but I 'm sure I am just stuffed with all sorts of manure, and no corn can get up ; for I teach here daily Latin, Greek, Algebra, Euclid, Logic, Metaphysics, Moral Philosophy, and then the boys are eighteen now, and are going up next spring for B.A., so I 've to grind.   Then I must try and finish an essay on Cowper which I have merely begun, also try and do some French, and besides all this I have what ought to keep me fully employed all summer, an examination in August for admission to the Hall by a Board which in its pride of novelty will, I suppose, pluck some of us.   For it I 've to get up all that I 've done in the University, and besides this Hebrew, and History of a thousand years.

PS.—Do write me a tremendous letter next time

crammed with yourself.   Speedily.   It's only 10d., not 14d.

To his brother-in-law, Charles Gibson

2 South Charlotte Street,
Edinburgh, 16th September 1854.

I've been attempting to drown distance and separation in the pages of Foster's *Essays*, and have in part succeeded. But what is reading him to hearing him read in those tones which never fail to convey his meaning ? And what is a pencil mark of approbation, or even a dull critique on the flyleaf of the book, to the sympathetic burst of applause, the subtle comparison, and the pointed application of the most abstract truths, which I have lately enjoyed ? After reading these *Essays* I think their great attraction is their depth of knowledge of human nature and the wonderful truths which are brought out so easily and yet so very forcibly ; certainly there could not be more sarcastic writing. All his arguments against errors of reason run into this form, and they are overpowering. By the by, in connection with your favourite, ' We come into the world crying, and every day tells us why,' Herodotus mentions a people of Indians who at the birth of a child do not congratulate the parents, but assemble to weep and lament—' Pretty notion,' as the Yankees say.

To J. C. Stewart

Anick Grange,
Hexham, 3rd August 1855.

Facts and time are rare things here, or I would have written you sooner. I suppose my letter must be just a description of the place. But there's nothing extra-

ordinary to describe. The buildings are new and look
very neat, the garden is a good one, the house is newly
oil-painted, the farm is quite English, having a great
deal of fat old pasture : these facts comprise all that
you would care to know. Since I came here, I have
been stalking about in all directions seeing what is to
be seen, and living the usual round of a life in the country :
up at 6, breakfast at 8, out till 11.30, read and despatch
letters, dinner at 12.30, after which I generally contrive
to read a little, then out till 5, when tea comes, after that
go and shoot rabbits till you can't see them, then come
in and take your supper and go to bed. That 's the style
for weak children. Dry enough, you will think, especially
when one has to lie at a hedge root for an hour till one
of these St. Swithin clouds sweeps past, leaving your
hay just as it was a week ago, and yourself tending to
bad temper, and all the ills that follow helpless distress.
Then you are in a mood for reflecting sagely on the resemblance of human life to a July day. I hope this will
find you in some rural retreat, at least in a place too small
to support more than one branch bank. (Speaking of
branch banks, the N. & D.D., Hexham, keeps no books.
but sends a daily state of transactions to head office ;
it 's surely a strange way of going to work.) I hope, if
you are in the country, that you have better weather
than we have here ; the glass is going steadily down to
much rain, as if it was November, and strange to say
the weather corresponds with the glass. Consequently
the strawberries are spoilt, and if it wasn't for a lot of
nice books that Tom has, I fear I would feel like a member
of a soaked picnic.

Have you read the *Memoirs of the Chevalier de Gram-
mont*, a dashing and I suppose true specimen of the
court of Charles II. ? A queer set of men and women
certainly ; they seem to have made up marriages only

that there might be duels, not children, as their fruit ;
Duke of B. makes love to the Earl of C.'s wife, the earl
challenges the duke, the duke runs the earl through
the body, and enjoys the society of the earl's widow
unmolested and with the stain wiped off his reputation.
I 'm glad there 's some change taken place in 150 years.
These old fellows were not so far on as the Greeks and
Romans, not only in this, but in agriculture, art of war,
and everything depending on or giving rise to civilisation.

I have just been down to Hexham, and being alone I
took my first gallop this year ; oh ! man, it 's magnificent,
I don't know how to describe it or what to liken it to ;
I should think it leaves waltzing with a girl you are
deeply in love with far behind ; it 's like some delicious
dream where you whirl in sweet company through soft,
sweet-smelling space, now and then gliding through a
rich, rosy cloud ; there 's something like it, if I recollect
right, in Shelley's *Queen Mab*, and in one of the *Arabian
Nights* tales. Moreover, this my particular gallop was in
a thorough-bred English lane, high-hedged, covered
half-way up with brambles and wild roses and honey-
suckle, and every ten or twelve yards rich old trees, and
on either side of the road broad, flat sward for tinkers'
horses and encampments.

Have you seen Tennyson's new thing *Maud*, or is it
not even yet out ?

To his Mother

2 MELVILLE STREET,
EDINBURGH, *8th December* 1855.

I don't think I have much palaver to-night, but just
wish to let you know how we are getting on.

We got a great lump of mutton from West Mains the
other day, which served us a fortnight, being done in

a variety of pretty little dinners. Marsh is going out
there for a week, but I can't get, as I must keep to the
Signet Library,[1] and could not spare the time at any rate,
as I have a thing to write for Dr. Cunningham, which I
must work at in the holidays. I enjoy his class very
much, but find Dr. Buchanan painfully prolix. However, there are some very fine passages in his lectures,
and I think his course is in itself more uninteresting
than Cunningham's. Dr. Duncan is going through Job
just now, and gives some most valuable notes, a good
many queer stories, and a great quantity of minor matter
difficult to carry away.

Mary asks if I continue my visiting. I do, and would
be very sorry to give it up, though I am oppressed by
the cant I meet with, and the lies, and most of all my
own insufficiency. Some one or two there always are
who seem to welcome me, and whether I can do them
any good or no, it does me much good to acquaint myself with people in their religious aspect, and also to have
some duty of that kind regularly to perform.

Tell Mary that I trust she will take this as an answer
to her letter, and I hope the arrangement may answer,
though I don't.

To the Same

2 MELVILLE STREET,
20th January 1856.

I again enlist in the Blues,[2] though it is later than it
should be on Saturday night, which I could not help.

I enclose a strange epistle I got the other day for you,
and wait instructions regarding it. Marsh and I know
nothing of the rich old coon that wants heirs, but would
be happy to make his acquaintance ; for I am sure I

---

[1] Which he was cataloguing.
[2] He frequently wrote on blue paper.

would give him my gratitude if his guineas would give me an hour or two more for study. It's just next door to despair to pass book after book in the library, and think of the store of information I might get out of them, and yet have not time to do more than 'Milton (John), *Paradise Lost*, roy. 8vo, Lond. 1712, 2 vols.,' and so pass him by. But such is life.

I have given in my Greek exegesis to Black, and am nearly done my Latin discourse for the Principal, for whom my love and admiration grow daily stronger.

Mr. Johnston, the publisher, and I have always a nice chat now on Sunday afternoons, as we are both there just as the bells begin ; so I am getting quite into his acquaintance, and like him much.

When are you coming here ? Marsh and I are always speaking about it now, but think you would be dull all day by yourself, unless you made calls all the time.

To the Same

2 MELVILLE STREET,
EDINBURGH, 23rd *February* 1856.

I am all right in health, though mentally very tired ; I have not had too much work this session, but it's too variegated for my taste. Two hours of temptation in the Library, three hours of trial with idle boys, and seven hours for the payment of nature's debts, teach me how little can be done in a lifetime. Had I my choice, I would sit for a year or two in one of the cells at the Library, and suck hard at the old tomes that just now stand teaching me what masses of knowledge is laid up there, and saying at the same time, Don't you wish you may get it?

I have got my discourses for this year read. My Latin one for Dr. Cunningham cost me more thought than

anything I have ever done, but I wrote it too carelessly.
Its character was therefore nothing very flattering.
He said there was a great deal of material brought to
bear well upon the subject, but the style was too curt
and the method was not such as is ordinarily employed
in such discourses. The only other part of my studies
that will interest you is that I have begun what I hope
will be a continued reading of the Fathers. I have begun
with the earliest and hope to get some good from a regular
study of them. I have read some of them before, but
never regularly laid myself out to get all out of them
there is to be got.

To his sister Andrea

2 MELVILLE STREET,
EDINBURGH, 5th March [? April 1856.]

MY DEAREST DOB,—You will see by that awkward
joining that the 'est' was a second thought (therefore
superlative, as second thoughts are best), a sudden out-
flow of feeling towards the little angel. (You don't feel
wings growing yet, do you ?) Your letter was delicious,
as good as (I might almost say better than) a smoke with
Davie ;[1] mind, it's not the smoke alone—it can't come
into competition with any mere sensual enjoyment. I
am not going to write you a letter, but I can't help saying
something to you. It's late now, and Marsh is sitting
at the fire chewing the cud of her dinner. I mean of course
by that, all that a dinner includes, *i.e.* spending from 4
o'clock to 9.30 at No. 65. I, unhappy, was dining with
Mr. R——, a man who has very little to say, but who
makes his bad memory counterbalance his bad imagination, by taking so long to remember the name of every
thing or person he wishes to mention, that his few scraps

[1] David Hogue.

of talk extend over quite a long space of time. Listening to him is, however, an anxious duty, as one fears he may hurt his brain in his fearful efforts of reminiscence.

I have a vanity, by the way, lately got : my old Greek Testament had got out of his binding, as books and curtains and all things else manage to do, so I got it very nattily bound in calf, gilt interleaved—but that is not all. I was showing it to —— last night when she was up ; the dear creature upon the spot, accoutred as she was, plunged into a promise to make me a cover of velvet for it ; picture that—you image, you ! Am I a happy man, or am I not ?

By the general style of this epistle you will have concluded, and rightly so, that the Session is done ; but not so I. I began on Monday last to get up at six. (I tell this to all my friends, not so much because I think it any great thing, for *some* people get up even earlier, I believe, but because I wish kind of to pledge myself to continue.) I have got such a jolly lot of work done this week, that I feel quite uppish in spirit. Three hours is a vast addition to one's day.

To his Mother

2 MELVILLE STREET,
EDINBURGH, 10th May 1856.

I must not begin all my letters by apologising for their lack of length and news and interest in general, but to-night is just like the rest. I'm tired, not so much with a week's work as with the Saturday evening's play.

Marsh has achieved her wish at last, and got a watch, a gold one too. The history of it is that I put myself into the hands of Whitelaw about it (as what else can one do, for you can't judge a watch by its face), and after calling on him two or three times, he at last had one which he assured me it was a perfectly marvellous piece of good-luck to fall in with, such as if I neglected, I would repent it all my life. So I asked him the price, which was £6, 6s. Accordingly I went to a lot of shops, and by a long process of induction came to the conclusion it was the best watch in the town for the money. It is an ordinary Geneva (gold), which has been worn for one year. Mine goes excellently well.

We have had to-day the first real fine warm day of the year, a regular Assembly day, taking the fat out of country members. The Assembly is to sit in the Music Hall this year, which will be much more convenient, though perhaps not so easy to speak in. Dr. M'Crie, you know, is to be Moderator. I intend to be there as often as I was last year, that is, never. I have little enough time as it is for study, and can't afford two or three hours per evening.

I have got through another room in the Signet Library, and don't know what they intend me to do next, but I suppose I will hear to-day. I hope they won't turn me off. It would be dreadful to have to take more teaching.

I can't talk gardening to you, or I would enquire judiciously after all the proper things, but I suppose you have begun your flower harvest already.

You would scarcely know Ramsay Lodge now, looking at it from Princes Street. There is an immense mass of stone (like nothing else than a fort) raised from the bottom of the garden to the level of the walk before the kitchen windows. There is to be a broad promenade along the top, and a statue of somebody, nobody knows who.

Old Mrs. Maclaren and Sir W. Hamilton are dead since I wrote last, as you will have seen by the papers, I suppose. They will find it difficult to fill Sir William's place. I suppose Fraser of the New College and McCosh will be candidates, both first-rate men, and perhaps make better students than Sir W. did.

To the Same

2 MELVILLE STREET,
EDINBURGH, *2nd June* 1856.

The 80,000 volumes are nearly catalogued now, and I am looking forward with some anxiety to the time when I shall for the last time put down the 8vo., 12mo., folio, or whatever it may chance to be. Mr. Laing has, however, been very kind, and is, I know, satisfied (though I say it, but it is to you) ; so I hope, if there is nothing more to be done in the Library, he may get me some other kind of work.

Dick Stothert and I have now two hours a day of work together to read books that are too dry for one of us to set face to, and we both enjoy it exceedingly, and find it more productive than any other work we do.

I must repeat my usual questions. How is Katherine, and the children ? Is the garden very flourishing ? as it must be if it pays you for the work you spend on it. Have you got a minister to please you ? You will think, from my way of asking, that I don't care for an answer, but I can tell you I think of nothing oftener than that little plot before the house, and the view from the dyke at the foot of the garden, which I wish I could see again.

To his sister Mary

2 MELVILLE STREET,
EDINBURGH, *21st June* 1856.

It will be a very dumby letter that I will write to-night, for I am very tired, but still I can't help at least telling you how very much I enjoyed your letter. I 'm sure I wish this was to say that you might expect me next week, for I am very sick of teaching ; at this time of year it 's just a perpetual scold with most boys ; but there 's still another month, so ' Once more unto the breach, dear friends ' must be my motto. My two hours in the Library is as good as a holiday, and gives me a relief. It 's so jolly to sit in my cell surrounded by old tomes, with no one to tell me that I am a nuisance and a useless old hulk. It 's a perpetual meditation to sit in the hall filled with the labours of mind since the beginning of the world ; it teaches one to realise the shortness of life compared to the extent of things to be known ; and at the same time excites one to make the most of one's few years, by showing what others have done,

I have no notion when they will wish me to take a holiday, but whenever it is, I think it must be spent with you. I wished very much to accept two very kind and pressing invitations, one from Captain Fordyce, another from Mr. James Macphail, but I fear that that will be out of the question. Marsh will soon be away now, I suppose, and so will everybody. I confess I am rather hoping that they will wish me to give as much time as I can to the Library, for then I will get some work for myself done, which goes on feebly when I have to teach four hours besides.

You can tell George I am doing my best to digest Blondel's *Apologia pro Sententia Hieronymi*, and find it very tough, though productive. I have got through Lokman's *Fables* (the Arabic Primer), and expect it to be useful, though I don't appreciate its value fully, I dare say ; but the fact is, if one goes right on with the present duty, it 's pretty sure to result in some *visible* use. I hope to get either the *Koran* or *Sinbad the Sailor* now—equally useful, I presume, for philological purposes, and perhaps equally true.

So long as I am at my desk I don't much mind what

I 'm working at, if it is work ; discontent shrinks from even
the resemblance of doing duty, but you may be surprised to
hear that there are very often times (especially such as this,
on Saturday evenings, or any time when I 'm idle) when
I am forced back to a mere argumentative faith, founded
on my apologetic notebook, the main argument which
will bear any strain being the testimony of the Apostles
to the Resurrection.   But this is not the faith which is
given by the Spirit.   Then in daily life, if I pick out all
the thoughts, words, or deeds, which by charity could be
ascribed to the influence of the Spirit, are they appreci-
able at all ? and if so, then there is to be deducted so
much as an allowance to be left for the cases in which
I may have made a wrong estimate ; and then what
remains ?   I very often feel that after all the belief that
I am forgiven is a mere impression of my own mind,
and that the heart is deceitful above all things.   In short,
I am just in a state that many thousands have been in
before, and of which perhaps you yourself may have
known something.   To begin to teach others, however,
when things are in this state at home is certainly pre-
sumptuous.   Excuse this long complaint.

To his sister Andrea

2 MELVILLE STREET,
EDINBURGH, 18th July 1856.

I have been intending for long, but never got to the
scratch yet ; but you are much mistaken if you think
that my letters are so few and short because I think little
of you.   The fact is, as you may see with half an eye, it
is because I think so much of you that I never dare begin
a letter unless I have lots to say, lots of time, and lots
of spirits, three things of great rarity with me.   But I
really wish just awful that you could come in and see
me, for you know I can't expect to come and see you this

summer, and I feel in no small degree vexed about it, for I have the talking of two ordinary years to tell you— things I can't trust on paper, things that one is betrayed into by either very high or very low spirits. I do hope some scheme may turn up to further my fraternal views ; but if not we must just translate to the future tense, ' What 's did *is* did, and can't be didder.'

I had a long walk with Stewart last night, the first since about Christmas. He 's a real nice fellow, far better than he makes himself appear to be. We had a great deal of religious conversation—a very rare thing for either of us, but I enjoyed hearing him talk in that strain so much the more for its rarity. He believes (and I think justly) that he is fitted for something better than a banker's clerk (though he now holds a situation which I don't think any one of his age ever before held), and finds it just as difficult as most of his neighbours calmly to believe that he is in the hands of Him who is alone capable of combining and arranging the fortuities of life so as to result in our best spiritual condition.

But *tempus fugit*, and I find I must follow the old rogue's example, as ten o'clock A.M. is in the paulo-post-future ; at all events, I don't feel in the infinitive mood this morning, though I have been dipping in the bound-less ocean, the saltness of which accounts for the ex-uberance of wit which I feel jumping out at my finger-ends, and which I hope you will find it your duty to laugh at as from your loving brother . . .

To his Mother

2 MELVILLE STREET,
EDINBURGH, 26th *July* 1856.

I don't feel at all persuaded that it is a fortnight since I wrote, and think this should have been to some one else, but I 'll remember better the next time.   Before you get

F

this, I suppose Marcia will have seen Anick, as she has so long desired. If so, make her sit down forthwith, and tell me how all the inhabitants are, and how the place is looking, and what she thinks of it.

My teaching is all done now, and I never felt so glad. I do wish I could either pick my own pupils or support myself in some other way. But I may be very thankful I have had so much, and if I am to have two more winters of it, I suppose it 's the best thing for me, or I would get some other work. Yesterday was the Exhibition [1] day, and all the boys in their white trousers and best jackets led me to think of all the trouble you took with me, and how little I ever thought of how I should behave to you in return. I hope that, though I did not work at school, yet the Academy contact gave me, involuntarily on my part, a taste for one kind of scholarship which I would not probably have elsewhere acquired.

I wish I could come and see you all, but as I have a very great deal to do before next session, I am glad that I am obliged to stay in town, though I often wish I could get the slip from time for a week or two and work and play at the same time.

Tell Marsh and Andie that if they wish to enjoy the *summum bonum* of Anick they must go down and lie within a yard or two of the Tyne and like Montgomery's hero 'stare on the skies' (not like him, however, 'ghastly and grimly ') listening to the ripple of the water.

To his sisters Marcia and Andrea

2 MELVILLE STREET,
EDINBURGH [*8th August* 1856].

I follow the alphabetical order here, you see, as it

---

[1] The name given in the Edinburgh Academy to the annual prize-giving and speech-day at the end of the summer term.

suits likewise the chronological order of your letters.
Don't imagine there is any degree in my affection.   No !
no !   You form a lovely double star in the sphere of
my emotions, which cannot be resolved from its nebulous
form at least at the distance which calls for epistolary
correspondence.   The fact of the matter is, I have not
time to write you as units, and as I have written you so
often I doubt if I 'll be able to get up one letter, far less
two.   You complain of not knowing what I am doing,
though I told you all my most minute particulars as far
as Monday.   Does it interest you to know that I have
this morning been finishing off (*i.e.* writing an introduction to) my exegesis for Dr. Duncan, or that I am
waxing wise in Hebrew synonyms, and beginning to be
bedewed with the beauties of Burke ?   And that Dick
and I have just got through *Lokman le Sage* for the
second time, and therefore conclude that we are Arabic
scholars ?   I suppose it will be more interesting to you
to hear that Laing is now gone to Cheltenham for three
weeks, so that ' young Dods ' is *booked* for the 28th of
August at least.   I am very glad, for now that I can't
get away, it 's all serene.

The ——s were up on Monday and Tuesday, when
we took a new walk up the banks of our paternal
Leith, enjoying the weeping willows (Eh, leisht ! their
tears were filthy), and the smell of the new hay, which
I can assure you quite quenched that of the old cats in
the sluggish stream.   We walked on till we came to a
ticket, the most impudent of an impudent race, stuck
smack on the footpath, calmly giving us to know that all
trespassers would be prosecuted.   We might have been
tempted to despise the law had not a thorny hedge on
one side the water and a floury miller on the other
awed us into obedience.   Yesterday I was caught in the
gardens by a shower, and as it soon waxed into the

regular old wives and pitchforks style, I betook myself
to the arbour, and sat there for an hour and a half reading the book —— lent me, enjoying the lightning and
the comforts of the cutty.   Afterwards I went down to
37 [1] to tea and had fine times.   They were just extra-
ōrdinar' kind, both of them, till at a quarter past nine
I thought it prudent to say the ' word that must be and
hath been.'

I have not been doing the extravagant at all since I
was left sole chink-keeper.   I got a Burke on the Sublime
etc.   The coon asked for 9d. for it, but yielded to my
better judgment and pocketed with content a tilbury.
I confess, however, I am meditating a *Confession of Faith*.
To return from the steeple to the *dust*, I have bought
16s. 6d. worth of shirts, as Kirsten has reduced me to
three at the wash and none to wear.

9.30.—I have now returned from 65.   It's a very
different place Queen Street without Mima and Nell.
Mrs. H. wonders why I won't go down and take
tea every night there.   She seems to think I can
carry five lexicons and a concordance in my waistcoat
pocket, and use them while walking with her children.
You two seem to be finding Anick rather a jolly place,
and no wonder.   I just wish I was with you all.   As you
say, Andie, I am quite falling out of your acquaintance;
but I don't think that is possible.   Make the most of
each other while together, and consider yourselves more
favoured than most of your fellows, if you can enjoy
each other's society for a twelfth part of the year.

You don't say how Mamma liked her shawl, or if she
liked it any way.   Nor do you say anything about Andie's
coming to Edinburgh.   Do try and make it out like
good creatures.   I 've not been in a bad humour since
the 25th July, but if you don't make out to come back

---

[1] 37 Northumberland Street, Mr. Dallas' house.

together, or in some style get Andie in, I 'll be dumpy all winter.

I feel as if there was still something I had to tell you, and that is why I continue to write, for my time is up, and as it does not seem to be coming into my head I must just cut it short. So with all the love of a solitary to all at Anick, believe me ever your sister-and-letter-loving brother . . .

PS.—Do write soon like good creatures, or you 'll drive me from my own *dear* home to the alehouse or No. 37.

To his brother-in-law, Charles Gibson

2 ALVA STREET,
18*th May* 1857.

I have just finished a sermon for Dr. Buchanan, which has taken me longer than ' the better half of two days,' and does not contain more good things than Mr. S—— would live fatly on for two months.   The text was a grand one, ' We know that all things work together,' etc., and I thought before I began that surely on such a subject good thoughts would rise spontaneous, but I have found that it is easier for a small writer to spoil a great subject than for a great subject to enlarge a small writer.   Also I have learnt, what I might have known before, that one's thoughts don't look so well on paper, and exposed to several pairs of critical eyes, as they do floating about in the luminiferous ether and secrecy of one's own brain. Thought is a modest muse.   If you court her away from desks and books and paper, she will perhaps receive your advances ; but when you ask her to name the day and be married to prose, she sends out some coarser-minded proxy for that kind of work, and when you think you have secured a pithy, pregnant originality, you put it on paper and find it—a very fine sentiment.

Marsh and I frequently take short excursions into

the unsettled regions of morals, and generally after dis-
cussing the causes of friendship, love, etc., come to the
conclusion that 'much might be said on both sides.'
One conclusion we came to was highly satisfactory, that
while most people suffer a pleasant delusion in thinking
their own relations the pleasantest people on earth, we
are sure that ours *are* so.   (The case being altered, alters
the case.)

To his sister Marcia

2 ALVA STREET,
Nearly August [1857].

[Dr. Duncan] is getting fonder of us every day, and
seems inclined to teach us all the languages living, dead,
buried, and a few that might be but are not yet ; and
keeps ominously before us a book printed in seventy-two
languages, and called *The Napoleon Polyglot,* towards
which he every now and then casts a loving grin, as much
as to say, How I wish I had lived at the time of Babel,
or been interpreter at the court of Shem.   You can't
blame me for being wordy when Dr. Duncan is the theme.

To Miss ' Mima' Hogue and his sister Marcia

ALL AVAY STREET,
EDINBURGH, 19*th August* 1857.

No letters since I wrote,
Feeling ever more remote,
I entreat you, twinhood, come
To your twice-bereaved home.

Now no Nelly eats my cresses,
No Mima shakes her raven
  tresses,
Empty stand the widowed chairs,
All is dark without the fairs.*

* A learned annotator (who did not always approve of this poet)
remarks that here there is plainly an innuendo to the effect that, while
all is dark without the fair, all is light within, a mere paraphrase of the
sentiment ' changeful giddy woman.'   It need scarcely be said that the
words may be differently understood.

My dear and gentle Sisterhood,—Don't be alarmed at the paper. It's a bit that's been lying for the last few centuries saying, ' What will he do with it ? '[1] and tempting me to write a novel on the subject, but as I have been forestalled in that as well as in some of my other designs, such as writing *Paradise Lost* and inventing the Steam Engine, I have just to send my old friend here into the world without a thereby hanging tale ; but as I felt sorry for the poor thing, knowing the said world is but a cold and hard-hearted stepmother, I determined to insure for it as much kindness as lay in my power by sending it to your protection. That's the reason of the paper. And the reason of my writing is that I feel a dissolving ecstasy in the air that whispers ' A letter, my boy, a nice long letter is wafted towards you, and by to-morrow morning will be seasoning your parritch with the cream of human kindness.' If it does not come, I can tell you you won't get a bit of this, so you know what you lose.

I don't know as I have anything to tell you, except that I am in very good spirits, and my spirits in a very good bottle. If you desire to know my manner of life, you can gratify yourselves when you come back, for I 've begun a diary. But, lest you die of hope deferred, I send you an extract to keep you up :—

> ' 7-8 Hebrew, Deut. xii., with LXX. After break-
> fast Hagenbach, Pelagian points, and Turrettin,
> vi. 6, ix. 7, x. 2. Then Murray at Portobello.
> DINNER. After dinner Gibbon, cap. vii. (Dio-
> cletian and colleagues).'

And so on. Highly interesting. My to-day begins thus : ' SLEPT IN.' The reason of that being that I was dissipating last night. I was out at the Robertsons' to

---

[1] Bulwer-Lytton's novel of that name was appearing in *Blackwood's Magazine* at the time.

meet two Sardinians, one of whom said he did not know English, and as he could not understand my French I concluded he had been born nowhere and knew no language. But when he gave me a long thing like a piece of tarry rope, and told me to smoke it, we got to understand each other—some—and walked about under a lovely sky till near the witching hour. The Robertsons were really very kind, and asked for all of you and every bit of you each most particularly.

Make George write, will you, and tell me what he is working at, or rather what he was working at, for I suppose he has ere this discovered that your company has asserted a rightful superiority to all work. Is he offended at me ? If so, tell him (in the language of *The Times*, 2nd column) : ' Write at once and send Fairbairn (with you) and all will be forgiven,'—forgotten too, he perhaps thinks, so far as returning books is concerned. I don't know how better to prove my love for him than by telling him again to read Sophocles. Would not I have been proud to pound the ink or forge the pens that wrote those plays. I wish I had some pupil that would make me do them more thoroughly. This is all about myself, as usual.

There has been a letter from Peg.[1] She has been drinking beer in London *trans lignum,* in which case I should think it is time Mrs. Laing took in (and kept in) a peg.

I 'll leave a bit here in case your letter has any questions to answer. So good-night to you both, as Curran said to the eighteen tailors.

Cunningham almost certainly, and Dick perhaps, is going to Germany this winter.

οἴμοι, δύσμορος, ποῖ τραπῶμαι ;
φεῦ, φεῦ, τί δράσω, δύσμορος ;
Je ne sais pas in the world.

---

[1] Miss Hogue.

To his brother-in-law, Charles Gibson

2 ALVA STREET,
EDINBURGH, 21*st August* 1857.

Had I been carried away by the rapture of the moment
and answered your letter as soon as I read it, I am sure
I would have given utterance to such expressions of
delight as would have made you conclude me drunk or
daft. You will *now*, too, more readily believe me because
I can, after repeated perusal, still say that it was a letter
(I mean in the Maclaren sense of the indefinite article).[1]
I won't try to tell you of all the delicate emotions it
raised in my savage soul, nor how it shed brightness
over my widowed condition, nor how I pitched into
my work after reading it with ' *re*doubled vengeance,' nor
how I sought for adjectives to apply to it, nor how I found
none worthy, and anon adapted to it your own words and
found satisfaction alone in styling it ' Yours, ay, emphatically yours.'

I wish I was out with you now ; everything I see
makes me long to be with you, and how I envy those
Irishmen I see tripping it on the light fantastic down
the London Road, or disposed in illigant groups at the
N.B. Station. To go to the Dean Bridge and see the
bawrley hervest is too much for me, though in certain
moods I find a kind of gladness in the torture, and go
and smoke away my feelings Eastwards. If all 's well
I am going to ask away next month, and I think I 'll get
a fortnight at all events. I must go to Anick a week,
you know, so I hope to be a week with you in the middle
or towards the end of next month. No schoolboy ever
looked forward with half the joy I now do. I think I
calc'lated my moments as much as most boys, but never
was I so eager to see you all.

[1] Mr. Maclaren the publisher was in the habit of using such expressions of eulogy as ' That was a man ! ' etc.

Many thanks for the reminiscences of my blue-jacket days.   Were I to write what I believe about the good you have done me, and what I would have grown up without your influence, your modesty would prevent you from believing the one half, and your affection would blind you to the truth of the other.   Of course you must feel that you are the only person who was anything like a father to my boyhood (the Dunse fellow wasn't such a dunse after all [1]), but if I were to go into particulars it would seem hypocritical conceit.   However, if ever I do anything well, consider that therein I am showing my gratitude to you.   I am not in a sentimental mood to-night, indeed I am scarcely up to my ordinary plain prose of feeling, or I might enlarge on this, but I hope we 'll soon be able to talk everything over more at our leisure.

Tell both Anne and Andie that I love them.   And that 's not nothing you may assure them on the word of a young lady whom I heard the other evening assert confidently that ' it is a very pleasant thing to be loved.'   I believe you, my boy.   How happy you must feel, you old creature, with that of a whole family, vigorously supplemented by the love of your most affectionate brother,

Write, write to   MARCUS DODS   for

he

is

lonely.

To his sister Mary

2 ALVA STREET,
EDINBURGH, 31st October 1857.

As Marsh wishes me to write to Mamma, and as I am in your debt, two very extraordinary circumstances, there seems to be a call upon me for something extra also ;   and therefore I address myself to a letter, and

[1] A man in Dunse took the pair for father and son.

intend to address the letter to you. And first I must
say that you are a brick for writing me such a nice long
letter, which, joined to two exquisite ones from Charles,
make me look upon this week as a kind of embodiment
of the Cowperian element in human life. I wish I could
write you a decent answer, that you might know how
nice it is to get letters from those you love, but after all,
the pleasure of writing such a letter as yours must have
been as great as that of receiving one from any other
person. Be persuaded to continue, and as you have
learned, enjoy ' the luxury of doing good.' You must
not be offended if this turn out either cold or brief, for
being on the brink of a clean sh–rt for dinner at the
Hogues', I feel much as a youth aiming his first plunge
in the sea on a March morning. Maggie has come home
from London, and added her kind, maternal grace to the
attractions of Tusculum. She has also added to my
stock of possessions something almost as delicious and
equally ætherial, viz. a dozen cigars, A1 as a smack of
London. Would that you were here to enjoy them
with me. Maggie brought spoils from the banks of
Thames, as if she were returning from the sack of Delhi ;
something for everybody and herself for all.

Of work I can say little, for the work I have been at
is chiefly making entries in note-books, committing to
memory (most faithless of trustees) bits of the Confession
of Faith, finishing my paper to the Exegetical,[1] and so
on. Of Hebrew I have more hope now than I have ever
had, and begin to hope, lovyerlike, that wooing I shall
at length gain possession of some of those *deliciæ* reserved
for those who add knowledge to knowledge. But when
I consider the time that I must be a hanger-on or dangler
before I can claim intimacy with the Hebrew muse, the
value of the reward alone keeps me from despair. I

[1] A New College Society.

can now see the merits of the language, and these are sufficiently attractive to overcome very great difficulties in acquirement.

You may be sure I feel, perhaps more deeply than you would desire, that this is my last session : my feelings on this subject, however, being, I suppose, much what you can fancy arise in the breast of any fourth-year's student, I will not spoil your imaginations by endeavouring to depict them. One thing only I may tell you, that very often there comes back upon me what Stewart said when I told him first I was going to study for the Church : ' Oh, man, you 're not good enough ' ; and though I don't think there should be much respect shown to the wishes of those who desire angels and not men to minister to them, it is but fair to expect that those who take upon them to be the teachers and ensamples of a number of their fellows, should be such as take good heed to themselves and to the doctrine.

Does George still keep salt-water menageries ? Davie's is increasing vastly. He has perch and loach and beetles and whales, and altogether quite a wonderful collection. He tends them as if they were the present resting-places of the souls of his grandmother and her progenitors, and watches them with a minuteness of observation that must have rendered him a capable author of a work on the habits of domestic fish, such (book, not fish) as his country would not willingly let die. But I am only wasting ink, so with warmest love to all of you here I sit . . .

To his brother-in-law and sister, George and Mary

2 ALVA STREET,
9th April 1858.

As I cannot accomplish a letter to you severally, I take advantage of circumstances, and make a matrimonial affair of it ; and each of you will consider that if the letter is pleasing in no other respect, yet it is in this, that it is the property of your partner.

My four years of the Hall are now past, and have irrevocably taken with them much I wish a thousand times to recall.   I am just *now* beginning to see what use I should have made of these years, and cannot but fear that when I have done with this life I shall have the same bitterness of retrospect.   But I do not wish to (nor can I) believe this, for I think I have already learnt where my error lies, and though it is yet to be rooted out, it is always something to know where to begin ; and believing that this knowledge has been given me for the purpose of taking steps in the work of eradication, I find hope in the thought that I will also be aided to the end.   I need not make any morbid revelations to you who know me sufficiently to account for any remorse I feel.   As to the work I am now nearing, I sometimes feel as if it was madness in me to go on, and other times I feel as if I could do as well as another : the mean of being a humble fellow-worker with the Holy Spirit is yet a condition *to be* attained.

I don't know if I told you that Sir Geo. Home shortly after his marriage sent me £5, with part of which I got Cramer's *Catenae Patrum Graecorum*, 8 vols. 8vo, Oxonii, and Calvin on the New Testament, your edition.   Have you any vacant parishes about you for a poor cove ?

To his sister Marcia

2 ALVA STREET,
EDINBURGH, 28th July 1858.

I got your letter a little ago, and I begin to answer it, though I dare say, after all, there 's only one question in it.   I did not get on at Abington well ; the people did not seem to care to attend, except one or two, and then when I did succeed in getting one or two to listen, they looked with such a critical, doubtful, unreceptive air that put me out in no small degree. However, I made shift to scrabble on my way. I lodged in the post-office, in a small, clean, comfortable room. The cream there is not 4s. a pint, and the mutton was just plucked from its native hills opposite, and as I was pretty hungry when dinner came in (at the stage when hunger becomes vocal and begins to moan and growl), I did the mutton justice.

I had the usual railway company : the two young men going back brown to their work in the city ; pater-familias with a brown straw hat and no end of gold chain ; two suspicious-looking characters and a nondescript or two ; also the newly married couple with bags and baskets as if they were already a family ; the young mother with her first sucking man, in this instance a revolting little lump of carnality whom I tried to redeem from a state of drunken stupidity, and at last by a *magnum opus* of a wink in the Shygo-growler style succeeded in drawing forth an intimation of mind expressed in a grimace performed by toes clad in green worsted.

Dr. M. is a nice old man like a thin Dr. Reid. He gave a red lotion and a box of ointment, and took 4s., and told me to call again if that did no good, which I thought did not sound encouraging. Unfortunately, when I saw him my eye was better than it had been for weeks, so very likely he would not think it bad. However, he has succeeded in making it much worse, and no doubt by the time I have finished the bottle and go back, I will be an interesting case.

I had a splendid walk with Dave last night, down to Granton, along to Cramond, and so home—b-e-a-u-tiful.

I went in with him to tea. Flisk is the way to spell the place, and Cupar-Fife is the post town ; I suppose, if you have a great desire to be aristocratic, you may indulge in Fliscque. Write soon at any rate.

To the Same

F.C. MANSE, FLISK,
CUPAR-FIFE [*4th August* 1858].

I thought, when I spoke of setting out to my hermitage at Flisk, that there was a mild joke in it, that it was a kind of professional way of saying that I was for a short season to be bereft of you and 65 and the other tops of society ; but I find that I was not a great monarch before I retired, so on looking behind me I find no train but a train of reflections and reminiscences only, for never was hermit more hermetically sealed up (there 's a joke there, go back and find it—stoopid). Do what I will I can't hear a noise but the ticking of the clock, and the boom of the wild bee, and the twitter of the swallows. When I blow my nose the startled rooms send back a groan, and when I try to vamp up a noise of a more pleasing description, I feel as if I were profaning the august stillness of nature's temple. Not a breath of wind, not a patter of rain, not a laugh of boy, nor shriek of girl, have I heard since I came here. The only sound that I have heard that really broke silence was a gunshot, and the hills, seeming glad to have found the rarity, and determined to make the most of it, fondled it and gave it from one to another till it died away in their caresses. When I went out to the back field to try if I could not see at least in the distance something like motion, the cattle came all round me as I lay, and sniffed at the discovery with the earnestness of those who have but one chance in a lifetime of taking stock of a similar species. I hear that I am only two miles from the Tay, so I am going to explore. It is a pretty place here, and an excellent manse, well built, well furnished and well provisioned, and I begin to think that a F.C. minister is a very comfortably living creature, that is if he has a commodious and pretty house, a rich wife, a thriving flock, and a contented spirit.

I made but a poor beginning yesterday so far as my own comfort goes. I let the people out half an hour too soon, at which they were far from being pleased. This was mainly owing to a rapidity of speech produced by a foolish flurry. I think I would get over this soon were I once settled and knew the people, but meanwhile it is a form of misery hard to bear, which makes me seriously and often consider whether it would not be better to rest content with teaching as my calling, and leave the sublimer occupation for those who are better qualified. I am not at all sure that the state I am in is just what every one who enters the office passes through. On the contrary, one reads of men who at once declare freely and with power the word of God. However, patience is the great Œdipus that every Sphinx opens up to. The present is not complete without the future, so for the future I wait, and in the present will try to find, not comfort and satisfaction, but work and contentment.

The two elders are both farmers. One of them, asking me to come and see him, told me he lived ' just over the hill ' ; and when I asked the other his place of abode, ' Oh, just over the hill.' I find, however, they are about two hours' walk separate.

PART II
1858-1864

PART II

1858—1864

(Age 24—30)

YEARS OF PROBATIONERSHIP

To his sister Marcia

44 BLENHEIM STREET,
NEWCASTLE-ON-TYNE, 18*th November* [1858].

My always delicious and well-beloved, and now far more so than ever, my dearest Marcia, however I thought it was all a joke my coming to this chimney, it looks very like a reality now, and I own a touch of sadness made itself felt as I unpacked my portmanteau a few minutes ago.

My lodgings here consist of a small sitting-room and smaller bedroom in a little brick house, one of a series of little dingy brick houses, which series is one of a grand collection of little dingy brick houses, the name whereof is Newcastle. Not yet having been in bed, I don't know what there may be there, but having had tea I can testify that it was very well, though you may tell Bobby there were no white ' cyakes.' The Misses Stoker are old ladies who were once in better circumstances, and of course I need not tell you that one of them is sickly (poorly), and needs to be looked after ; the other is active, and looks after her and everything else. This seems to be the way of the house. Eight shillings a week is what

I am to pay, and I dare say I shall be sufficiently comfortable. Mr. Miller was here for a long time this afternoon, and I am to have a walk with him to-morrow. There is not gas in this house, which is a bore.

This is, as you see, a miscellaneous letter, but I will write you more anon. Of course, I occasionally feel very queer when I feel separated from you all, unable to speak to any of you, but if I thought I was to be of any use here I would not for a moment dream of being dull. Indeed, at rare times I feel content to take this world altogether as a time of work, and look to another for enjoyment, and if only I thought I could work to purpose, this feeling might become predominant, but experience of myself has not made me sanguine.

To his Mother

44 BLENHEIM STREET,
NEWCASTLE, 22nd November 1858.

I arrived here all safely and sadly, and am pretty comfortably set down with two old ladies who are very attentive and kind. Mr. Miller, too, is very friendly ; but blood, as Tom is fond of telling people, is stronger than water, and I feel very considerably from home. Were I on some business that needed only my hands I would be in good spirits enough, but I am eaten up by an anxiety which had I foreseen I think I would have chosen some lighter profession. I hope this will wear off, and that when I make some friends here, I will be able to live in greater peace ; but my heart travels enviously from Alva Street to West Mains, and will not settle contentedly in No. 44 Blenheim Street. Those two days I spent with you were in many ways very delightful, and if possible, I must try and get back at Christmas, though I fear that will not be, as Mr. M. is not by any means robust. I preached twice yesterday, and will have to do so next Sunday too.

I need not say how continually you are all before me at your several occupations, from carpets upwards. I would just bathe and luxuriate in a circle of friends just now, and don't know whether to wish the bitterness of solitude away, or to wish it to remain till I can suddenly drown it in some wished-for company. This is, indeed, our life of work, and at times I feel as if I would be content to have it so if I could do something, and at last win a rest for which I had been duly prepared.

To his sister Marcia

44 BLENHEIM STREET,
SMOKEBOX, *Life*, *6th Day*
[*23rd November* 1858].

MY INEXPRESSIBLY DELICIOUS MARSH,—To picture my feelings at the receipt of your letter may be the aspiration of future men of genius, but is altogether beyond my ambition. The very thought that I still have it in my left tail pocket beside the *Olneys*, and can at any moment summon it thence, makes my old seated heart knock at my ribs and my sluggish blood flow faster. It came, however, to renew pain in some measure, for now that I hope it is past, I may tell you that I have been in a terrible way since I came here. Dejection, depression, prostration, these words express it not, but I now know what it means to be *sick at heart*, body and mind together pained and mutually lacerating one another. A bitter past, a dumb, mute, blank present, and a blind, black future meeting at once are not good company for any one, and nearly made me fly from them anywhere. I cannot, even if I wished, analyse my feelings, and say precisely where or what was my disease, but I feel that it all resolves itself into the old Calvinistic

affair of the natural man.   To be serious, I wished to
find what I had in me, and I came here with some hope
to be successful in my search, and I have been.   I have
discovered within myself a degree of dependence on the
things of this life I had little idea of.   It 's one thing
to profess to be a citizen of heaven, and another to be
bereft of everything on earth, or to feel that you must be
clear and loose from everything on earth.   As you may
imagine, I 've read almost all Henry Martyn, where, as
you say, there is much for me—more than ever.   Indeed,
much of it I have read and re-read, and diffused through
me, but I believe it has helped to sink me.   To see him
able to give up all, and to feel myself clutching at the
merest baubles, is a painful humiliation.   The bit you
notice I had marked and noted.   I could excuse myself
in some measure if my earthliness was after his sort.

I do not wonder that I feel pained when the thought
comes across me that during all this weary life I may see
you only now and then.   But if you knew me you would
not wonder that I am often dull and sometimes on the
verge of enduring melancholy.   If you knew my utter
unfitness for my work, you would wonder at my choice of
a profession, and I would wonder at it myself if I did not
know the darkness of the views and the obliquity of aim with
which I entered it.   All this has come up on me just now,
for here I am before a vast evil, an evil that cries out for
remedy, that exposes its sores, and cuts you to the heart
with pity.   And what can I do, I, who have not even got
the length of self-forgetfulness ?   I could do something,
and I hope I shall do something, when I learn to be the
servant of Christ.   But I feel it a fearful thing to be at
once set down before this vast work to be done for Him,
and at the same time have my heart and all my affections continually asserting themselves, and by their
refusal to let go their objects letting me know how I am

scarcely at all His servant.   It is indeed a life of self-
denial this, and I feel as if now for the first time I had
even a dim view of what it is to be not one's own, to me
a heart-rending lesson, a long and bitter lesson, one I
would gladly exchange for fasting, or scourging, or what
asceticism you will.   Let me keep my own will, let me
be my own, aim at my own idea of holiness, aid myself
with my own props, and I would do most things.   But
this is the hard thing to learn, that in *everything*, from
this moment for ever, I am not only not to get my own
will, but I am to desire not to get my own will, to will
to be controlled by another wholly and unceasingly.
This has to me at times all the pain of dissolution.   It
is indeed a dying to this world.

> ' Death ends indeed the cares of life,
>   Yet shudders life when death comes near,
> And such the fond heart's death-like strife
> When first the loved one does appear.
> For, where true love is wakened, dies
> The tyrant *self*, that despot dark.
> Rejoice then that in death he lies,
> And breathe morn's free air, with the lark.'

Were love not the executioner, indeed, he would never
die, and he is a tyrant of a thousand lives.   But I must
say no more of him, and ask your pardon for sending you
all this.   Only I wished to trace my feelings, and no one
but you would I dare to trace them to, and so it has
come to pass, tumultuously, I dare say.

Maggie's hymn was most excellent, winning the inmost
feelings.   Mima's text preached me a sermon.   What
would I be without you all ?   If ever I do anything the
reward will be yours.   Separation is not only robbed
of all sting by Christian hope, but itself strengthens the
hope that robs it.   What a thought, that we all, who
love each other's presence so well, shall when all is done

meet, better able to love, and never to part ! What a
balance, the joy of eternity to the trouble of time ! It
is not much that is required of us, after all. At the
most, pack a few years as you may, they are rapidly
going. How wretched then it will seem to have bargained
for self, to have saved self, to have pleased self.

But I must tell you some of my news. I now know
some of the people and like them. I have also an acquaintance who has got his thigh broken in two places,
and has lain on his back for 13 weeks without peace of
mind or body. I found six of his mates-on-the-line up
in his room shifting him—touching enough to see the
burly, strong, work-begrimed men helping the poor
feeble fellow that had so lately been one of them. I am
of course going to circulate *Lights for the Line* among
them. There are some others of whom I might tell you
if we had a fireside instead of 120 miles to talk across.
I like the town notwithstanding the dirt and smoke and
noise, and though I fear I won't have much time for study,
I will have lots of contact with people.

I had the prayer-meeting to-night, and one of the
district ones to-morrow, and two services again next
Sunday, and school between. Mr. Miller had me at tea
last night, when I made great friends with the girls, one
three, other four years. At their request I made myself
a bear, and extracted an eye from the brain of one of
their dolls ; proofs of my ability to fill the see of Durham,
if they had the appointment. They are nice little
beings. The Misses Stoker are very good to me. I
dare not cough, for they instantly charge me with having
a cold and threaten gruel. They bring in my night-shirt
and hang it before the fire nightly, and I get on nicely.
Only this desirable residence of theirs has many of the
disadvantages of a country house with all the smoke of
town. It is like Gilmore Place, the street. Mr. Miller

evidently expects me to stay some considerable time, as he has been taking me to visit a lot of the people, and so on. It's now to-morrow morning and I must work, though I have hosts more to say.

I can scarcely get up any sympathy for you, do you know ? You have work you can most thoroughly overtake, and you have Queen Street. Of course you have trials, and after all, yes, I do feel for you, when I consider you. But while our better minds entirely adopt and welcome this system of things, how thankful we should be for everything. How triumphantly should we pass through life if we only knew this, that we are saved sinners.

If Bobby can get my skates exchanged for ones that would fit him, he may take them as a Xmas present. He should get a good pair and not be done. I don't want him to be plaguing Charles just now. If he does so, he is to consider the gift as half (one skate) from Andie, as she gave me mine.

I suppose I may send my love to the three *little* M——s, if not to ——, and whole boilers full to Queen Street, hot as Midsummer, fresh as Spring, and rich and ripe as Autumn, and by no means nor in any respect whatever resembling Winter. Now I must stop, really. Be grateful to the Hogues for me. I feel Dave's influence here, and make up to all sorts of chance people in his fashion and enjoy them. What a civil world it is so long as you don't tread on its corns or call it bad names ! Now good-bye, though to leave you is a rending of heart to . . .

To the Same

44 BLENHEIM STREET,
NEWCASTLE, 2nd December 1858.

MY DEAREST AND EVER DEARER MARSH,—Henceforth I renounce all attempts to express my gratitude to you

for your letters.   I felt tempted when I had read your
last just to come right away and hug you.   It was
full of lies, but, as saith my Lord Bacon, the mixture
of a lie doth ever add pleasure.   And do please have
a headache next Saturday that you may send me just
such another.   I had one from Charles this morning,
which knits me to him as I never was knit before, full of
the purest affection and encouragement.   I have not
been able to write to Dave this week, and must indeed
curtail this, the only letter I 've got written, as I have
a very great deal to do here, and my time greatly cut up.
Mr. Miller, you know, takes me three or four hours a
day visiting in the most unsatisfactory manner—gossip—
and you may fancy me going groaning along and thinking of lots of sick people I might be visiting to some
purpose.   But those he takes me to are *without exception*
kind (Mr. Marshall, the editor of *The Express*, sends me
his paper daily), and were we seeing them for any end or
purpose there would be very great pleasure.   But when
there is no profit can there be pleasure ?

Yesterday I had to go to the funeral of the man I told
you of.   Before he died I had read out of Peg's *Olney*,
' In evil long,' and had a good deal of talk with him
about it, but when one finds it so hard to keep from
self deception, to judge of others is what we dare scarcely
venture on.   But to think of the altogether inconceivable
difference of the two states, one or other of which he is
now in, and to be in for ever, makes one feel the necessity
of timely urgency in warning and winning men to think.
When one comes face to face with these things, what a
secondary and almost contemptible thing learning, etc.,
seems.   I never saw a human being in such a state as his
wife was in, screaming so that I heard her before I got
to the house, and so out of possession of herself that I
never felt more the need of some spirit of almighty

influence to persuade and control the mind. If I see
many scenes like that I 'll soon be old.

I 'm tempted, you see, to tell you of lots of people you
can't be interested in, for there is no one here you know
except me, and they are the complement of me. I wish
I had an old friend or two, and still I feel it rather dismal
when I prowl out at dusk (I 've got into a habit of so
doing, as if I were going to meet you) and see the comfortable fellows going *home* after their work, and the
doors shutting with a fine, satisfactory, inclusive bang, and
yet letting fancy in to see his Annies and Marys clutching
his legs, and so on. This is not the dungeon or the
stake, but neither is it altogether what the flesh ($\sigma\acute{\alpha}\rho\xi$)
would desire. However, I am often *very* happy, and
always contented, and you are not so good at an
impression as Mim if you thought I was anything else.
I told you all my mind in my last letter, partly for the
reason I gave, and partly because if you are not here to
keep me from being sometimes a little down, I think
it 's but fair you should help me up again, and your
letter certainly did so.

The names I go by here vary with the rank of the
namer. ' Wer young meän ' (last a dissyllable), ' The
Assestent,' or ' Mr. Miller's curate.' Mr. Miller calls me
' Dods ' (sometimes Mr.), never ' Young Dods,' however,
as he thought I was 30 to say the least of it. Misses
Stoker are very kind, and I am quite as comfortable as
' wer young myan ' need be. I don't dislike the town
by any means, there is much to love in it and much to
do. All that was said of its ungodliness was, I fear,
too true.

Give all my usual loves, as I feel no abatement, but
rather find my affections to be of the india-rubber order,
so that the further I am from you the more tightly I feel
bound to you. And don't be so awful nice to one another

on Saturday nights. I am now finding how true it is that you may not poke a man's fire till you 've known him seven years. For if that be too long a time for introduction, certainly it is only the warm feelings of a *very intimate* acquaintance one may freely stir up and refresh oneself at.

Now I must stop, for I have to rush out and see a poor fellow lying with consumption, a cabman, age 21, and it 's already getting dark.

I am almost ashamed to ask you to write me another rouser in answer to this, but I really am your ever more affectionate . . .

To the Same

44 BLENHEIM STREET,
NEWCASTLE, TUESDAY [*4th December* 1858].

This is a business letter, and not a reply to the exquisite packet of this morning.

I wish just to say that it seems impossible for me to get away just now. Mr. Miller would, I know, be anxious, especially as neither he nor I have been altogether up to the mark of medical certificates lately. I believe it 's the anxiety here that won't let me fatten and thrive, and I hope, when I get used to seeing and hearing and acting in the right way (if one ever can), I will be better. Meanwhile I know Mr. Miller would make up his mind I was going away never to come back, if I left town. Just this morning he told me the office-bearers want me to stay for three months. He urged them to name a longer period, he says, but they would not venture beyond their funds. He has given me some useful hints, or advice rather, about preaching.

Don't be telling Mamma that I am not well, nor anything about the sad side of this place, for she has a bad enough idea of it already. I tell you all my troubles, though I feel I am laying open my weakness, because that is *one* of the heap of advantages of true love (and of old friends ever new), that it is constant even when faults are in sight. (This is what makes me so trustful in Peg. She knows me, I feel, better than most do, and yet likes me better than most do.) The sublime of this, of course, as Foster would say, is in the love of God to man.

I do rather pity my poor books, but you and Peg will be tender. Handle them as if you were lancing my eye. Those that are in the lowest shelf of the room press keep at the top of something, as they are most likely to be needed, not the folios, but Turrettin and the octavos. Don't let Gesenius's grammar, a square flat book, that lies on Liddell and Scott, go deep.

To the Same

44 BLENHEIM STREET,
[? *9th December* 1858].

MY MOST INCOMPARABLE MARSH,—I have an awful lot of things to tell you, but they 're all fighting which to be first, and so I don't know where to begin ; and time runs on, as it 's past ten already and tomorrow another visiting day, eheu! By the way, you must have misconstrued some part of my last letter, or I must have been even more than usually given to lying, if I said the people were uninteresting. The visits I might say, but that very much just because the people are interesting, and I feel they could be so nice did one know them really, that it makes it a wretched affair to be merely introduced and *hope* to see more of them, and talk for a few minutes of things you feel they care as little about as you. I think the congregation rather a model affair altogether (assistant included, of course). A great mass of them are visibly in earnest, and the elders doing their work thoroughly, visiting and praying with the sick, according to the

apostle ; and in church they could not be more attentive ; upturned faces is the prospect when the eye rises,
and all as kind as if they had doodled me when I was in
petticoats. I have been at tea at one or two of them,
once at the Railway Station! But don't think I am
dissipated, for the last time I was out to tea I was home
at 5.10—at ten minutes past five, not in the morning,
observe, but in the afternoon, and it was not yesterday's
tea, mind, but to-day's really, the ' tey cyakes ' still hot.
The Blandford St. district is the most discouraging and
flesh-trying part of my work. To-day a woman told
me she had no time to speak to me. She had a sick
friend in the next room she must go and see, and when
I asked as engagingly as I could if I might see the sick,
' No, it wasn't convenient '—and such. The young men
of the congregation keep well together. They have a
debating society, and many of them teach in the Sabbath-
school, which is large, and I am going to have a class
of them on Sunday mornings for Bible, and another of
boiler boys, or lads rather, who would not condescend
to a Sabbath-school.

But think of it, Tom was in on Monday for some hours,
very jolly, and he bought me a Paraffin lamp (right
reading is ' Varra fine,' or, according to the etymology,
Paraphaen, *i.e.* more brilliant than common), as I said
I was going to get one. The candle is dismal, and flickers
so, my eye was getting queer. I need not tell you Tom
was grumbling, as I have told you he was in town ; but
by the bye, you should have seen the old ladies and the
lamp. Fear of fire is their hobby, a kind of pyrophobia ;
that 's why they don't have gas, afraid of a blow up.
And when I was pulling the cork out of the flask of oil
they retired to the other side of the room, evidently
believing it to be a concoction of bottled explosions
warranted to go off whenever the cork was out. Had

they known it, they would have more justly dreaded me,
for, as you may guess, I was strained to the last button ;
one absurdity more, and I 'd have gone off with a terrible
bang.

I wait with great excitement the account of your
decision. I have ceased to try and decide what you
should do, for each letter you seem to be on some
different tack. I sympathise with your indecision, and
wish I could help you ; indeed I can't get off feeling as
if I would find my name, or should find my name,
stuck up at the poor's-house gate in the list of men
who have deserted their unprotected females. But you
have your two M.'s to advise you, ' trusty and well
beloved,' and no mistake.

I must tell you of a touching (and it struck me peculiarly Northumbrian) saying I heard the other day
from a poor old woman who wished her paralytic husband
to be allowed a seat near the pulpit on the Communion
Sunday, as he is deaf and does not go to church, and is,
indeed, a Deist (very common in Blandford), but she
thought seeing the tables covered might do him good.
' For eh ! ' she said in a faltering voice, almost in tears,
' it is a lovely sight.' Poor body, I could have cried
myself to think of all she has probably passed through
for that man, praying, as she said, night and morning
for him, and he now old and almost out of hail with his
infirmities.

I preached to-night in preparation the sermon I told
you I was writing, and Mr. Miller thought it ' very
precious.'   There was none of Archer Butler in it, for
though the text was the same the subjects are not.
My subject was the *necessity*, from the very nature of
things, of pain in following Christ. I give you Mr. Miller's
opinion, because I was heartily glad he was satisfied, and
because the expression reveals the man.

I am to be at Falstone on Sunday for Mr. Stewart, who is coming to assist. Tom is going to drive me up. When kindness has to be demonstrated in *deeds*, Tom is a dab.

The little Millers are very nice, especially one, a fat little bundle that skirls and never tires (neuter verb, remember) being tossed up to the ceiling. Now I must really stop. I need not go into my mental states, or I will become too subjective in my preaching. I am the same stupid, selfish old being I ever was, skipping from self-complacency to despondency. At the same time, I thankfully own Newcastle has done me good many ways. Rainy, as you say, is worth thinking of, and often I do. Twelve strikes.

I have got two beautiful illuminated scrolls (I think for the West Mains nursery)—6d. at the *Church's* Repository. People here, as you know, speak of one '*going to church*' as quite another affair from going to your John Knox's, or your meeting-houses, or your dissenting chapels of any kind.

Now this is becoming wicked, and I must go work. I feel very tenderly towards Mrs. Hogue, but of course you need not tell her that; and I am frequently reminded of Mr. Hogue when I hear the organ of the chapel opposite begin to boom, or when I discovered Arminianism in a tract I was just going to give away—a *Kelso* tract, too—but (don't tell Mrs. Hogue or Frank [1]) I am going to give it away notwithstanding.

To his sister Mary

44 BLENHEIM STREET,
NEWCASTLE, 16*th December* 1858.

I should have answered your most refreshing letter with more fraternal haste, but I find I am other things

[1] The Rev. Francis Gillies, minister of St. Stephen's Free Church, Edinburgh.

AGE 24] YEARS OF PROBATIONERSHIP 113

than a brother here, and when I sit down to write a letter the visions of sick people that should be visited and the skeletons of sermons that want their leanness clothed skip before me and shout to me to be brief. Your picture of home was delicious, and came to my lonely old heart like Hook's Elixir of Life, or I suspect, if the gentleman will pardon me, with a much more reviving efficacy. You *are* a sister, and so is Marsh, and so are they all, all sisters. George may say what he likes, but I have him there ; he can't be your brother, and I am ; and since I have been sent away here among strangers, I have been forced to seek consolation in hope, and dwell with unspeakable complacency on the thought that life is short, and that in a very few years we shall all be gathered together with our love deepened and un-interrupted. I am, however, getting a great number of acquaintances here, as the congregation is large, and besides them I have some men who, according to the Newcastle custom, go to no church. I have a great deal to do, for though Mr. Miller takes the forenoon now, I have a Wednesday prayer-meeting, and classes, and hosts of visiting, and then all around on every side un-claimed ground where one might labour many lifetimes. I feel as if I were rooting here, though, of course, there is little *reason* to suppose I will be a permanency.

I have just written one thing since I came here that I think you would care for ; it was in preparation for the Communion, on Luke ix. 23 : the self-denial I made the formal self-renunciation which is the fundamental trans-action of a man with Christ, as well as the habitual subduing of the will to the higher will of God. Mr. Miller liked it and ' Stephen ' best of what I have done. I feel a very great helplessness being set to subdue the devil and destroy his works with 27 pages of sermon a week. But I sometimes get hold of the belief that it has been

H

appointed so, and that the foolishness of preaching may be the wisdom of God.   I feel most hope when a man is prepared by sickness to hear the truth.   There are some strange characters here—clever fellows utterly regardless of religion, and hosts of the most debased beings you can well fancy to be men.   It's a gross, material, fleshly place.   The πνεῦμα has the worst of it here with the σάρξ.

Give George my love, and tell him I now sympathise with his years of solitude, and scarcely grudge him your company.   If I knew any *femme* who would be willing to share a very small lodging in Newcastle, and the sorrows of a stupid and desponding person, there is no saying that I might not follow his example, but as such females are not common occurrences, there seems no fear of that at present.   Ask him if he ever wished himself a handicraftsman, a writer of deeds, or even a carver of bacon or leather, or something that had no more responsibility or risk than a dexterous manipulation could prevent, or the expenditure of a few coppers cure.   A teacher of youth seems to me now to be a most enviable personage, and the worst of it is I am not so thoroughly convinced that this is wrong as to make me at once resist the idea; for I find it hard to persuade myself against so many evidences to the contrary that the ministry is my true vocation.   Now, Mary, don't be grieved at this, for I am in a much better state of mind just now than ever I was before, greatly owing to this smoky old town, and that most delightful of moderns, Henry Martyn. Excuse my selfishness in this letter; it will of itself convince you that it is from . . .

To his sister Marcia

44 BLENHEIM STREET,
17th December 1858.

Though your last was cream-laid, bordering on the buttery, this must be brief and I fear not the soul of wit either, for the more time I spend here the less I seem to have to spend elsewhere, and the terrible idea of single sheets once a fortnight flits occasionally before my horrified fancy. I am determined, however, to resist the insinuation as long as I can, and sit down now regardless of many things that say they should be done.

I have become acquainted with a most extraordinary being since I wrote last. He was in Stephenson's, of course, as almost all the men here are, and cracked his breast some six years ago throwing a heavy hammer horizontally, and ever since has been the subject of a series of diseases, which he describes with horrible minuteness. He fancies, however, that his sufferings are a kind of private atonement, and he is now, I suspect, very near his end. He reads great hosts of medical books and others, Rollin and so on. But he is invested with a kind of wildness, as if he had been into some world where different forms of suffering are known. He is very happy, indeed exulting, as if he were a kind of hero, and it's very hard to help him. He knows his Bible *thoroughly*, but never went to church, and is indeed a fine sample of the Newcastle workman.

There is a woman too I know you would like to see, Widow Eltringham, a strange history, the end of which is that she, a tall, spare woman in a worn black dress and apron, and a wee shawl pinned tightly round her body, teaches about twenty ragged children, penny a week, in what is notoriously a heathenish part of the town. There she lives in her little room, holding fellowship with God, while surrounded by filth, blasphemy, drunkenness, and all that is vile.

I just fear now to probe the people I visit, for one or two steps of their history is sure to land you at some fearful thing. Fancy one woman losing five grown-up sons (all she had), two of them killed ; another a husband and a son the same week, and so on. And so many whose whole life is anxiety and a struggle with poverty and wicked relatives.

You did not send a bit of Rainy last week. Give me at least one good thing to stir me up, for I hear none like his now. Tom gave me hawful blowings up for want of animation, and did not like me so well as at Hexham, which I think, of course, was a mistake on his part. I am quite reconciled now to go and be lost anywhere and am, I hope, getting shut gradually of my unutterably despicable self-seeking and vanity. At least, the form of vanity at present is, I believe, more sensible if not more pure. I would be willing to go to a desolate, unknown place, because people there would know *nothing* of me, and would not be making offensive hobservations and hurting my pride. You have no notion what it is to get selfishness exterminated. It 's like Charles' quicken grass, everywhere and always coming up. It 's as if one had fed on mutton all one's life, and then tried to pick it out from flesh, blood and bones.

To the Same

[44 BLENHEIM STREET,
NEWCASTLE, ? 23rd December 1858.]

It was very thoughtful of you to send the 2s. to Mrs. Eltringham, but as there is a collection for the poor of the congregation on New-Year's Day, I will add a little so as not to let your particular object be altogether defrauded, and yet save my own feelings and hers by presenting your sum. She is one of the ' poor of the congregation,' but being poor in spirit also, she is happy. When Mr. Miller asked her how she got on, she said *she knew no want*, quite innocently, in a way that rebuked me thoroughly.

I have to get up something special, of course, for a

New-Year Day's sermon.   I am writing at the Transfiguration to-day.

That Dundas [1] was wanting me again revives many old feelings, and made me think how nice it would have been had we all been together still, for teaching seems to me now to be most paradisaical employment, and I used to enjoy Dundas' hour very well.   I fear I am more fitted for educating intellect than soul, and should have left this to those who have more of the element itself.

To the Same

44 BLENHEIM STREET,
7th *January* 1859.

You won't look for a very entertaining letter when I tell you that I begin it because I have fairly run aground at my sermon, and turn to you to try if the very thought of you may not kindle me a bit.   I wish you could come and spend your evenings here, especially as there is an unoccupied chamber that is always suggestive of addition to my fireside.   I spent my holidays in what philosophers say is the very height of ecstasy, unconscious pleasure, for I had no time to be conscious that holidays were going.   I have been very well, though, lately, and am getting quite fat.

The people here are so very kind.   I wish you knew some of them.   If I get Dalkeith I 'll be very, very sorry to leave here, but I feel quite plastic in the matter.   Mr. Miller I am becoming much attached to, and then I am getting used to the harness more, and take things as they come better than at first.   A great proportion of the congregation is male—mostly very intelligent.   I am to begin a youths' class on Sunday morning next, but

[1] An old pupil.

Mr. Miller has been asking some fellows to come much older than I anticipated, so it won't be a sinecure.

Thank Andie very warmly for *Standish*, which I like very much, and I would be glad to know a Priscilla. How jolly it must be having her (Andie, not Priscilla) with you. I scarcely felt sorry for you going back to your work under the circumstances.

By the bye, was Peg one of the ladies present at the giving of the funds to Dr. Cunningham ? It was just not quite what he deserves, but the direction was good and *very* honourable to the Church. When a man is rewarded for self-sacrifice, it shows a high principle in the rewarder, as well as in the rewardee. I suspect he won't write any work now, though possibly this may tell him to be quick. He should be nominated ' Grand Councillor and Senator of the Free Church of Scotland.'

Tom was in—just for a half-hour—the other day ; still, it was refreshing. I wish Tom and I could get through the upper crust, I am sure it would be turtle doves below—at present there is only a kind of smothered cooing that comes muffled through. Tom seems to be always wishing to make one believe he has no affection at all—a thing he won't readily succeed in doing.

I have been out every night this week, often at two or three families the same evening. Every one is so busy here in the day-time that there is no seeing them except at night, but it cuts up work fearfully. I do *no* reading except for my work, and very little for that. I rather fear Dalkeith would be the very opposite of this— that I would have too little practical and social work.

Mr. Miller knew Mr. Gillies well, and often speaks of him. He has a good deal of affection about him as well as Mr. G. He does not think Frank has done himself justice, and believes he would have stood higher had he not been so fluent, and more dependent on scratching of head and biting of nails, and surveying the heavens, and perusing vacancy, and all those infallible methods of extracting sermons from stones and thought from matter, that such a poor stagnant wretch as I have recourse to.   Sometimes I feel as if I had already emptied myself, and must retire to darkness and cobwebs like a bottle of 'waccum.' What comes extempore from a man goes extempore too, I feel, but then what sticks in one does not stick in another, and the only conclusion on this, as on all other matters, I feel quite certain of is this, that the world is a *riddle*, and that we passing through it are somehow separated chaff from wheat.

Now send me a great screed, and make Andie eke it out and tell me how Dr. Bruce is holding through the winter, and try if she can't get a receipt for making and delivering sermons like his.

Now if I don't stop just now I will need to stop short on Sunday, for I have not nearly finished my treatise : it 's terribly difficult to write sermons, it 's quite against my flesh. I would enjoy writing dissertations, on subjects theological or other, but there is always a struggle to get along in a discourse *to people*.

To J. C. Stewart

44 BLENHEIM STREET,
NEWCASTLE, 11*th January* [1859].

I select this sheet in some measure to represent my gratitude for your letter, which picked me up and set me on my legs, not by any means that I hope to fill it, so don't be alarmed. To be conscious that I have a friend like you comes across me with the most pleasing sensation the world can give, and then it is followed by the still deeper joy of reflecting that it is not altogether what the world gives, but that our friendship will be continued and augmented a hundredfold hereafter. Many, many thanks for so *feeling* a proof of your friendship as your letter. Man, I wish I had your facility of thinking so that others may be benefited ; how often I envy you your brightness and fluent conception when I feel the utter stagnation of my own thoughts, a stagnation compared to which ditch water seems champagne. I really feel for the people sometimes, listening to what I inflict on them. Of course it 's truth I tell them ; but then some have a way of filling you with wisdom by as simple and easy a process as eating one's dinner, while all that I can do is to give them tough, uncooked ideas, that will let them exercise their own powers of digestion before they receive the strength the truth contains. Fellows talk of finding their natural talent, of cultivating their gift, and of following the path their nature bends to. I am inclined to believe my natural talent is to do nothing and to be nothing, and were I to seek the work I am fitted for, I might spend my life in the search, and die without the discovery.

Your advice to read *White Horse* [1] comes to me with much the same romantic air as an invitation to lunch and smoke pipes on the banks of the Zambesi would. I have no time for much that I ought to do. Your advice as to men you would think I was following fully, if you saw me here. I am not uncommonly visiting from 1.30 to 10 P.M., and certainly I am seeing life (and death, which is more to be pondered still) in very diverse phases. I get on wonderfully easily among the families here, but in almost every one there is work to be done—a son who does not go to church, and who scoffs, and is being destroyed ; a husband who drinks ; a wife who is suspected of the same ; a mother to be consoled for the death of five

---

[1] Probably *The Scouring of the White Horse* (Cambridge, 1859), by the author of *Tom Brown's School-Days*.

sons, grown men ; a father who is hopelessly sunk in low spirits, because his business has passed from him.   There is every variety of wickedness, and there is scarcely a family that does not feel it in one way or other.   There are hosts of young men, the majority of the congregation being male, a very pleasing difference from most con-gregations.   Going to church, you know, is not the thing here at all ; a man tells you plainly, and at once, that he rarely has seen the inside of a chapel.   Certainly all this is a new ' 'sperience,' but how to purify it all, that 's the difficulty.   You speak of mingling with society to impress upon it what is good ; but the die, you are aware, must be harder than the metal, and I feel much a Mr. Pliable.   If I were strong and manly, and what I ought to be, it might be useful to mix with other men ; but as it is, I find myself very little impressed (permanently) by them, and I know I do as little in the way of impression.   I am naturally like you in one respect, I see a great deal of truth on both sides of a question, and this tempts me generally to side with the opinion expressed by another, unless it be some very cardinal point, and these are not found canvassed in drawing-rooms.

I am glad your sister likes Galloway, though I have no doubt *you* don't like the gal-away by any means. Give my love to your mother and Jessie, and write to me very soon, like a brick, and believe me . . .

To his sister Marcia

44 BLENHEIM STREET,
January 1859.

I have just got home at half-past ten, having been out since half-past twelve—not writing sermons, as you may imagine, but visiting all sorts of people ; one a man drunk in bed, who said he had been to hear me preach,

but corrected himself, saying 'Na, na' (he's a Scotchman),
'ye didna preach, ye read'; one an admirer of mine (a
real fine fellow !), who, however, is not immaculate, but
is grievously complained of by his sister for sitting up
reading and smoking till four in the morning and sometimes past it.   She has only three remedies for his evil
habits—grace, a good wife, or Australia.   But you
should know something of them ; they are a brother and
sister of the Misses Mouat who have a boarding-school
at Newington.   They are real nice, the sister a very
devoted creature.   There are many people with whom
I will be sorry indeed to break acquaintance, if at any
time I have to leave.

But, Marsh, I 'll never be a preacher unless some great
change comes over me.   I like the work now, but I have
the same indecision as ever, the same doubt as to whether
I might not do more good in another way, and so on.
I hope in time these questionings will answer themselves.
I believe my love for you influences me.   You cannot
imagine what drawings I have to those years we have
been together ; it seemed so fit a thing that it does seem
like sacrilege to put an end to it.   Perhaps there may be
an opening for you and Mima among the young ladies
of Dalkeith.   By the bye, had Mima any impressions
about Dalkeith ?   Let the oracle speak : I feel, as I told
you, most unconcerned, and hope that when the time
comes I shall be grateful for whatever comes.

Andie has, I suppose, gone back again to her work,
I hope with a cheerful and unresigned spirit ; if she
is still with you, or if —— is within hail, you may
tell them Gosse is to preach for us on the last Sunday of
this month.   There is a man here of a very kindred spirit,
a Dr. Richardson, quite different from Newcastle, and
his wife delicious, such a beautiful couple.   Dr. Richardson got him to come.   I am going to preach, you may

tell Mr. Hogue, on Sunday morning with instrumental
music in Mr. Pottinger's, a Baptist who has gone to
Edinburgh to supply Dr. Jonathan Anderson's (or
Watson's, is it ?) pulpit. Did I tell you I had begun
a young men's class ? It promises well so far as numbers
go. There are a great host of men in the congregation,
far more than women. I am glad to hear Dykes is at
Leith, and hope it will develope him, and fit him for something better still. Of course he will be liked wherever
he goes.

Continue to send me something of Rainy's—either a
mere outline of his sermon, or a thought or two. It gives
one a jerk.

You have no conception of the schemes I have to lay
here : to-morrow, for example, I have to go and try
my powers of persuasion on two talented (really so—their
works are their witnesses) young men who go to no place
of worship ; they live excellent lives, and are very
dutiful to their mother. Then I am expected to be able
to induce sons to support their parents, daughters to
forsake the chapel their sweethearts attend and come
back to us, to find work for young fellows, to inveigle
young ladies to visit districts, and to soothe old ones
who have taken offence and gone to other churches (an
awful deal of that), to transform a heterogeneous mass
of conflicting (you have no notion what a place for fighting this is. You mind a kitten we had that crammed
its head into the queerest places, under the fender, and
so on ? That 's just the way one does here, and I have
often to sit and hear histories of the most petty quarrels
and squabbles, whose only relief is that they put me in
mind of your stories) materials (v. 6 lines back) into one
compact and devoted Church.

Hexham is expected to be vacant soon, but I 'd rather
be here than there a very long way. Dalkeith has the

disadvantage of having a number of country people. I find it much easier to preach to townsmen—they don't need so much explanation.   It is on the 6th of February I am to be at Dalkeith.   I don't expect to be more than one night in Edinburgh (perhaps I might walk in after service, though I do not know that that would be seemly).

I hope Mamma won't leave West Mains till I see what is to become of me, for, of course, if I do get Dalkeith it will be a very practicable scheme for her to be with me.

To the Same

44 BLENHEIM STREET,
NEWCASTLE, 21st *January* 1859.

I have not got written last night as I should have done, and I feel when I write anything but sermons in the day-time that I am much a thief, so you can make your conclusions.   I wrote to Dave, too, this week, so you'll get some of his ; and besides I intend to send you a paper in which you will have the felicity of seeing both your Northumbrian brothers acting as chairmen on the same night.   So I don't think you will growl.   Get the 65ers to contribute again this week, and also Rainy.   I like his bits very much.   If I could preach like him—I suppose if I could I would growl still, so I must not covet. What a good thing it is that contentment is a thing that is within our reach, and so much more effective a remedy for small gifts than getting up a step higher—a thing altogether beyond our reach, so I 'm in for contentment and work in a corner.   I am well content with my work just now, and very much fear (though of course I should not) that it 's more suitable than anything else I could get.

The young men's class is jolly—such bricks to give one a right answer.   One of them called last Monday, and stayed nearly three hours.   He has been through very deep waters, poor fellow—tender-hearted and naturally sceptical, but is, I hope, rapidly coming to the truth : but I need not give you sketches, as I can't paint. That poor fellow Greggson is in a dreadful way—body and soul.   Every breath is a groan, and when he coughs it just seems to come tearing up from the remotest and inmost fibres of his body : and so he lies week after week.   Then he has read far beyond his education, and sees everything confusedly—has lots of ideas, without being able to connect them in order or system.   His wife complains that when she speaks to him he answers her so as to frighten her ; then often something I say makes him cry, he is so weak.   I feel lamentably unfit to help this and many other cases that need.

I wish you knew Mr. Miller's three year old ; she is quite a character, and she and I are great friends.   ' Do you love Mr. Dods ? '   ' Yes, I *do*.'   But I am afraid she is one of the facts that sadly contradict the song, ' Oh ! say not woman's love is bought,' for I believe her love to me is somewhat of the barter order.   Her demands are huge, and she seems to look upon me much as she would look on a felicitous invention that could at her pleasure become a swing, a baby-jumper, a camel, or a writing-table, and were I to refuse to be as Protean as her desires, I fear the answer to the above would be ' No, I *don't* '— in equally forcible tone.

I have a D.D. hearing me every evening.   I can't say it has much effect on my preparation ; the largest element in my audience is still the sisterhood.

To the Same

44 BLENHEIM STREET,
NEWCASTLE, 27*th January* [1859].

You will divine, I dare say, that I am in a good humour to-night, and so I am.   To think that this is the last of my 1st Newcastle series is not a little elating ;

but, moreover, I have to tell you what I know you will be glad to hear, of two young fellows, I don't know if I told you of them before, Allison by name, and at Hawthorn's factory—never go to a place of worship, but have come the two last Sunday evenings. I discovered this to-night when I was going in a very heartless, hopeless mood to try again to persuade them, and I have had a two-hour discussion with them on conscience, revelation, etc. One of them is a most superior fellow, draws most beautifully, reads extensively (so do most of the workmen here), and argues most pleasantly, being able to see when an argument is sound. The young men have come out capitally to the morning class ; there are 23 now, and I have promise of some more. But surely I told you all this before; it seems as if I had scarcely been once asleep since I wrote. I have been bittling away at my sermon this week with more than usual vehemence, as I am advertised along with Gosse (! how he 'll glory, decent man—it 's not often your F.R.S.es and such have an honour like that put upon them), but in consequence of trying to write something worthy of an advertisement, I have almost failed in writing anything at all. Mr. Miller and I are to meet him at tea on Saturday, to which I look forward with considerable pleasure.

I have been out all day to-day since dinner, and it is now half-past ten ; but we made some nice visits in Blandford St. Mr. M. went with me to all that I thought hopeful ones, and two or three seem disposed to come to church, and indeed promised in a way speaking of performance. I store up a lot of things to tell you, but I always forget them all when I come to write. All the nice things that happen, you know, I docket and title ' This for Marsh.'

One old party in the congregation made me such a

rare gingerbread loaf, I almost could have thought it
was from the fingers of Anne. How she discovered my
weakness I don't know.

I had an invite to Monkwearmouth, which is vacant
just now, but of course I at once declined on the ground
of inability to take two services and to re-form the congregation, which has sadly fallen away. The church
there is a very nice one. My text for Sunday is ' This
mortal must put on immortality,' emphasis on ' *This*,'
but I am not getting up to it. I feel as an apprentice
bricklayer would feel if set before a block of Parian marble
and informed that a Venus lay concealed there if he
could find her with his chisel.

Now I must begin to finish for the usual reason. I
hope you have got a letter begun, not only for first
Tuesday, but for the Tuesday after I come back, for
mind it must be a tremendous affair : fancy me—rejected candidate—just dried my first tears—a sleety day
—dull trains—anxious heart—etc., etc.

To the Same

44 Blenheim Street,
Newcastle, 10th *February* 1859.

It was truly nice of you to send me such a delicious
little note, and if it is any satisfaction to you, let me
tell you it was eminently successful—cheered me more
than I could have thought possible. My first impulse
was to sit down at once and tell you what a brick you
are, but as my rule (derived from the mother's side) is
not to act upon impulse, I delayed. In this case I regret
I did so, for now I have such a cold in my head and
general stagnation, I scarcely can get up steam to do anything. The hymn you sent was almost as nice as the
note it came in, and I have read them both many times.

The smiling manse and the inhabitant thereof of whom you speak are all very nice, but where are they ?   You speak of the wife as if you had some definite knowledge of her—have you been reading my hand, or consulting a witch, or casting the stars, or how have you hit upon her ?   I rather avoid looking into either your future or mine—my constitution predicts for me long struggles against many things, and were it not for Peg's text (for which thank her), 'Trust in the Lord, and do good,' which calls me to work for others now, and leave *then* to God, I would be even more wretched a being than I am.   It seems often very astonishing, almost incredible, that through all our complacent resignation and morbid forecastings and such abominable feelings, God should love us and deal with us still.   Suppose we had thrown upon our hands one or two (not to mention a world full) of such misconstruing, suspicious, sulky creatures as we are !   You think you have your share, and indeed I do feel for you, but then if to do good rather than to be happy is our life's intent, you are in your right place. It is a grand thing, a thing to be prayed for, to be convinced that our calling here is to work and suffer.   This prepares us for everything that tends to depress, and makes us rejoice still more in the rest and enjoyment we *do* find here.

Your appearance, half-headachy, half-sad, is always rising before me, and I could wish you had not so dejected an air.   When I think of you working away all day and coming home to not very exciting evenings, I wish I was with you, if not to lighten, at least to share the dismalness.   For myself I have not pictured anything more pleasant in life than those years ; give me three feet round the fireplace, and you in one of the said feet, and I could forget all beyond.   My more happy thoughts of you are in the company of the 'admirable and incomparable.' They too follow me here, and I have found to-day not once only, but oftener than usual, that my reading was mechanical and my thought 'N., *nihil*, nothing.' Mrs. Hogue pursues me with her sayings and admonitions, I walk with Dave, cautiously debate with Mr. Hogue, see Nelly laughing at my would-be wisdom, Bessie ecstatifying, and so on.

Mind, Marsh, I mean you to use the pounds I left with you for a few of those things you could luxuriate in if you had all your salary to yourself. Now don't be nasty and say this is nasty of me, but just do what I ask you for once. You may even lay it up for capital to begin the great boarding establishment on. Of course I would like to have a grand house with a suite of rooms for you and a boudoir where you might cultivate the muses, etc.—but *quand on n'a pas ce que l'on aime, il faut aimer ce que l'on a*—at least, that's the style for getting cheerily through.

PS.—I have been elaborating a theory founded on 'All things work together,' to show how by the very nature of things a proud man ought to have the pride taken out of him, a zealous man have his zeal tempered, and so on, by passage through the world ; it would suggest to Mima the idea of my certain failure at Dalkeith and all other places, for of course a vain man should have the vanity taken out of him.

To the Same

44 BLENHEIM STREET,
17th February 1859.

I must try and get writ to Bobby, so I must be brief to you, and therefore to business. Topmost comes the information that I am not the man for Dalkeith. I expect to have further news from Dr. Macfarlane to-

I

morrow, and will then tell you who has got it, if it comes before post. Spare your pity for some more needy object, for I don't feel in the very slightest degree cast down. The fact is, till I get more experience and more fluency in practical applications, I am not fit for a charge even so little rural as Dalkeith ; and as most of the people here are satisfied, and as I can *more* adequately at least supply their wants, I am glad to be here. I find the prayer-meetings very difficult indeed. I feel that the people are just getting nothing. I can't get on at that familiar and edifying exhortation that Mr. Gillies excels in ; this I do hope I will improve in ; otherwise——

I don't wonder now that you were anxious about my beginning preaching, for this week I purposed giving them ' All things work,' and thought I would have time to write another sermon, but really when I read it I stood, or rather sat aghast, and have been writing hard to renew it, and when I consider that what I now write will seem in a year's time equally absurd and unprofitable, I (to say the least of it) do not feel gratified by my inference. To be convinced I was a child six months ago is also to be convinced I am still very young.

In answer to your enquiry as to longings :—

> ' Then this desire of nature is not vain,
>   She covets not impossibilities ;
> Fond thoughts may fall into some idle brain,
>   But one assent of all is ever wise.
>
>   .   .   .   .   .
>
> Will seeking good finds many middle ends,
>   But never stays till it the last do gain.'

I must say good-bye, which understand in its original acceptation, *vide* Trench, page unknown. Give them all my kindest love. I won't particularise any, lest I be drawn to go over them all, and stultify my own intention,

P.S.—I open this to say I have just had a very flattering epistle from Dr. Macfarlane.   He has written to Lewis of Leith, he says, recommending me, which is peculiarly considerate.   If you just think of the circumstances you will acknowledge it to be so.   If I come to Leith after all, it will be jolly enough, but I can't help being exceedingly thankful of these months here.   What a fool I would have made of myself had I gone to Leith instead of here, where I have got ground down to purpose, I hope.   I must not, however, be setting my heart on the old seaport, sacred by the memory of the most delicious of brothers-in-law.

To the Same

44 BLENHEIM STREET,
NEWCASTLE, 24*th February* [1859].

But talking of poets, I was nearly made a poet of yesterday all unbeknown to myself, for being called upon to preach at Hexham, I obeyed the call, and on reaching the pleasantly lying and ancient city, I found myself in the midst of the most lovely scene I ever saw in February.   It was 7.30 A.M., and fresh as April, the brown lands speaking of everything strong and solid (Giles thinks my sermons will be ' moral dumplings,' a kind of religious stickjaw, I suppose he means ; this was not the solidity suggested), and then the birds, oh ! Marsh, the birds, just like a decoction of the essence of Milton, Tennyson, Cowper, Charles, and your sweetheart, pouring through one's soul, and then the buds on the apricot tree just white all over with blossom, I wish you could have seen it.

As to Leith, I had a fluster for two minutes when you first told me of it, and yet I see many delicious things about it ; but as to competing with Laidlaw in the matter of preaching, there are a good many things I would sooner do than that, and one of them is to stay here and go on with my work. You know there are some very striking adaptations in my being here—too many to enumerate. I feel like a fellow that's got into a new, well-fitting coat—there is a certain queer smell about it, and a something that is not altogether comfort, but still the motions are free, and he feels sure that when the first gloss is off it will be a pleasant wear. Reading is no objection here, you see, and I get on with all the people, and like them well, and have considerable sympathy with them, which I fear would be hard of forthcoming in Leith. They are so different, the people here. As for the advance it would be, and prospect of landing in Edinburgh, I can honestly say that I do not feel that at all : if work is to be done, *of course* one place is for one and another for another, and by what each has so will each be judged and receive. Even the anxiety to study half the time is wearing off here. I am learning to live and learn and work, instead of playing at places. But don't think from this that I would not be delighted to get Leith ; if I be asked to preach, and if (oh ! shadow of a hypothesis) I should be asked to stay. You know it's very plain, when you take a calm, unfraternal view of the matter, that people accustomed to Freer and Dykes would not be satisfied with ' young Dods.' There is a vanity that extracts praise from the common cour- tesies of life, and turns into compliments the partial flatteries of friends, but I am not surely come to that, and though I sincerely believe that you and 65 like my sermons, I am not so bereft as to imagine that I am on the same shelf as Laidlaw and Dykes ; and if you divest (only for a moment, if you please) yourself of your consanguineal ' spirit of uncritic,' you will not be very urgent in your desires for my coming to Leith,

Here the people have had no experiences of the young Free Church, and listen with the most exemplary patience to what I can produce, and are content.   Canterbury or Salisbury, as you say, would be the thing ; you could have rooms in my palace then—and I am getting quite confused as to my Presbyterianism with preaching here for all the denominations.   If my heart was habitually and thoroughly in the work I would not care one atom where I was, but to be professing to serve Christ and Him alone, and to know yourself to be filled with *all manner* of things hostile and hateful to Christ, is a wretched matter.

I intended to wind up Leith in a sentence, and I find I have wound up my letter in it.   I think I could get a call to the best Baptist congregation here—a very large and wealthy one.   I have preached once, and am to go again, and though I doubt whether the people would depose their own minister for my sake, there is some talk of his going away.   Should I go in ?

This is Friday morning now, and I have just received a missive from Dalkeith signed by some elders and deacons and so on, telling me not to cry, like a dear, for I did very well considering, and had the votes of 6 out of 8 elders, 5 out of 7 deacons, and 10 out of 13 Sabbath-school teachers.   I suppose I must reply in a gentlemanly manner admiring their good taste ; it was very kind, though, of them.

To his sister Mary

You won't mind there is such a place as 44 BLENHEIM STREET,
NEWCASTLE, 28*th February* [1859].

If I did not know I could still address you as my ever dearest Mary, I would not address you at all ; and as for giving reasons for my silence, they are too many to be entered on.   I prefer to state the matter syllogistically in the form of a dilemma : if I have been so busy with duty all this time that I have not been able to find an hour to write to you, I must have been very good, good beyond the common either of myself or of most other men ; and if I have had time to write to you and not done it, I must have been wicked beyond the common, I hope of myself as well as of others.   I don't care to choose either of these horns for reasons that will probably suggest themselves to the discerning mind of my sister.

I wish I had Markie here to banish my solitude, though I am getting hardened to that as well as to many other things which, I fear, I ought still to be soft to.   I feel that already I can look on the wickedness of this place (which is very open and abundant) with a much more callous heart than when I came. Sickness still impresses me, and death, of which I have seen much here.   Surely I will never be able to think death other than a very fearful, or rather awful, thing.

I like the work ;   at least that is my deliberate choice ; but to waken on a Sunday morning and think the service of God a weariness, and wish I had been anything but what I am, and finding that this temper does not vanish with one rebuke, or two, this is most tormenting, and fills me with thoughts I need not describe.   I trust this will die away, and that my whole inclination shall be on the side of the labour, and that in its most spiritual aspect.

There are some most interesting people here, and had I you for a ' society ' (in yourself) of district visitors, I could direct your energies to where there is work to be done.   I am encased here in work, dense and deep on all sides : reading for amusement or meditating for want of something to do are things that were, and I sometimes wonder if certain books shall never again be looked at

by me. Virgil, for example, I have had much to do with ;
then am I done with him *for ever* ?   Am I to part from
the old creature and never again meet him ?

Why did George not write ?   Shall I make him jealous ?
Yes ; good for him to curb his evil passions.   I had a
two hours' talk with P. H. Gosse the other night.   He
has a son not eight years old, who knows all the shells
as ever growed, and has discovered some private species
of his own, which his father publishes in his new work
with no end of triumph.

Now I must stop.   If ever I am Archbishop of Canterbury or hate Milton's *Comus*, I may alter in my affection
for you.   Till then, however, I may safely promise to
be . . .

To his sister Marcia

44 BLENHEIM STREET,
NEWCASTLE, *3rd March* [1859].

I think Thursday must be a day unfriendly to the
muses, for I always find I begin my letters to you in
consequence of sticking in my sermon.   In the present
instance I have been labouring to describe a half-
hypocritical party, and as I have not been able with
any good conscience to use any of my usual models
(you and the M.s and Dave) for this copy, I have come
very badly on, and at last limped so manifestly that I
thought it better to close till the muse choose to return.
Now shall I say anything of your last letter, or refer
you at once to Longinus or Burke on the Sublime and
Beautiful ?

There was a congregational meeting last night whereat
it was decided to ask me to stay five months longer after
this month : a quite spasmodic effort this, as the people,

even when I came, were growling about the extra expense, and as they had been giving Mr. Miller assistance for two years now, it is scarcely to be wondered at. After the five months, infinite space, I suppose! However, the congregation is increasing considerably, and that pleases the people, and that makes me comfortable, and in that case it is easy to feel what always ought to be felt, that *here* (wherever that may be) is the place for work. But Leith—Marsh, why did you ever tell me about Leith ? And now that these fine Spring days are coming in, and it 's warm and sunny, a little sociality would be appropriate ; but it does not do to devise so subtle a happiness as I sometimes do. Out of fine weather, and Pegs, and such like, could you not knock up a future worth living in ? And what would probably come out of it ? It has been coming upon me often lately, at funerals and so on, that there are certain things in presence of which it is right and healthy to be mournful —a strange state of things indeed, but still the state we are undoubtedly in—' Blessed are they that mourn, for they shall be comforted.' It breeds sympathy this, too. One is tempted to ask what is the *use* at all of harrowing up your heart by sharing or viewing other people's woes ? Why not get away from them to sunshine and peace ? But that does not seem to be the right way of matters even when one can lend no practical aid—that is always on my mind here. I have only to walk one minute, just round the corner, and I get into the thick of inevitable sadness— At this point I judged it better to go to the thick of it than sit talking about it. It was two then, and now it is eight, and I have had tea, but as this is almost all I have done to-day, I won't be able to write much more.

Thank —— for the picture, and don't tell him it 's beastly, and just about as like you as I am like Apollo. I 'd as soon think of cutting off your head and sticking

it on my chimney-piece, as putting that up ; but I feel
his remembrance of me in a very tender way, and if
I could photograph, I 'd send him one of the Sultan's
Engine and Carriage, which are exhibiting here just now.

Fancy if we had spiritual bodies in our present state
—if every evil thought and disposition was registered
in the face—what a dreadful thing that would be !
Where would beauty be found ?

If you can direct me to anything more exquisite than
the 13th Psalm, I will follow your direction with a happiness not often attaching to earthly pursuits.

I suppose the Leith people think Sandeman the man ?
Pottinger the Baptist *is* going away, and I am to preach
there next Sunday morning.

What is Mamma to do ? It would be useless to ask her
here, would not it ?   I would scarcely ever be able to
speak to her : it is only at dinner I get time to dip into
' the suggestive.' [1] I am rapidly becoming illiterate.
And I don't know how she would suit this place : they
say the street is very dull and smoky. I think she
should go to Glenluce. Then the people here are not
the easiest to deal with : a mistake in grammar will
almost cause a disruption. ' And more than so,' as
' the suggestive ' [1] says, Tom would have her off in a
twinkling.

Friday morning.—I have just received your note and
its enclosures, all delicious. Surely the postman must
feel the wiser and the better man for having such things
in his hands. Many thanks to Ailie [2] for the collect : it
shall go up beside the other and ' be my solace day by
day.' Not that one should need a solace other than
what one always has before one as the great fact of the
world, the death of Jesus Christ, but then this is applied
in various ways at various times.

[1] Foster.   [2] Miss Alison Hogue.

I need not say I am not sorry about Leith : it does seem strange that there should be work that I could seemingly do in Leith and work for you in Edinburgh, and yet that we should not be together, and I am tempted to reflect that had I stayed in Edinburgh, I might have got work there. But then I don't reflect any such thing, for I know these ' ifs ' have all been considered, and besides I have no doubt I am giving and getting far more here than I could at Leith. There are more people to be worked upon ; and then I have nothing here but my work, and that I find is also good. No distraction but what I create. This will, of course, wear off. Some of the people I could become really friendly with in a social as well as professional way : one of them, Mr. Mouat, I would be tempted to spend hours with. He is the man that can't sleep till 4 in the morning, and that knew I liked poetry by the way I pronounced my consonants, that has a good deal in common with Stewart and with Charles, has a thorough contempt for the Newcastle people, and thinks I should be in an Edinburgh church. This is probably giving you no high idea of him, but if you could meet his sister who is in Edinburgh just now, you would fall in love with her.

PS.—One of Mouat's remarks to me the last time I saw him was that the Bible never threw him into a brown study. This remark arose from him stating that —— had recommended him to read the Bible at nights by way of breaking himself off sitting up (which —— looks on as a crime—a lust of the flesh he will never give in to, I dare say). On reflection, how very injudicious a thing, as if the Bible was the sleepiest of books. Mr. Mouat said he had taken the advice, but not even *Blackwood* was so *suggestive* as the Bible.

PS.—My text this week is Matt. xxiv. 5 : the false

Christs I particularise are repentance, knowledge that
God has planned a way of salvation, religious observances,
and the spirit that says ' Oh ! but I am not deceived by
any of these things.'

To J. C. Stewart

44 BLENHEIM STREET,
NEWCASTLE, 7th *March* [1859].

I would have liked to have gone into an elaborate re-
futation of your last letter, for, as no doubt you will sigh
to hear, I am convinced your ideas of pulpit eloquence
are somewhat incorrect. There are just a few things,
however, which render any comparison (or reasoning
from analogy) of pulpit to other eloquence inadmissible.
The object is not only to convince, but to instruct also :
its occasion is stated and ordinary, not extraordinary
and rare—this I think of very considerable moment.
Could you yourself sit under ——, or would you not
ere long rebel—' Am I to be the audience to this, week
after week am I to be the object of this exciting address ? '
Thus far had I got three days ago, when pain forbade
me to hang my head any longer, and so I had just to
yield ; for what one of Livingstone's savages said of
hunger, may well be said of pain, ' A very great fellow
is he.' My lip has been rivalling any gourd or melon
in rapidity of enlargement, and by aid of fomentations
has at last *out*grown itself, discharged, and is in the way
of mends. Your *Saturday Review* came most acceptably
—the very thing—but don't you notice in the style of this
generation a threatening of degeneracy in the shape of
that refinement which obscures thought ? How often
a writer seems to be calling our attention to his language
instead of openly and Englishly telling us his mind.
Had you ever to read a sentence of Addison twice to

discover his meaning ? Had you *never* to read over
again a sentence (or, at least, a clause) in *The Saturday*
or *The Times* ?   But I don't know, and therefore will not
say, that this is all fault, but rather I am inclined to
believe that there is nowadays a greater *accuracy* of
thought than in many former ages, and for the convey-
ance of that a more educated phraseology is needed.
I don't at all refer to allusions carefully dug up and
presented off-hand, but simply to the current abhorrence
among literary men to state what they think in the most
natural and easiest comprehended way.

.This in intention is a very long letter, but really I cannot
write with much pleasure to-day, even to you. I wish you
were here to have a crack with, or that there were private
telegraphs of very easy working. I own it is shabby
to send you such an answer to your last, which did me
good many ways.   Do write very soon again, like a good
fellow, and mind, though your advice about preaching
was not all to my mind, there were things in it that
roused me considerably.

To his sister Marcia

44 BLENHEIM STREET,
NEWCASTLE, 10*th March* [1859].

MY MOST TRUSTY AND BEST BELOVED MARSH,—Your
letter was almost the only thing I was caring about on
Tuesday morning — having scarcely shut my eyes
on Monday night, and getting up with a lip about
the size of half a dozen, the thought that it was Tuesday
morning was more soothing than all the fomentations in
Europe ; and then when it came with Mim's interpolations
and Peg's appendix, there may have been bigger men
and taller men, but there was not a man in Newcastle

with a bigger lip and higher spirits than I ; that is certain. I begin to think myself much a Job minus the patience, and the daughter Jemima and a few other items in the shape of flocks and herds and eloquence. The pain in my teeth and cheek was ' hawful,' just as if a company of little fiends had formed an association for rope-making, and had commenced among my nerves. After I saw what it was going to be I got Livingstone's Travels, and set to work to be ill, and did it in very delicious style (minus sympathy), got my pan of bread and kettle of water as of old, and read away at intervals. The nights were rather a different affair, however, but I would strongly recommend to any one that is not *seriously* ill to read Livingstone ; to see the way he threw off fever and all kinds of things, and would not give in to ' nothink ' (as Miss Stoker says), makes one cheery. The Stokers have been very kind, but have no id*ea* ! They were going to mix a large quantity of mustard in the poultice.

I had a letter from Dr. Bonar asking me to go to Leghorn for some time to assist Dr. Stewart, who is ill, but of course, as it was not a permanency, I could not accept. Would not it have been rayther nice to bask ' under an Italian sky,' and to see Greece, Palestine and the Nile, for you may be sure I would not have come back without seeing some of the Lions of Eld. But I suppose there is more to be done here, so three cheers for the dear, dirty old boiler-makers and the Stinks of Canny Newcastle.

Many thanks for your notes of Smeaton (a very fine fellow is he). I could have known very well whose sermon it was—some of his sayings to his class are in it, ' Have no *public* but the eye of God ' ; and he is always waging war (why, I don't know) against high-churchism.

If, as you seem to believe regarding yourself, and as

I believe regarding the family generally, there is lacking a conspicuous talent for anything particular, we should congratulate ourselves on this, that we are conspicuous in having better friends than anybody else. About the talent, however, to omit personalities, what of John ? Surely he has just hit upon his right profession. I don't suppose (from what I have heard and seen) there could be a much better draughtsman than he, and Tom's farming is becoming a very notable thing : both of them were left to choose for themselves as nature bid them. Tom, I suppose, was a farmer from his nursery days, John an engineer as soon as he could think at all, but you would find it hard to say what I was at six, or at twelve, or at twenty, or now. The premise seems very distinct, ' unstable as water,' the conclusion I shudder to think of. A student I could be, I think , I would be glad to retire from the surface of society and dive for pearls, but to set them and make them of use, real, practical use——(that score means what 'the suggestive' means by his). But all this is dismally subjective—but mind, be you subjective. I like you best when you are, though I don't think it best for you to be so.

But as the world said to the Makololo when they came to the ocean, so my letter says to you, ' I am finished, there is no more of me.'

To the Same

44 BLENHEIM STREET,
NEWCASTLE, 17th March [1859].

DEAREST AND BEST,—(Quotation, mind, from your loving Peg), I am afraid you are sinking into the depths of subjectivity. Come out, I say, come out ; go work, and do not meditate : I am believing our whole habits of life are heterodox and to be revolted from.

Now lest I forget, ask my private physician in what quantities I am to take rhubarb and soda ; the porter I can better regulate—anything under a hogshead a week, I suppose.   I am going into cod liver like a shark, in a vain attempt to get up some muscles.   I never was so sleepy in my life before, and feel as if my backbone was india-rubber, my head a leaden or paste bullet, and my arms and legs bags of sawdust.   As for my ' *desideratum* ' —oh, no ! we never mention it.   However I have been consoling myself with a lecture on Shadrach, Meshach and Abednego ;   and noble fellows they were, if I could only tell people so in plain terms, and persuade them to go and be like them.

You are perfectly mistaken as to my idea of Job.   I would as soon think Dave a ghost as Job.   Of course the book is a poem, but the poet was not such a misguided creature as to pass over all the great personages already inhabiting the popular mind, and make a hero of his own ; the same as Homer wrote an *Odyssey*, a poem full of fancy and fiction, but all gathered round and taking interest from the well-known (already well-known) hero Odysseus.   The Dean, begging his pardon, has got half an idea through some review of a German critic, I should think.   There is absolutely no *reason* at all against Job's reality, except the name, which *some* think means ' persecuted,' and *therefore* (observe the strictness, the inevitable certainty, of the reasoning), therefore the book is all allegory.   After blowing away this reason, Hirzel says :   ' Ein weiterer Grund aber, Hiobs Existenz in Zweifel zu ziehen, ist nicht vorhanden.'   Luther expresses pretty much the view taken by all real critics (like our own Lowth and modern Germans) :   ' Ich halt, das Buch Hiob sei eine Historie und darnach in ein Poema oder Gedicht gebracht, das *einem* widerfahren sei, *doch nicht mit solchen Worten*, wie es beschrieben ist.'   Shakspere's plays or Milton's account of *Paradise Lost* is very much the same kind of composition.

I had a letter from Dave on Saturday, which I have answered in a way that I wished to be affectionate, but that was only dry. I sent him a *track* which I liked. I have great pleasure in looking at his picture, really more pleasure than I remember to have had from any picture. He's a nice fellow, and these fine nights I feel much inclined to be off and have a walk with him. I could not help (as a last resource) asking —— to go a walk to-night, the whole country, you know, bathed in moonlight. He stared—so much for having a wife and children at home! I don't think I would care much for a wife that would not care to be out in the moonlight. He has given me a little book that belonged to M'Cheyne. Mr. Miller thinks I would be pretty sure of a call from the Baptists, if I professed my doubts as to the efficacy of Infant Baptism—but that, unfortunately, is one of the few points on which I am rather inclined to be dogmatic. A nice large congregation and some *very* nice people.

Friday morning, and a note from Mr. Miller saying he has had an attack of bleeding, which, though stopped, will make it unsafe for him to preach, so here am I in for two sermons besides my own and my class. Really it's refreshing—makes one's spirits jump a little. I had a great lot more to say, but of course I must just stop, as I'll need all my time. Alas, for Greek, Hebrew, German, or Cyprian. The Greek will, I hope, keep itself up now, but oh! if you have influence with one divinity student, tell him with authority to study Hebrew when he has time.

Now, Marsh, I am ashamed to send you such a vile little scrape, but a youth called last night who has ideas about man being a Trinity, because he is made in the image of God—a real clever fellow, and had he been educated would have been something ; but that's the thing here that ruins them. Be thankful for your education : mind, you are *very different* from what you would have been without it. I was thinking about you much last week, and am very penitent for all my glumpiness, and wonder if I would be as wicked to you still if I had another chance. I hope I may get it at any rate.

To his Mother and his sister Marcia

44 BLENHEIM STREET,
NEWCASTLE, 31*st March* 1859.

I must write to you in a family capacity, as I have not time to send such a letter to either as each deserves. I fear, indeed, it will be but a meagre one as it is, for I have been very busy this week, and not spry. I was glumpy this morning, and Mr. Mouat called and asked me there this evening, so I went, and have been resuscitated. He is a strange being and most lovable. I had a long walk with him after leaving, so I did not get home till past eleven, but it did me good. He has seen as deep into the well at the bottom of which truth lies as most people. Besides being a painter and a skilful photographer, and a maker of really most superb drawing-room screens, he numbers among his works the building of an organ. He has not it here, but sent it to his Edinburgh sisters, who use it constantly, and say it beats the professed makers' ; so, I suppose, there will be some musical genius about him too. He is the only person here I have yet found with whom I could become Davidic, but he is, of course, a good deal older than I am—34, I should think.

Rainy's note you sent was nice, only if we wait till our desires are pure we will never pray at all.

K

I wish Dr. Cunningham was here for a week; he would go back and append some fierce denunciations to his lecture on the Arminians. Everybody here almost is Arminian, and won't get out of it.

Dick Stothert is going to New Pitsligo, a station, so that if Sir John Forbes could worship in a schoolroom, he would hear a good sermon.

To his sister Marcia

44 BLENHEIM STREET,
NEWCASTLE, 7th *April* [1859].

DEAREST AND TWO THOUSAND TIMES BEST,—I think the best way will be for me to write this to you to read to Mamma, as I find it is not an easy thing to write to two people at once. Your last was delicious, only I expected some more advice about Rainy[1] : just three hours after posting my answer to him I was offered the *Superintendence* of the town Mission here. It was an Episcopalian who was kind enough to mention me to the Committee, which is mostly Episcopalians. There are eight missionaries, and I dare say it would have been very nice accompaniment to John Knox work. I told them I was engaged, and also that I am too young, all the missionaries being well on, thirty, forty, fifty, and so on. But had the offer come a wee bit sooner, I suspect it would have transmogrified my intentions, as I feel almost as queer in prospect of leaving Newcastle as I did when I just came. The weather is delicious, and everything coming out—only it's awfully hot, worse than Paris in July. Mr. Miller is the most sanguine man I have had to do with; the moment I mentioned about the offer of Mission work here, he turned on the street, and without a moment's reflection went back to the house of Dr. Sang,

---

[1] *i.e.*, about Mr. Rainy's invitation to the writer to come to Edinburgh as his Missionary.

the offerer, though I protested all the way that I was
engaged, and would not and could not draw back.   He
devised some beautiful trap to waylay me, which has not
yet been successful, and never will, I expect.   Then,
you know, throughout my protestations he was sketching
pictures of me settling here and getting you to keep
house, etc., etc.   He has an immense idea of you, but
no notion of where your good qualities lie, so he is always
coming out with things about you that make me laugh,
they are so unlike you—(supposed expressions about
my health and so on, you know).

Awful reminiscences of the smells of the closes and the
filthy odour of dirty human flesh come across me ever
and anon ; but it won't be so bad in reality, and with
the agency you speak of, no doubt I 'll be well backed.
But I am determined to go into the thing soberly.   Things
here are all tempting me to stay now—out to the West
the country is beautiful, and then, as you observe, Mouat
is a darling.   I think you and he would get on first rate.
You know them at once, you know, not only in the way
you know all the people here at once, that is, in the way
of being quite free and affectionate, but you know themselves, what they are, and what you may always expect
from them.   Then there are *lots* of other people I have
got very fond of.

I was over at Widow Eltringham's yesterday, and she
was speaking about Winslow's book you sent.   ' Eh !
the comfort there was in yon little book.'   She is not
well, thinks she is breaking up, and has not a soul to
help her.   Every time I see her she strikes me as being
the very type of a dame schoolmistress—an oval face
and sweet eyes, with a sternish mouth, above the middle
height, light made ;   and she always goes and gets the
neighbour's baby (a thin, white, dirty little object) to
show me, and sits hugging it, calling it ' the darling ' (as

if it was !) and ' Eh ! what hearts they must have to hurt
a little thing like that.'   I like to have a talk with her.

What you feel about Greek should be tempered by
remembering what you must have lost in gaining it.
Think of the time an Oxford man spends in acquiring it,
and cut this out of the time you have had to study, and
it will leave you minus a good many things more useful
to you.   I own that often when I have been peculiarly
delighted with any nice thing in Plato (my only joy here,
except occasionally two lines of Æschylus), I have felt
a misgiving for the share I had in stopping you, but the
above consideration has always reassured me of my
rectitude in the matter.

P.S.—' How beautiful is rain '—it 's been pouring, and
Miss Stoker enters, ' It 's quite a mild day, and a *beautiful*
rain.'   How absurd to laugh at a poet, then, for using
the expression.

I have been getting violets from everybody, though
Dave's astonished me most.   I feel very helpless as a
recipient of flowers—just one quick feeling of delight,
and then the feeling of a confirmed bachelor who gets
a young baby to hold ' for a minute or two.'   I don't
know where they go ; I 'm afraid I don't like to
inquire.

To the Same

44 BLENHEIM STREET,
NEWCASTLE, 15*th April* [1859].

I have been thanking you so long for the second
volume of Butler that now that it has come I don't feel
at all the gratitude I ought.   I took it quite as a matter
of course.   Mamma's share in it, however, was unexpected,
and her I most cordially (as Dr. Gordon would say) thank.
But think what comes with it in the same *letter*-bag—

2 vols. *tall* 8vo of Sir W. Hamilton's *Lectures* (24s.), the
Metaphysics, from W. and J. D. Fordyce, and a letter
from Peg. Now say none of them are gentlemen, do,
if you please. Of course, I felt it my duty to spend
almost all Monday and Tuesday in reading them, the
more as I expected to get a holiday on Sunday, but
instead of that I find I am to preach twice (as always
of late). I have a sermon to write this time, and no
time to do it, and am in a gross and clayey frame
besides. To-day I had pledged with Mouat, so he has
been photographing me all day, and to-night I am to be
at tea to meet some wonders, so I don't know what's
to become of me.

I have not heard again from Rainy, so Mr. Miller thinks
the proposal of staying here for two months must have
frightened him so that he has done with me. I hope
now Rainy won't let me stay here ; it is very uncomfortable being between two places, and to feel utterly
unfit for either and more of a beast and a hypocrite
and a goose and a spoon than anybody else you know.
Davies was, no doubt, a philosophical poet, but I cannot
concur in his sentiment that we are just 'well mixed
bodies.' I feel, indeed, inclined so far to believe him that
the soul is mixed up in a most distressing way with the
body ; but this I would call 'ill mixed' rather than 'well.'

Thank Bob for his letter, and tell him I am looking
forward with pleasure to some *noctes Horatianæ*. If I
did not think it was abominable I would here put, Should
I not be a teacher ? But I dare say I would just be as
discontented therein.

I have been looking into A. Butler, and think I would
have had an even higher idea of the man had the second
volume remained an *ignotum*, for I see there are the same
ideas very much ; but it's as grand as the first, quite.
They are almost all Charity sermons—the rogues have

known who to get to make the people come out with their purses.

I know this is mean in the extreme, but what more can a wretch do that has neither time nor anything else ? It 's just on post time, so I must bolt, though ashamed to call myself your loving brother . . .

To J. C. Stewart

44 BLENHEIM STREET,
25th April 1859.

I blame myself very much that this letter has not long ago performed for you the last act of friendship in lighting a consolatory pipe, but you must take some of the blame yourself, for had your last letter been less excellently refreshing, it would have been answered sooner ; but time after time I have delayed till I could do it justice —vain hope, I find—and now that I am fairly shamed into writing by the reproachful appearance of your letter lying unanswered between Augustine's *Confessions* and the *Olney Hymns* (my unanswered letter department), I feel as unable as ever really to answer yours. The weather, neither, is favourable to the corresponding muse (an omission, by the bye, in the ancient list ; from which fact you may make deductions, and on which you may even write a treatise, and would do so if you were, as fortunately for yourself and your friends you are not, a Dawes or a Keightley), but if you have never been in Newcastle at all, still less in the north-west of Newcastle, with a south-east wind blowing, and, least of all, with the addition of a close, constant rain, I need not try to describe the weather, for any description would give you a false impression.

I am glad to say that I hope our epistolary efforts will be soon changed for the easy intercourse of personal presence, for Rainy has asked me to come and be your Missionary, and I have accepted the invitation, though

I look forward with no small fear to the work. Of course
I will need to alter my style of preaching entirely. My
sojourn here has been all I could desire, with the single
blank of old friends, but it 's good for one to be thrown
out from all one has been unconsciously depending on,
and be set to work in a new and very different sphere.
Your sister Maggie I have often cordially sympathized
with, for the softer sex can't repel dulness by those
resources open to us—promiscuous society, reading-
rooms, pipes, etc.

There is one fellow here whose company I have culti-
vated, as he puts me considerably in mind of you (is a
heavy smoker and makes me smoke—similarity No. 1),
though in some things he is very different. He has great
taste in literature, is a thinker in the modern style, has
common-sense to an uncommon extent, discrimination,
and many other very excellent qualities, and was unfortunately obliged to sink them all in the tea trade.
He has no fondness for business, so the consequence is
he is neither one thing nor another ; but I don't know
why I should detail to you a man you never saw nor
probably will see. But then, as I hinted before, what
can one say on a drenching Monday evening ?

And here enters my brother Tom, so farewell to letter-
writing, and believe me, my dear Stewart, with tender
recollections of you all . . .

To his sister Marcia

[? NEWCASTLE, early in 1859.]

By the way, what horribly heterodox ideas you have
about reading ; you might as well want to taste to-day
in your mouth all the dinners you had ever eaten as wish
to remember all the ideas you had ever had. Thank you,
no. They have given you strength ; following an argument gave you some additional ability, and though the

memory of it is gone, the ability is not, unless you have turned lazy since, which you have not.

But I wish I had time to write you about this, for it is one of the few things I have clear opinions of my own about. Believe this, that very, very few people can read ; almost everybody can read history, travels, science (objective instruction), but very few can read books calculated to strengthen their own minds, to increase their subjective power—such books as Butler, Foster, and scores more. Many can understand them thoroughly and answer any questions on them, but they can do this without having themselves *thought through* what the author has thought ; now you must do this if you would acquire some permanent good from the thoughts of another ; they must not remain *his*, they must become yours, not ideas which you have got from him, but thoughts that you have thought for yourself (under his guidance of course). Ponder this, and I believe it will do you good.

To the Same

100 LAURISTON PLACE,
[EDINBURGH], 22nd July 1859.

This is not to grow to a letter, but is for the most part just to thank you for your epistles and to say that your desk has come, along with a pot of some confection or other. The desk I won't say anything about as I suppose you will prefer making your opinion of it yourself by unbiassed observation.

Nothing has happened since you left, and if you want a summary of domestic intelligence you will find it in Eccl. iii. 15.[1] I went towards the High Street on Wednesday, but turned away when I got near it, my head being like clay, my heart like gall, and my blood like boiling

---

[1] 'That which hath been is now ; and that which is to be hath already been. . . .'

verjuice ; so I passed the greater part of that day in the Grange Cemetery.

I have no time, or I might prolong this. I dare say this should have been to Mary, but I do not think I 'll write to her again till I can give some better account of myself. I am out of the tub, but the sight of all my hopes (for life, at least) vanishing into thin air—not vanishing altogether like Alfred Jones, but hanging about to mock me—makes me still bad and wretched. I suppose one must make up one's mind, however, to be wicked, and mean, and vacillating, and to be content. I learn to know the difference between feeling and senti-ment—also a painful lesson. Also I begin to have a far-away perception of what is meant by humility—a most disturbing perception to . . .

To the Same

100 LAURISTON PLACE,
2nd August 1859.

BEST BECAUSE DEAREST, AND MY OWN VICE VERSÂ,— Don't suppose I am so bad as this. I have answered your note long ago, but giving it to Peg to enclose to you, she has scragged the whole correspondence, and what she has done with it I don't know, and I suppose no more do you, and all the compensation she offers is this inside.*

Of myself *silentium sat*—I don't mean that *silentium* has sat upon my lips till Mamma is wearying for you to come back, though this also is true, but as *verbum sat sapienti*, a word is enough to a wise woman, so *silentium sat omnium sapientissimæ*, something less than a word is plenty for a woman that's wiser than the whole truck. (N.B., by the way : ' Main truck ' is the answer to a question you asked me long ago at dinner one day at the Hogues' : if you 've forgot the question, of course you don't need the answer.)

There were a lot of very fine things in my note (though

not so many as in yours, which I consider about the top of all letter-writing), so you can't expect that I should again perform in the same style, and so soon. Thank Andie for her little note, but tell her that sentiment is one thing, feeling another, and that while the one may do for preaching on, the other must be the backbone of deeds. Tell her also to walk through this age with a legible ticket before her and in her own heart, ' BEWARE OF HUMBUG.' Oh ! to be true all ' zrou ' !

Just one thing. How easy to say Throw your heart into your present work. That is (if honestly done), forget all you ever hoped, cut short all you have ever prepared, and thus naked of preparation and of hopes go and instruct and comfort !

* [The enclosure.] I should have told you that yesterday as I was heaving along I espied in the distance a figure with hand extended and mouth distended, which of course did not disappoint me in proving to be Professor Smeaton. He as usual led me to believe that I was the man nearest to his heart, and indeed there is literally no room for him *showing* more affection even to his wife ; as for himself, I much doubt if ever once in his life it has occurred to him that there is one George Smeaton presently a dweller on earth, who needs to be cared for.

To his sister Mary

11 CASTLE STREET,
4th December 1859.

After your yesterday's letter was posted, Mamma got very rapidly worse, and suffered a very great deal. I wish you had been here to help, but I am glad you did not see her tossing uneasily from side to side, and sometimes trying to get relief by sitting up in bed. Marsh is very much worn out, last night especially being most painful.   We would both like a long talk with you, but I suppose that cannot be.   You may interpret my feelings by my last letter.   I can't write more now.

PS.—It was at ten minutes to six this morning that Mamma died.

To the Same

11 CASTLE STREET,
EDINBURGH, *8th December* 1859.

We have just come in, having left our Mother beside her aunt, and more I can scarcely say, for this whole week, and more than ever to-day, I have been flooded by emotions of such diverse character that I can scarcely discern what is real and right, and what is morbid and false.   So much delight is given rise to by seeing Tom and Charles and Katharine and Andie, and such a true repose in the kind, kind affection of Maggie, and then the reflection, What is calling out all this ?   But I can't tell you what Maggie has been to Marsh and me at this time.   Every one has been very kind, but she more than all.   Charlie Stirling came in and followed with us to the grave, and Robert Gordon and Cousin Tom and Davie Hogue.   But we will tell you all when you come, which I trust you will be able to do sooner than you speak of. Katharine intends staying till the middle or end of next week, and would like very much if you could come before she goes away.   Now Mary, do try and come.   Then if you do, Marsh will never be alone till after the holidays, for you will go out with her to West Mains.   You will excuse us pressing you to leave your own home at such a time, and I know you will do all you can to be here next week.   Write, please, immediately, and say when we may expect you.

We were all very much disappointed that George could not get.   He was so much with Mamma, and had so true an affection for her, that we feel his absence a great blank. I do trust that those feelings of affection that are so quickened at a time like this among us, may be perpetuated and constantly increasing.

I can't write any more, but do try and come, and say at once when. I know George won't grudge you.

Mamma lay as if she slept—the complexion being noway changed.

To his sister Marcia

[Begun at Birdhopecraig, Northumberland, and finished at Hexham, *February* 1860.]

Believing with a faith passing the faith of some who count themselves faithful that in the course of my travels I will reach ('sometime—far off—at last' [the poets, particularly the laureate]) an envelope, and a Queen's head, and a post-office, I make the most of my opportunities this Saturday night (the wet and windy exit of a windy, but fortunately not wet day), while you are, I hope, all sitting cracking, a select, pleasant and refreshing-to-think-of company, and begin to answer your letter, which can never fully be answered, for it called upon those feelings that lie deep and far down in the heart, far from the lips, and that silence best expresses, or only these three words, I love you. Did you ever observe that ' love ' is the only fitting copula of a first and a second person, or do you despise a grammatical way of putting the fundamental law of the human universe ? The solemnities of the subject I leave again to silence, whose offices in this world are many and important.

You do not at all know (now really you don't) the full pleasure (and also the pain) of receiving a letter, for you never received one from yourself when you had come to a desolate region at the end of a twenty-six mile solitary ride, and had taken in at one glance all the comforts and discomforts of a queer little room that you are destined to know better, and even intimately, by inhabiting it for a time. Had I been to preach immediately after reading your letter, the other candidates might have said good-bye to Birdhopecraig. Let me say ' What a brick you are ! ' and what masses of good you have made over to me, my duck, in your lifetime, nuggets more precious than those of Australia—of high spirits, hope, energy, calmness and the breaking up of a rocky heart to flow into pleasant affection for every one. This is not sentiment, it is truth. It is my view of you as seen by heart and mind, alone here as I sit, where paltry sense cannot distort.

Here I am once more in the habitable parts of the earth. I started yesterday at eight and got down here to dinner, but too late for the post. This is market-day, so I am going to prepare something, as I have to hold two meetings this week up yonder, one on Thursday, the other on Friday. I had one on Sunday evening, and am to have another on Sunday evening next. So you see I am popular, and as it is only for one week that I will ever have the chance of experiencing this part of human affairs, I go with the tide for this week. I think of Spurgeon and his thousands and compare them to my tens, and draw conclusions.

Katharine and I had long confabs about you yesterday, resulting in the usual conclusion that Providence does more in this world than planning. Kathie [1] wants me to send you an apple by post, but reflects that everybody would eat it, so your share might come to be of the smallest. She sends you a letter.

I got on grand with Miss Hope,[2] but fear I indulged in

---

[1] His niece, daughter of 'Katharine' Dods, just mentioned.
[2] His hostess at Birdhopecraig.

a little sentiment about her rheumatism and her cats.
She is an extensive proprietor in this species of live-
stock, having two to lie in the oven on one side of her
fire, and one whose tail may be seen disappearing into
the depths of the boiler on the other. Which accounts for
the milk in the cocoa-nut, that is to say, for the frequent
' curn '-like specks in the bread, and the marks on the
beef made by incisors that never saw Sheffield. The
room was comfortable enough, but taught me to appreciate the free air, the ornament, and the fine lightage of
the bigger room outside. Good-bye. I am longing to
see you and the rest.

To his sister Andrea

11 CASTLE STREET,
EDINBURGH, 18th April 1860.

I have not time to write a very long letter, so I don't
take an extensive acreage of paper, as you see. It 's
just before tea on prayer-meeting night, not a propitious
period for letter-writing, but I must thank you for your
birthday present, which was more acceptable than any
other you could have devized, I can assure you. There
is one of your epistles (a leaf of it, at least) that I keep
in my journal and read very, very often, and I would
write you oftener to tell you how I value you and all
that concerns you, but time is not long enough for all
the nice things, and I am lazy. I might have written
to you oftener, but men—or I, at least, am selfish.

I have not much to do just now. I write a sermon per
week and a prayer-meeting address, and read some.
Sunday is the hard day. I rise responsible when the rest
may lie at ease, and have generally, always I may say,
to preach twice—not in Lady Glenorchy's, but somewhere.
Then at night I have a class of young women—about

two of whom are spokesfemales for the lot. It 's a true
British meeting, a representative Assembly. I like the
work very well, only there 's too little to do and too little
for doing it. I could not go and hear Gladstone just
for poverty—every penny that is not used up in living
is devoted to books, and of pennies that go that way
the number is easily reckoned, for I have just bought
three books this year. But all things are good, and
poverty teaches like the rest. It 's an experience, however, not to be desired.

I would like to send you Marcia's letters if I could
spare them. It 's dismal without her, very, though I sometimes think I both work and am better when living alone.
I wish you were here ; I think we could get on, though I
have a vast deal of brute in me—an almost unconquer-
able deal. Willie Jeffrey is away now too, as I suppose
you will soon discover. He went in good spirits with his
bones and his medal : he has, of course, the self-con-
demnatory growling of most young men before they come
out of their tubs and see round them. He will do—I
have no doubt when his mother sees his medal, she will
think he has done. I have not seen the Hogues this
week—as I am resolved to work and live on work while
I can. To-morrow, however, I hope to go and be re-
freshed. Now this is a shameful little morsel for your
great lump, but I am really unable to say more, so believe
me when I say that I am . . .

To his sister Marcia

11 Castle Street,
Edinburgh, 19*th April* 1860.

Let not your last letter be repeated unless you wish
me to take the telegraph express to Cheltenham. But
after all I daresay you may growl away, there 's nothing
like getting it all out, and to-night I could outgrowl the

whole tribe of bears, not because of any particular grievance, but just because I am in the mood. I am naturally a cannibal, and I find now my true vocation to be in the South Sea Islands, not after your plan to be Arnold to a troop of savages, but to be one of them where they are all selfish and lazy and brutal. Why I have been born to be a Christian when I would have made so savage a savage, is one of the marvels : '*omnia exeunt in mysterium*,' a favourite adage of yours, by which I have always taken you to mean that in whatever direction you choose to follow your nose you are sure to come at last (and the last is very shortly) to an ocean, boundless, fathomless and uncommunicative. I know one reason for your growls and one for my own, and as you give promise of being the better for your growlery, I do hope the same for myself ; but the amount I suffered in the second prayer-meeting to-night was really trying, and if I am a probationer much longer, I will either be able to bear a good deal or—— However, I have made it my almost incessant prayer that I may get work fit for me, whatever it be, and I believe I will : meanwhile I go on. I have come to very nearly the end of my sermon for this week, so I am looking forward to some Plato.

Your algebraic question lies before me (as reviewers say), but what to say about it I don't know, except that the answer is quite right, and that if you will try it with numbers instead of being on your p's and q's, you will see the meaning of it better. [Formula.] That is called approximation, the answer coming always, so long as you find yourself inclined to work, nearer and nearer the truth. Unless the book gives a good explanation, don't bother either yourself or your pupils about it, but go on to what is within your understanding.

Poor James, how I do pity him, and how I do pity

the masters that could ever dream of putting him to
Latin before he knew Hebrew even, not to mention
English! Tell John I am very sorry indeed to hear of
his being several times dux, and hope to hear of his
being dux only once, and that he is never any place
else at all.

To the Same

11 CASTLE STREET,
EDINBURGH, 23rd April 1860.

This is not Thursday evening, but I found my claim
to write to you on the ground that I have been at a
prayer-meeting at Leith (for one of the elders). I was
dismal all day, have done scarcely any work, have talked
horrible things within me, and been worse than ever,
and you will expect to hear that I was wretched at the
p.m. If so, you will be disappointed, for I never got on
so well, easy and complete, quite satisfying myself ; any
further attempts at solving the problem of myself I ——
leave to posterity. One thing I will append to 'We cannot
kindle when we will,'—'We do kindle when we won't.'
This being the preaching week here, I am to be at Kirkcaldy on Sunday, and as they are wishing to get a colleague and successor to the minister there, it does not
require the discernment of a Palmerston to see that I
will be looked on as a candidate, and it will not fail to
strike you that this is my last chance ; but they won't
listen to a man who reads, so what is he to do ? I 'm
in a fix ; I do believe if I don't get this, I won't get anything, and yet if I get it——
Did you give Mima any instructions about being good
to me before you left ? for she is sometimes unusually nice.
I just saw them for an hour on Saturday, as Innes wanted
me down—down I did go at eight, and stayed till 11.45,

L

with Laidlaw and Knight, a very pleasant time. They are superior fellows all, to me at least.

On Sunday I met —— coming from Rainy's and going to read *Pilgrim* to one of her blind people ; luckily I was in a bad humour, or I would assuredly have embraced her and called her my own, which she is not. I say truly and with deliberation she did me more good than Mr. ——, whom I had been hearing ; she is a little sunbeam, a medicine, a star, a fountain, almost a Marcia ; at least your loss is worse because it includes the loss of her. And while this and a thousand other things make me bewail your absence, I have only found one cause of gladness in it, and that is (for you will like to know it), that it teaches me to know how much I love you, and that 's nice. So when anything comes up glumpy and makes me wish for you, I just trip up the sadness, and supplant it with the gladness of being sure I love you much, much. You are the only person I have felt this to strongly and consciously ; many people I have sought to win the love of, and delighted in the consciousness of that, but no one whom it seems so satisfactory to me not only to love, but to know that I love. But one gets deeper into things, and thereby learns what a depth lies yet beyond.

Having finished my sermon early last week I read the first of Plato's dialogues and found it far easier and even more delicious than I expected. I could have made a good translation of it when I was in the heat of it, but ' 'tis past.'

Now I would like to sit and write all day, but as that was not a part of Mr. Davidson's engagement, I must just stop. I send away this because I want to hear from you immediately. I must go away out to-day and make a great visitation.* Ever your wretch. . .

* One feels quite grand when one cannot do just

whatever one likes—our great sovereign Duty, aren't
we proud of your livery ?

To the Same

11 CASTLE STREET,
FRIDAY, 27th *April* [1860].

About Kirkcaldy, I saw nothing else for it ; to commit
is absurd in my case ; to talk would not do, as I would feel
so ashamed of myself that I would have no freedom ; so
I had resolved to take ' The Temptation ' and ' The First
Fruits,' and deliver as much as I know and read the rest,
and leave myself to their tenderness.   My present comfort makes me possibly too indifferent to the result ; then
if I went to Kirkcaldy, what of you ?   But if the one is
arranged, I suppose the other will be.   You know there
must be girls to be taught where I go.

By the bye, why could you not spare one of the stamps
that came in yours for the outside ?   Did you think that
twelve inside = at least one out ? for the postman either
did not see the twelve inside or did not agree with your
valuation, and made me pay 2d.

To the Same

[11 CASTLE STREET, EDINBURGH.]
Sahara, past the Oasis,
three days' journey [*May* 1860].[1]

BELOVEDEST,—Innes was up last night.   He's a
brick, but I was unwell and in dumps, and though he
stayed with me, walking till nine o clock, I said scarcely
anything to him the whole time.   However, he thinks
rowing would be a fine new kind of exercise, so I am to
introduce Sandeman and him to Granton next free
night.   I was telling him about our night there,
Monday last, so glorious I feel as if you must already
know all about it.   We went up as far as Cramond

---

[1] Three days after his sister's last letter.

Island, and took possession of it, and had grand pulls. I think I 'd make a fine fo'castle man, but the salt junk and sleeping with twenty others—talk of a room to yourself!   I 've been reading Carlyle last week, the *Sartor Resartus*, and it 's just like the first bathe in summer.   I *wish* you were here to read it too.   I had to let myself out somehow, so I took it down to Mima on Saturday, and made her read a lot of bits.   It 's beyond a short description—do come home quickly and get it read.   It has come to me just in the very month I needed it.   I 'll send you some extracts.

I am to be at Mr. Gillies' on Sunday morning, and intend giving them ' In your patience possess ye your souls.'   It is not so good as others I might give them, but one must have some regard to reputation.   Last Sunday was very pleasant.   Dr. Alexander, though paralysed, is very nice, rough, simple, strong, old school, bound up in a little girl four years old that the wife of his old age died in giving birth to.   But the congregation is huge and important ; argal, I am not the man for their money.

Growl away like a good 'un, and I 'll outgrowl you. Had I written last night, you would have had a fine specimen of me. I felt like Shakspere's old men, ' a plentiful lack of wit, together with most weak hams.' I mixed myself some Gregory, however (not without quoting ' no wife to grind his ——'), and am better.   It is dull work this, though.   Again I say I would not mind it so much were it only my hands that had to work, or my head ; but when it 's me myself it 's harder.   But as Carlyle says, let us consume our own smoke.   What *is* the use of growling, after all ?   *Was* I made to be happy or to be pleasurably comfortable all my days ? Patience, patience.   You will probably get the bits of Carlyle some day during the week.

The weather here is superb. 'No speck nor stain obscures,' you know. Tell A—— her *British Workmen* are doing their best to better twelve families in Greenside. It often makes a visit a vast deal easier, quite a different thing, to have a pretty paper to give, and that costs something.

If you are going to send texts I 'll send you one that will last you all the year and more—χαίρετε ἐν Κυρίῳ πάντοτε· πάλιν ἔρω, χαίρετε, Rejoice in the Lord always : again I say, rejoice : then notice the connections on to the end of the paragraph. I am not, however, going to allow myself to write you a lecture on it.

To the Same [1]

[? *May* 1860.]

'It is very mournful, yet not useless, to see and know how the Greatest and Dearest, in a short while, would find his place quite filled up here, and no room for him.'

'Detached, separated ! I say there is no such separation : nothing hitherto ever was stranded, cast aside ; but all, were it only a withered leaf, works together with all ; is borne forward on the bottomless, shoreless flood of Action, and lives through perpetual metamorphoses. . . . Rightly viewed no meanest object is insignificant.'

'I too acknowledge the all-but omnipotence of early culture and nurture.'

'Any road will lead you to the end of the world.'

'Obedience is our universal duty and destiny ; wherein whoso will not bend must break : too early and too thoroughly we cannot be trained to know that Would, in this world of ours, is as mere zero to Should, and for most part as the smallest of fractions even to Shall.'

'From poverty does the strong educe nobler wealth.'

---

[1] The extracts begin without introduction on a sheet of notepaper, and later develope into a letter.

' *Frisch zu, Bruder!* Here are Books, and we have brains to read them ; here is a whole Earth and a whole Heaven, and we have eyes to look on them. *Frisch zu!* '

' Not what I Have but what I Do is my Kingdom.'

' Like a very young person, I imagined it was with Work alone, and not also with Folly and Sin, in myself and others, that I had been appointed to struggle.'

He quotes an old, kind proverb, ' There is always life for a living one.'

' Thus did soft melodies flow through his heart ; tones of an infinite gratitude ; sweetest intimations that he also was a man, that for him also unutterable joys had been provided.'

' To consume your own choler, as some chimneys consume their own smoke ; to keep a whole Satanic School spouting, if it must spout, inaudibly, is a negative yet no slight virtue, nor one of the commonest in these times.'

' With Stupidity and sound Digestion man may front much.'

' The painfullest feeling is that of your own Feebleness. And yet of your Strength there is and can be no clear feeling, save by what you have prospered in, by what you have done. Between vague, wavering Capability and fixed indubitable Performance, what a difference ! A certain inarticulate Self-consciousness dwells dimly in us ; which only our Works can render articulate and decisively discernible. Our Works are the mirror wherein the spirit first sees its natural lineaments. Hence, too, the folly of that impossible Precept, *Know thyself* ; till it be translated into this partially possible one, *Know what thou canst work at*.'

' Always there is a black spot in our sunshine : it is even, as I said, the *Shadow of Ourselves*.'

And a great deal more which would give you an Indigestion were I to send it.   Fancy the book the uniform style of which is very little less brilliant than these gems. I wish you were here to read it too, and for other reasons.

I can't write you a letter to-day, as I have copper-coloured clouds hemming me in on all sides, even above, owing partly to an idle week just gone, that is, a Platonic and so on week, partly to mine ancient restlessness, and partly to the deepening and still deepening sense of my brutality.   I think you are about the only person (on deliberate survey) towards whom I have ever acted from love : you do not know how selfish I am, you do not know what selfishness is and can, until you know me, and it has brought me into serious scrapes and sins that drag after them the usual vile train of shame and heartlessness and pride.   Were I to tell certain friends of mine what I am, they would aghast hold up their hands and say ' You in the Church ! '   Tell me, if you can, if this is honest, this way of life.

But I have no time to begin to growl, and I will write you a letter on Thursday, probably in the very best spirits imaginable, for this also is a part of me, a wavering-ness that if it secures I shall dip into the black, secures at the same time that I shall also dip into the bright. It 's pleasant truly to go about among people with the clear, home-pressed consciousness that many of them already justly despise you, and that if others do not, it is only because they don't know you.

Now you need not think of me as dismal, because I am not.

To the Same

[11 CASTLE STREET,
EDINBURGH, *May* 1860.]

Here is, I think, something confirmatory of what I said, or what I was thinking at any rate, a week or two ago ; probably I expressed it better; this is from *Sartor* :—

' But indeed Conviction, were it never so excellent, is worthless till it convert itself into Conduct. . . . Most true is it, as a wise man teaches us, that " Doubt of any sort cannot be removed except by Action." On which ground, too, let him who gropes painfully in darkness or uncertain light, and prays vehemently that the dawn may ripen into day, lay this other precept well to heart, which to me was of invaluable service : " Do the Duty which lies nearest thee," which thou knowest to be a Duty ! Thy second Duty will already have become clearer.'

You will know also how I applied the following :—

' Fortunatus had a wishing Hat, which when he put on, and wished himself Anywhere, behold he was There. . . . Were a Hatter to establish Himself, in the Wahngasse of Weissnichtwo, and make felts of this sort for all mankind, what a world we should have of it ! Of him would I purchase, were it with my last groschen.'

This, too, you may make several things of, religious and other :—' Remember what an umpire Nature is ; what a greatness, composure of depth and tolerance there is in her. You take wheat to cast into the Earth's bosom : your wheat may be mixed with chaff, chopped straw, barn-sweepings, dust and all imaginable rubbish ; no matter : you cast it into the kind, just earth ; she grows the wheat,—the whole rubbish she silently absorbs, shrouds *it* in, says nothing of the rubbish. The yellow wheat is growing there ; the good Earth is silent about all the rest,—has silently turned all the rest to some benefit too, and makes no complaint about it ! So everywhere in Nature ! She is true and not a lie ; and yet so great, and just, and motherly in her truth.'

Good this, isn't it ?

To the Same

11 CASTLE STREET,
EDINBURGH, 10*th May* [1860].

BEST OF SISTERS,—It just strikes me as I begin to
write to you that this is a duty I never weary of, and
it strikes me as a proof how singularly excellent a
creature you must be to have such power over my
affections, or to prove that I have affections at all. But
what is to become of me if you are always to be away,
this style, I don't know. However, I must not growl.
Let us consume our own smoke. (This, you observe,
is my present motto.)

Innes was up last night. We walked out to the
toll (Dean Bridge), and then along George Street, and
down to his lodgings. We had much talk on whether
a man be responsible for his expression, whether
expression in the father becomes feature in the
child, etc., etc. He has lent me Vaughan's *Harrow
Sermons*, which are not, I would say, quite up to Arnold's.
I like Innes for his steadfastness, and hope he may do me
some good that way.

I lent Stewart *Sintram*, which I have been draining
lately. I wonder I did not more thoroughly delight in
it before ; also *Aslauga's Knight* ; they are both of them
what every young man ought to have deep into him.

It is, as I said, Friday morning, and I have already
been at a prayer-meeting which began at 7.15. Now do
not omit to let H—— know of this, and ask her if she will
not let us hope the Free Church may become Christian
if we go on in this good course. It is to be every morning
for a week.

Since coming home I have got your letter, and *cannot*
say how it went all through me like an injection of new,
healthy blood : I cannot tell you of it, for the English
language did not take such letters into account. I met

Mima yesterday, and held her for a time in converse,
though she was as usual busy : she has always, she says,
been seeking for time to write, but has, as you know, not
accomplished it.   I knew I would find a fit present for
her ; I fell upon a German Hymn Book at an old book-
shop, clean and nice, with 1560 of the best for 2s. : that
beats yours.

I rejoice to hear James has been again delivered to
our glorious nursing mother nature, and feel persuaded
that had they kept him at ' mathematics ' much longer,
they would have made an integral calculus (freely rendered, completely a stone) of him.   The account of your
walks does me as much good as if I were taking them :
the very words ' fields, trees, brooks, meadows, Spring,
pansies, *England*,' what freshness they bring to the
withering heart.

St. Peter [1] does speak to me, but pride is the awful
poison of life.   One great want of our lives is that we do
not take the word of God as His Word speaking to us.
We ask for assurance of this and that, when, dear me,
here is God telling us all about it the whole time, not
loudly repeating what He has spoken, but from eternity
to eternity *always* telling us eternal truth.   Would that
we had ears to hear and hearts to understand !   Surely it
is by realising this written word and the Word incarnate
to be the present voice of God addressing us singly that
we are to reach that gladness and constant contented
assurance that the words of man give us.   I think there
is a good deal in the *eternity* of truth—not only what
will be true for ever, but, taking eternity as the Now
that is always, truth that is true now, and by the word
spoken to us now.

I wish I had time to send you some Platonic extracts ;
perhaps through the week I may do so.

---

[1] A picture of St. Peter walking on the sea, which his sister had
recently given to him.

I fear I must come to a pause, though did the course
of this world permit, I would very gladly wear out the
day talking with you.

To the Same

11 CASTLE STREET,
EDINBURGH, 17*th May* 1860.

MY DEAREST OF WOMEN,—You are the most encouraging of persons ; each of your letters does me
more good than its precursor, and while it thus gives
me the grateful though scarcely credible assurance
that you are improving, it tells me also that I am
not hopelessly bad ; for how can I be so when I have so
long and increasingly loved you ?   Love is a saving grace,
saving from as well as covering a multitude of sins ; and
though it is heterodox to believe that the good works of
another can cover my sins, yet it is true that they may
prevent me from sinning.   Salt again.   I wonder when
that sermon will be finished.

I have heaps to say to you that has been boiling like
a volcano all the week (and, indeed, I had to give it vent
by a little safety-valve * that I enclose), of which this
ought to be the crater, but the bells are chiming for
Assembly, and I must go this year ; it won't do to be a
heathen any more.   Then I dare not trust to-morrow,
for Charles will be here, and that means not much
towards letter- or any other writing.

Tell H—— that I have not missed one morning meeting, nor have ever been late : surely I may go and hear
the Dean, at least, on the strength of this purification ;
might I ?   Dave calls us the Early Christians.

You asked me a question, by the bye, that I 've never
answered, about body, soul, and spirit,   I believe there
must be a difference, as the *vox populi* makes one, as, *e.g.*,
we would call M—— and M—— choice spirits, S—— a

rum soul, and C—— a trifling body; but speaking seriously, theologians have distinguished them, especially
Olshausen, whose hobby it is to keep it up continually.   The spirit is the highest part of man, that on
which the Holy Spirit rests and operates; the soul is
something like the heart, only joined with this there is
the idea of vitality—a man as he is born is a soul (study
1 Cor. xv. 45 [1]), but really what is intelligible and true
to a Greek is utterly unintelligible in English.   I believe
that the marrow of many of the finest passages of the
N.T. is wasted on us, but if any light breaks upon me,
I 'll send you a slice of the beam.

The Assembly has put me into a wicked frame; I 'll
never be a Churchman, it would kill me; I hope dinner
(that 's my time for Carlyle, you know) may refresh me.
If I had been born without pride I could have been more
comfortable; the second birth comes to be a most
seriously practical affair.   If people would listen to
sermons with a dash of bitterness in them, I would give
some vigorous ones just now, but rather, I suppose, I
should preach one to myself on bitterness.

* [The safety valve.]   I must not omit to mention
that in one of the morning meetings an elder being
asked to pray did so, and including me in his petitions
desired that I ' might have no confidence in the paper '
—was it not rare ?   There 's hopes of me yet, you see.
I am sorry the meetings are done, though they were not
specially nice at all, yet an hour so spent is a good
foundation for a day's work.

You seem to be getting on better now, or do you hide
your complaints ?   Don't do that, for there is a satisfaction in getting your growls and thinking, ' Now she says

---

[1] ' And so it is written, The first man Adam was made a living soul;
the last Adam was made a quickening spirit. '

this to *me*, this is her heart ; had she been writing to some one else, she would have spoken through a mask.' What would be my ideal of a letter would be a transcript of all the ideas that had been most interesting to yourself throughout the week, using ideas in the widest sense so as to include feelings and all the rest of it, spirit, soul, and body.

To the Same

11 CASTLE STREET,
28th May 1860.

I go to Kennethmont next Sunday, and am going to read one and preach one, and do my best, I suppose. Though it is out of the world, I do think I would rather just go away there than stay on here hanging between heaven and earth.

I had a long, long talk with Charles, but the worst of him is, as a helper to me, that he believes so clearly in Satan's personality, and lays such a deal to his door, whereas it 's my very misery that the thoughts that arise and dwell within me are my own—that this abominable disposition, and this other, are *me* and not another. Of course, God is our God to teach us to do His will, and His Spirit is good to lead us into the land of uprightness, but the weariness and the abasement of finding out all one's own blackness, and of never getting visibly better !

For the mere sake of *getting on*, of being nearer my work and promotion, and of being settled to the work of my life, I own I am not very anxious for a parish.   I know very well that my *man* can grow here every bit as well as elsewhere, and it 's to grow we are planted here for—and if I am to be left here to fight out this difficulty, then I must, and it may and ought to do me good too ; but how to do it, and what to do !   Advise me, if you can, taking me at the very lowest you can imagine, for I am worse than that.

How will these strange connections we have formed with one another, and the difficulties we have brought one another into, appear to our view reflected on them from a future life ? One thing, Marsh, this may sour and sicken you at the whole affair, men, women and all together, but I believe we are all for your good, and the more so if we can get good out of you.

To the Same

11 CASTLE STREET,
31st May 1860.

It is now past meeting time. Innes has been up. I like him growingly. He has left with me a very nice article of his. I did not get on well at the meeting to-night. I am not getting any better at addressing people. I can read to them, and I can write, but it 's not in my nature to speak to more than two. Surely something will soon settle this important question of whether I am to preach or not. I am very seldom, if ever, in low spirits about this ; it is not a thing to be in low spirits about. I don't think it is my fault (that is, my fault as compared with other things I would call my fault). I have tried pretty hard, and if it is not to be, something else will be, that 's all. To share a lodging with you and jog along from hand to mouth would not be a life to be resigned to ; we should rather think not ; but many things make me desire to be a preacher. The great reasons weigh with me ; then surely Mamma would like it, and when I think of all she did for this end I do strongly desire to get a church.

But would it not be nice to go on as we have been ? But then something black would be sure to come ; and it isn't the nice that has the deciding voice in the matter.

To the Same

11 Castle Street,
7th June 1860.

I got to Kennethmont with difficulty, feeling at every stage further and further from everywhere, especially from Cheltenham (which I beg to advertise the Greeks and all others whom it may concern is the true centre of the Globe).   At last I got there late at night, pouring rain (but we are quite used to that now, beginning to become amphibious).   I put up at a small farm, where they fed me lustily ; the cream, you might have felt its healthy influence at Cheltenham, and lots of it.   Well, I was wickeder that Saturday than even I am often, and on Sunday I was cold as Kane, and preached to them as if I had been thirty years their minister, and was getting rather tired of the berth.   A lot slept, which it struck me was uncivil when they had asked me to come, and at my own very considerable expense.

The manse at Kennethmont seems very nice, and is larger than the church.   I don't think they liked me, except an old man, and one young man, especially his wife.

Innes I have seen a good deal lately, and Sandeman kept me walking George Street backwards and forwards for two hours last night, enforcing on me a certain style of preaching.   I called for Smeaton also when I came home, and as he was going out he asked me to go with him, and took my arm a long way ; was not he good ? He thinks Kennethmont the very place for me 'with my studious habits' (eheu !), and is going to write and call them all sorts of bad names if they don't take me.

. . . the Spirit is the only Preacher, the only everything for us to live and work by ; how grand if one could be habitually and actively willing that He should do and be in us what He is always so willing to do and be! Sometimes it strikes me with a kind of sudden rapture how these words 'with a pure heart fervently' shall be fulfilled in our love to one another hereafter. How good must He be who, knowing our enmity, has given us such power of affection, natures so capable of intense delight. Could one only always believe this goodwill of God, how easy it would be to love, serve, and enjoy Him. What are the minds that can see, and not see this love, the hearts that can feel, and not feel this?

To the Same

11 CASTLE STREET,
EDINBURGH, 14th June 1860.

It's no use thinking, however: μηδὲν μεριμνᾶτε, which is, Be careful for nothing; would that I could do likewise! Each week just now is convincing me more deeply of the unfitness of me and the ministry. But I have done a good deal of work at Plato and one thing or another this day or two. Plato is all that you have ever heard of good of him, truly wonderful.

I have written a sermon on ' Be sure your sin will find you out,' but it is not what I expected. Had I courage, or would it consist with decency, to give them extracts from my own autobiography, I would have preached effectively. I can't understand why Augustine's *Confessions* are not *universally* read; they seem to me to be just *the* biography, and I am strongly inclined to write a new translation. I know it could be no better than others, but there ought to be lots circulating, and I don't know of any that circulates at all. Now I must stop this most uninteresting, dead scraping, hoping that the rain will follow my example, and let me get out to visit my flock which is not mine. Of course, I will tell you the certainties about Kennethmont whenever I know them.

I have been thinking of trying to write an article for *Macmillan's Magazine* on ' The women who have loved us,' but of course it would be a failure like the rest of me. But what Carlyle says of Johnson is true of most : ' It was needful for him, at all rates, to know that outward profit, that success of any kind is *not* the goal he has to aim at.   Pride, vanity, ill-conditioned egoism of all sorts are bred in his heart, as in every heart ; need, above all, to be cast out of his heart, to be with whatever pangs torn out of it, cast forth from it, as a thing worthless.'

Now my trustiest and ever and altogether to be loved, believe me, though not your clever and wise and good and steady and pure, yet your most affectionate brother . . .

To the Same

11 Castle Street,
Thursday, 21*st June* 1860.

I feel inclined to begin ' Dearly beloved and longed for,' but out of respect to Mrs. Hogue and some more I do not, though it is rather hard to be cut out of all the best phrases in the English language.   I 'm not going to be hypocritical, however, and call you anything else, for that is what you are to me just now.

What in the world made you give me Venn ?   I 'll sell it and send you the book I get in exchange ; I think that will be about the right thing to do.   I am not by any means sure I 'll like him.   I have only just looked into it, but I fear he is not the man for me ; has he not a great deal of pushing assurance ?   The letter to the young back-slider is first-rate.

Next winter lies in the thickest mist—what you are to do, and what is to become of me—but I can't say I often think about it.   Mr. Bruce (old King David) wants me to

M

go out to Auckland, and I fear there 's no work nearer to be had.

I don't think I have any news this week. I have been hard at work on 'How long halt ye between two opinions?' I took tea with the Fordyces on Monday evening ; they were just as kind as could be, James offering to get me books out of the Advocates' Library as many and as often as I choose. On Tuesday they called for me to go down and see a Rifle Match among the Advocates. William kept first for a long time, but after that Hubie Hamilton[1] crept up and got before him ; they all did excellently well, rarely missing at distances of 400, 500, and 600 yards. It would have done Napoleon good to see them.

The weather is now beautiful here, and we had a jolly day last Saturday visiting the Channel Fleet, Innes, Sandeman, Knight and I ; it was real prime.

To the Same

11 CASTLE STREET,
EDINBURGH, 23rd June 1860.

Just a line to ask you to advise me. They want a teacher of English Literature and Classics in the College department of the Glasgow F.C. Normal School. Work four hours a day, five days a week, ten weeks' vacation, salary liberal. Ought I not to apply ? Remember these are the very things, the only things, I have a shadow of proficiency in, or am likely ever to be good at. The only three classes I took prizes in were Greek, Latin, and Literature. Now I less grudge to ask you to think about this, as you have no lessons to make your head ache. But let me know soon what you think. I have written a long letter to Tom stating the case fully—a

---

[1] Sir William Hamilton's second son, who was at the Edinburgh Academy with the writer, and afterwards became Sheriff-Substitute at Edinburgh.

graduate is preferred. It does surely seem work much
liker me than my present ? Does it not ? I need not
write long to you, for you know me all already. I recant
every wicked thing I said about Venn ; I have been
looking at the letters towards the end, and like them
immensely better.

To the Same

11 CASTLE STREET,
EDINBURGH, 26th June 1860.

So far from thinking you the most unsympathizing
of sisters, I would challenge all sisterdom to produce a
more sympathizing, or one who sympathizes to better
purpose. I am very grateful for your letter ; it and
one from Tom much to the same purpose have decided
me not to apply, though I am not by any means finally
convinced either by what you or he says that I am any
better fit for, or as well fit for preaching as teaching. I fear
there is among us much unwise and wicked, as well as
some good ambition for works which nearly concern
and *visibly* promote the kingdom of God. One thing
I know, it was wrong in me then to choose when I did ;
whether my evil has been turned to good, remains to be
seen. Whatever Paul says of the law in the 7th of
Romans I have found true of the ministry ; no doubt
it is holy in itself, but in me it has revealed and *excited*
an amount of sin that has slain me. Other people with
stronger natures may have, doubtless have, endured
a great deal more, but I could not have endured more
misery than I have done since I began to preach. When
I look at the two years as a whole, I cannot but wonder
how I have got through so long ; the mercy is it comes
piece by piece. Sometimes it seems as clear to me as
noonday that I ought at once to give up (a much lower
degree of persuasion would have been to Bunyan a voice

from Heaven). I know that no man's sufficiency is of himself, but I can't *accept* ; to-day I do it, and to-morrow I am unable ; this is my nature, and grace does not expel nature in a day, but only at best in a lifetime ; and the prospect of a life's work in which there will always be the strongest temptation to my besetting sin, or at least the keenest sense of it, is enough to make me dull often. I know that I cannot now reasonably expect success in any line of life, because I don't deserve it and have done what I could to hinder it. Few fellows have made a *messier* start, a more palpable flounder than I. What often riles me is to see fellows getting on fine, and just every way in themselves better men than I, and me missing all their goodness and at the same time all their comfort and usefulness.

But why are all my letters to be of this style, and I suppose mere repetitions of what I 've told you before a score of times ? I can say to you, ' Be not righteous overmuch,' be not too tender to me, for I am the more tempted to prolong my growls. And this is a birthday epistle ? *Sic.* What can I wish you other than what I wished Mima on hers, that she might become younger and younger year by year, renewing her youth with the life that the more it is lived the younger one grows ?

Do any of you want something to read ? If so, get a hold of *Eric, or Little by Little*, by Farrar, and you won't be disappointed.

' Dr. ' Jeffrey came in while I was in the midst of this at 9 o'clock this morning (an early excursion train). I have been with him all day, as he seemed to have no one else, and no one else would miss me or my work. Now it 's past dinner, and he lies smoking on the sofa ; a nice fellow, but he 's so different from me, I wonder we get on so well.

Your letter this morning was, I think, better than any

of Venn's I have seen, a very long way, but I must stop. Ever your beast . . .

PS.—Without this advice of yours and Tom's, I would *certainly* have applied for that situation.

To the Same

11 CASTLE STREET,
EDINBURGH, 28*th June* 1860.

I have done scarcely anything all day, and written no sermon this week, but for conscience-comfort I intend to get up something before the week runs off. I have made no application, nor intend to make any, for that situation, though the salary is tempting—£250. The teaching, however, is of a different style from what I have been used to, and I will wait till, if you have to think of me as a teacher, you may think of me in a position more of a kind with Arnold's. To have been his ' shell ' master must have been worth living for ; but like the porter on the Scottish Central, I think ' this is the queerest world I ever saw,' ' and I having had some experience in worlds,' etc., etc., a facetious porter might have continued.

Do you know, and are you anyways suitably impressed with the knowledge, that your last letter was a very wonderful and felicitously expressed compound of judgment, piety and affection ?

Clark, the publisher, came up to me to-night after the sermon, and walked along a good lump with me. He first asked me if I knew German, and seeing what he was at, I at once said No, explaining to him that I had never been in Germany, nor had learnt it with a teacher. Then he told me that he was now to publish *The North British Review*, and asked me if I would write an article. I think, you know, he made me this offer quite as much from the flush of his own prospect of increased business as from

any idea he has that I would be a worthy contributor.
However, I told him I would gladly try my hand if he
would give me a subject.   He told me to take any, and
write one before November (!), which is the first quarter
of his publication.   Now Marsh, I am going to bother you
again—*think* if there is any book I could review, *i.e.* any
subject I could write on which would connect itself with
some book, will you, and tell me.   For you see, I would
like this kind of work ; it would pay.   I am glad now
I did not ask him for work before, as it is so much nicer
to have it offered.

I don't think there is any other bit of news to tell you.
I have seen neither Innes nor Sandeman this week.   But
my love for Augustine helps me through much, and I am
studying the Psalms, or at least beginning to read them
with some small observation : many a delicious morning
I had at Newcastle with your little Psalter.   I fear I was
better then than now.   I don't think you were.

Would it do to take that new subject, Plato, for an
article ?   That would give an impetus to my reading of
the old gentleman.   One thing to be remembered is, in
a first choice of this kind, that I identify myself with the
department I choose, not altogether, but probably.   The
only other thing I ever thought of doing in this way was
to take up the Fathers, one by one, and give a summary
of their lives, teaching, spirit, and so on, an article each,
beginning with the apostolic (your old friend Diognetus),
then Clement, and so on.   Give me your ideas, please.
You see, that would lead me to reading more professional,
and yet that reading for which I am best prepared.

This is another selfish letter, but you are my senate
as well as my sister, my circle of friends and my intimate.
I would like to give you some bits of Augustine, and I
dare say I just will.   There is first of all the often-quoted
one, ' Thou madest us for Thyself, and our heart is rest-

less until it repose in Thee.'   There are two very fine
paragraphs which, however, I think occur in the *Manual* ;
one sentence of them is ' *Whither* do I call Thee, since I
am in Thee ? or *whence* canst Thou enter into me ?   For
whither can I go beyond heaven and earth, that thence
my God should come into me, who hath said " I fill the
heaven and the earth " ? '   Then a truly magnificent
paragraph : ' What art Thou then, my God ?   What,
but the Lord God ? . . . most merciful, yet most just ;
most hidden, yet most present ; unchangeable, yet all
changing ; never new, never old ; ever working, ever
at rest ; still gathering, yet nothing lacking ' ; and so on.

'What am I to Thee that Thou demandest my love,
and, if I give it not, art wroth with me and threatenest
grievous woes ? '

' In infancy Thou did'st nourish me according to Thine
ordinance whereby Thou distributest Thy riches through
the hidden springs of all things.   Thou also gavest me
to desire no more than Thou gavest ; and to my nurses
willingly to give me what Thou gavest them.   This my
good from them was good for them.   Nor indeed from
them was it, but through them ; for from Thee, O God,
are all good things, and from my God is all my health.'

This quoting from Augustine reminds me of a scheme
I once had of comparing the autobiographies of Augustine,
Bunyan, Halyburton, and *Sartor Resartus*.

To the Same

11 CASTLE STREET,
EDINBURGH, *5th July* 1860.

It is not evening yet, but I have fairly run aground
in a lecture I began on Monday, and of which I have only
succeeded in writing four columns, *i.e.* one third of the
whole thing, though I have been sitting with my pen in

my hand with the most untiring and exemplary uniformity.

I sometimes find myself thinking that you have had
so much worry and work in your life that now you should
surely (and will) get some easy thing to do. As if what
comes after even threescore and ten years of labour and
sorrow is not *also* labour and sorrow.

If I treated you as you deserve I would stop here and
write no more, for I can write nothing but misery and
dryness. But I don't think I will treat you as you
deserve, as I have very seldom, if ever, hitherto done so,
and incoherence of action being one of my aversions
(because one of my great temptations), I won't depart
from my practice.

I had a note from Kennethmont saying I am not to be
asked there again if they are perfectly aware of it ! You
know, all these congregations that refuse me shape
themselves (to me) into a person, let their head fall
knowingly on one side, lay their finger on the right lateral
extension of the nasal instrument, and deliver themselves
as a jeering oracle might be disposed to do : ' You are
not the thing for this,' ' Not quite,' ' No, we are not
reduced to that yet.'

I must confess to you. I have bought books lately
to the following amount : Owen on the Holy Spirit (folio),
1s. 6d.; Warren's *Blackstone*, 1s. 6d.; a translation of
Augustine's *Confessions*, 2s. ; but if you knew the amount
to which I have been tempted, you would think the self-
denial of Francis of Assisi luxurious and indulgent compared to mine. (I got Herbert's poems, too, for 10d.—a
nice little copy, not very correctly printed, but that only
makes you read the more carefully.)

To the Same

11 CASTLE STREET,
EDINBURGH, 12*th July* 1860.

MY DEAREST AND DISTRESSED SISTER,—Many thanks for your growl.   The lees, sediment, bottom-mud of your mind even, partakes of that deliciousness that belongs to you, so that it is refreshing to drink of your turbid mutterings and utterances, as of your lucid and undefiled wisdom.   But I trust you are settled by this time, and are so expectant of your holidays as to be enjoying them in anticipation.   It 's very queer to think of you *beginning* again, but fresh starts have their nice, as well as their nasty, ingredients.   Only, if I go away, eheu!   I am going through to Glasgow on Sunday first to preach as a candidate in Jonathan Anderson's old congregation. The present minister is disabled, and is not expected to preach again.   Whether to desire success or not, I do not know ; of course it is my duty to do my best.   The one thing that has struck me as an advantage is that you could be with me, the one disadvantage that the work would be heavy, as I believe the congregation (besides being a city one) has fallen away greatly.   But why speculate ?

I have a good deal to tell you this week, though not of very great interest.   First, because last, I sat last night till the grave, grey light was laughed out by the merry sunshine, or rather I lay in bed till five this morning, reading *Westward Ho !*   I have a kind of fancy you have read it.   I hope you have not, for if not you have still a book to read.

Well, Cunningham has been in town, the same as ever, lots of fun and great throbs of affection, and many qualms of conscience.   I was at Main's on Monday and met Sandeman, and we sloped at nine, and had a long, long walk, he prelecting Metaphysics : he 's grand.

To the Same

11 CASTLE STREET,
EDINBURGH, 19*th July* 1860.

I am feeling more and more done, and if this Glasgow thing comes to nothing, I don't see why or how I am to hang on longer ; physically I cannot, and morally and spiritually I have been done long ago.   I never preached better than at Glasgow ; it is a nice church, very, but only about 180 people, so that each might have had a pew.   This, of course, makes the idea of a call rather terrific, as how could I ever increase them?   They have been going all about and hearing ordained men—Dykes, etc., but seem very hard to please, so it's very likely that it is all past that I have to do with them.   I was very hospitably entertained by an old bachelor in lodgings.

To the Same

11 CASTLE STREET,
WEDNESDAY, 8*th August* 1860.

Your letter was, as usual, invigorating in the extreme, and I needed it, for I had an awful day before me.   A very short while after I had read it, Dave came up to get me to go with them ; and what on this side of the world made Dave resign himself to a holiday, you 'll ask ? Why, you should be aware that yesterday 22,500 riflemen appeared in the Queen's Park to be reviewed by Her Majesty, and so many people were there that I supposed all Britain must have come, except my own personal friends, whom I did not see, and as many as had to be left to keep the machines in England from running off with themselves and the country.   It was very grand to see hundreds of thousands gathered together (for literally there were hundreds of thousands—two of them, at least).   Mrs. Hogue would not go, her only reason being, so far as I could make out, that she expects to see more people at the day of judgment.

The town, of course, yesterday was crammed to suffocation. This day, however, will I fancy prove an emetic ; it 's a day that makes one grateful—not for itself, certainly, but for yesterday, during which it only rained thrice. You can scarcely see the Castle to-day, and the spire of the Assembly Hall may have been run away with during the night for anything eyes can say to the contrary. Still, I am in one of those hopeful moods that can fancy the glories of a summer day in 1861, only this hopeful mood partakes slightly of the sombreness of the day, when I reflect that we were to have gone to Granton this evening and had a row. Why I should be in a hopeful mood bodily, I don't know, and hopeful moods are things to be accounted for with me. I 've done a jolly day's work, but that is the consequence, not the cause, so possibly it may be because you are not coming home so soon!

I don't say anything of the review, because you may see all about it in the papers, if you care ; and though a very fine story might be told of how we slid down the hill, and how we cheered and laughed, you are aware that story-telling is your department and not mine. Suffice it to say that the volunteers, having excited our admiration yesterday, have excited our sympathy to-day, so that now we are bound to them by what we are told are the two firmest ties, and they have gone out of town thinking themselves no end of patriots, each battalion not for a moment doubting that it was theirs that was the Queen's admiration, and leaving us quietly of opinion that had it not been for us on the hillside, it would have been a very dull and flat affair. The town must have looked very strange yesterday with nobody but Mrs. Hogue in it (during the review), but I don't think there was any one to see it.   I 'm kind of vexed I did not come up to inspect, only I 'd have been sure to have been suspected of some felonious intent—had there been any policemen to suspect me.

Bessie is very anxious you should be home in time for the great event.   I think now of giving her a *Lyra* like yours, and that would be cheaper than Tennyson ; especially as I was on the point of getting a 7s. book for myself, so it would be only 3s. to her and 7s. worth of self-denial to me, which is cheap at the money.   Be sure and say what you think of this, for I ought to give it now.

Last Saturday Dave was at North Berwick, so I went down to Granton by myself and took a boat, though it was blowing a perfect hurricane, so much so that it was taking spray off the inside of the harbour.   I would not have gone down had I thought it was so windy ; but when I got down I did not like to be beat, so I went into a snug little punt and nearly tore myself in two rowing about, till I thought the old cavalier Carbajal's ditty most applicable :

'The wind blows the hair off my head,
Two at a time it blows them away.'

It did me a great deal of good, for the day before I had been sympathizing with *Hypatia*, feeling as if all my inside were scraped with oyster shells, and since I have been strong.

To the Same

11 CASTLE STREET,
EDINBURGH, 16*th August* 1860.

This place is deplorably deserted, for nowadays it is not the gentry, but everybody, that goes a-rusticating.

However, though some days pass without my saying
a word to any one but Agnes, I am in considerable force,
and have been writing with an energy that rarely visits
me. You see, I have all the work just now, and that gives
me lots to do. Don't think I am by any means a slave,
for I 've evolved a theory, which is that I can do as much
in four working days and two holidays as I can do in
six working days, and in accordance with this theory
I have been at North Berwick twice since I wrote ; and
so entirely just do I find my theory, that I almost believe
I might halve the week, or as holidays are so helpful,
possibly six days' play would be a better preparation for
Sunday than six days' work. But no doubt you will
rather desire to hear of the practical development of the
theory.

On Saturday, then, I went down with John Edgar by
the excursion train (1s. down and up), and having taken
some photographs of Tantallon Castle we all left in a
fishing-boat for the Bass. They were almost all sick,
as the breeze was right ahead. Dave even was bene-
volent to the sea-monsters. Nell was divided between
terror and squeamishness, till the latter made her resigned to anything. Peg, John Edgar, and I were much
in our usual. I had no time to be anything else, for
I took an oar and found keeping pace with a lusty young
fisherman needed the whole of me and my exertions.
We had four oars coming back, and sail too, for we were
expecting to be late for the train, and as three fishermen
were pulling pretty hard, I was nearly black in the face
by the time we got in. I, of course, enjoyed the sail
far more than the Bass, but the rest seemed to prefer the
rock. But really there was nothing very wonderful on
it : the geese were so tame that you could touch them—
not always with impunity, as one clawed Beenie. The
sandwiches were good, and plenty of them, as Nell had

made a vow never to eat again. The sky was superb, and the sea glorious. We wanted Mima and you very much, but we all pronounced it to be one of our best days. It did me a vast deal of good. On Sunday I found myself sitting bolt upright in the pulpit, not slouching as usual, and Mrs. Hogue declared I was more vigorous than ever she had heard me.

Encouraged by these facts, and by the further information that Dave was taking a holiday on Tuesday, and a very pressing invitation from all of them to go down, I got up a little before four on Tuesday morning, started a few minutes before five, and walked to Longniddry (little more than 13 miles), saving expense in railway fare if not in shoe leather, caught the train there, and got to North Berwick about 9.15.   Dave and Midge met me, and then we all sallied away to the harbour and saw a fleet of fishing-boats set sail, then we scrambled on the rocks, where the girls left us, and Dave and I had a dook, such a one—souse into the clearest water I ever saw, so much so that what seems three feet deep is fifteen.   I state a sober fact, that you may really form an idea of its transparency.   After dinner we got a boat and pulled away out, but there was a swell, so the girls wanted us to turn ; but as the day was very splendid, we lay to in a quiet bit and enjoyed.   Here a number of boats (sailing) passed us, and almost without exception the fishermen offered us a ' tow.'   It is evidently their kindness, the thing they can do for a stranger ; like giving a snuff, it costs very little to them, and shows friendliness.   We did not take a ' tow,' as we thought they might tempt us to go too far down.   But how shall I describe to you our after tea walk to Dirleton ?   I really cannot, but if you are here before the trips are done, you must go and see it.   I never saw any village at all like it.   Of course the day was favourable, but I could not help wishing that John and you had lodgings there instead of a house in Leeds.

I should have told you one of the jokes of the Bass day, a very characteristic one.   Bessie was all for a sailor's life.   Our first hundred yards or two of sail, she would be a fisherman were she a man, to dance across the main, that was the life for her; you 'd have thought, in short, that Adam [1] had been a lieutenant in H.M. Navy at the least,—but a change came o'er the spirit of her dream. It was the suddenness of the thing that was so amusing; she had scarcely finished a triumphant sea-song, when her mouth was filled with far other sentiments.

Kindest love to John.   I wish I could be with you some of your evening walks.   Love at a distance, however, is better than companionship without it, so let us be thankful and hopeful; and believe me ever more and more you most affectionate brother . . .

PS.—I call myself ' yours ' with very often a pleasant after-thought that I am yours because in a great measure made by you—at least the good of me.

To the Same

11 CASTLE STREET,
EDINBURGH, 22*nd August* 1860.

MY DEAREST AND BEST,—As I desired that this should be an extra long letter, so it has come about that it will probably be extra short, for this morning I received from Anne two lengths of butter and two friends—the butter to remain, the friends to melt away.

Let me tell you of my own ongoings, at least of my bright ones.   On Friday evening Dave waylaid me and took me by dint of serpentine reasoning to North Berwick.

[1] Her future husband.

We had a jolly evening, though it was late before we got down. Then on Saturday we went to Pressmennan Lake in a long cart; awful the jolting. I never was so thoroughly tired in all my joints; the rack can't be altogether different. The way was very delectable, and the place itself lovely.

On Tuesday I was not the genuine *testudo*, or real turtle, as Bobby now says, so I went to Granton all alone, or rather myself alone, and took a boat and pulled like a sea-dog for an hour, taking some pleasure in going past and round about a beautiful little yacht in which a fellow was luxuriously reposing, and fancying he was ' whopping all creation.' I won't say how much wind there was; you may calculate. All else that I have done is on blue ruled paper, cut into squares, and headed ' Labourers in the Vineyard.'

Last guess—why are the citizens of Edinburgh as clever as Goldsmith? Of course you don't know, nor does any one else, so far as I know, but they have made a *Deserted Village* of this, and a good many *Travellers* to boot. A sad conundrum it is, I can assure you. Somebody advises us, if we want to rise to distinction, to begin by not being ' born vaguely,' as in a large town. I am sure the child that added to our numbers in this city would be heard of just now. The people who meet you lift up their eyebrows astonished, as an Englishman might be astonished, if in search of the source of the Zambesi, to meet an English lady in full crinoline and ribbons, tripping it over the wilds. When Miss F——puts a padlock on her door for six weeks, I wonder whom you may hopefully call on. I hope soon to be able to lock my desk and go like the rest.

My Friends—I am proud of them; I would be proud of myself if the saying were just, ' Judge a man by his friends '—but it 's not.

To the Same

11 CASTLE STREET,
EDINBURGH, 30*th August* 1860.

How strange it is that when we have most to tell we use fewest words. I having something to say, you may expect a very short letter. I have asked away for two Sundays, and intend to start for Anick on Monday morning to be there for nine days, so I hope you may be there too that I may get at least a glimpse of you. Another nine days I hope to be at West Mains. It is jolly to think of, only I wish I deserved it better that I might enjoy it more ; however, I am resolved if conscience say a word about the matter to spiflicate it, or jump into the Tyne and drown it, or ride away from it on the grey mare. I 've heard of a host of vacancies lately, Huddersfield, Lewes (jolly, eh ?) and Dalston, all English, but so far away I don't like to risk going.

Innes has been up a great deal lately. On Saturday he came for a row, but I had work and could not do it, which cut me to the heart. Just as I was settling after tea on Monday and feeling prepared for any amount of work, in he comes again with his calm, unsurprised way, and hooked me off to the Canal, where we got a first-rate boat and a little boy to steer us through the bridges. Innes can't row, and nearly killed the boy with laughing, besides nearly drowning us all with crabs, which he is pleased to term crustacea. We did, however, get back again in the boat, and so improved that two boys actually bet a ' maik ' whether they could keep up with us. It was past ten before we separated, having discussed everything. I had long designed a party of him and Crichton (next door), and as Peg had given me a pot of delicious jam I had them to devour it on Tuesday. They left early (8.30), but we did make good use of the time,

N

and if yours only came off half as well, you were very happy.

I have been rather lucky in the jam way lately, for the other evening I was lying out of the bedroom window while tea was infusing, and thinking how good a landlady Mrs. A. was, and having thought that into me and felt grateful thereanent, I came down to tea, when in walked Davie embracing a jam pot and uttering ' For you '—you mind the exactness with which he delivers messages.   So when this is done I will just go and lie on the leads and think again, and renew my supply.

Your answer will, of course, catch me on *Tuesday*, I say on *Tuesday*, at Anick, and you, I hope, will be immediately on the back of it.   We 'll possibly have a talk if we meet. Now good-bye, for I 've lots to do.

To the Same

11 CASTLE STREET,
EDINBURGH, *4th December* 1860.

A letter came from Birdhopecraig which I would en-close, but it may be needed yet, so I don't.   By it I was asked to go for two or three weeks to Birdhopecraig as a candidate, which I have declined to do, in the first place because I think it is rather too much of them to ask when they intend to hear other candidates, and in the second place because of course I could not leave Bobby alone. I have offered to go on the 23rd or 30th, or both, which surely is as much as they can desire.   This may give them a scunner at me, but I did it advisedly.   I went to Smeaton, and he said, ' Go at once and stay as long as you can '; but I talked him over to my view, and he thought if I went some other time for them it would serve the same purpose.   He told me also he was much pleased with my paper and will put it in the earliest number if Dr. Cunningham's article does not spin to too great a

length. He was never so kind as to-day, took me by
one hand and put his other round my shoulder, the
position I have always thought very pretty in tales of
the last century, but never realised since the *palmy* days
of Hubie Hamilton.

Mr Davidson gave me a tremendous lecture to-day
about my delivery, and advised me to go to Melville Bell,
which I believe is all in my eye. If I could get a man
to put warmth into me, and utterance, in Paul's sense,
I would deliver wonderfully. But it vexes me all the
more when people talk of my delivery, for I feel all the
more deeply it is not an external thing that art can overcome, but my nature that is not a preacher's nature.
However, if I go to Birdhopecraig, I must preach, and
they must be satisfied ; and if I don't, I suppose there
will always be ' life for a living one.'

To the Rev. J. C. Macphail

11 CASTLE STREET,
EDINBURGH, 10*th December* 1860.

If you count it a pleasure to receive a note from me,
you reap the fruit of your own generosity, for I write to
thank you for Culverwel, to say I have enjoyed it very
much and benefited, I hope, somewhat from its fine
spirit, and lastly to advise you that I intend despatching
it at once so far towards you as the chambers or dwelling
of Mr. Nicolson. I did write a thing on Plato, not for
Clark, as he probably distrusted my ability on second
thoughts, sensible man, but a kind of conglomerate,
sick-headache reverie, which Smeaton, most easy-going
of editors, has received for *The British and Foreign
Evangelical*, in which it will appear as soon as Cunningham
comes to a colon and lets anybody else get in a word.

I have no prospects, except that Birdhopecraig is

vacant, and I am to preach some day, but I can never get up any hope where there are candidates. I can hardly be with Mr. Davidson much longer. How can I preach well when I only preach to them once a month ? Of course I am getting a great lot of study that I could never have hoped to accomplish in a charge, but whither does it tend ?

Have you yet preached to your young men ? And is your own class as thriving as ever ? I would like very much to hear how you get on, but I have some notion of what a town minister's life must be, so I do not press you to answer this. If, however, you should happen to receive the book, which is possible only (as the probability of a book coming back is in the inverse ratio of its value), you might acknowledge receipt of it. Tell me also of Simeon's laurels.

Remember me very kindly to Mrs. Macphail and your brother, and believe me, my dear Mr. Macphail . . .

To his sister Marcia.

11 CASTLE STREET,
EDINBURGH, THURSDAY, 20th December [1860].

As to your proposal to return I have only to say in words what your proneness to falsehood has made sufficiently familiar to your ear, ' That 's a lie ! ' You can be of no use in the way of nursing me ; I never could be nursed, and can't learn now, and I am beginning to believe that *for my complaints* the best cure is to walk about and do your work as long as you can, and sit down afterwards, and when you can't sit, go to bed. But I am far better to-day than I 've been.

Innes was up last night bringing me two of Clark's vols. to review, which I would very gladly do for the books themselves without any extra silliver. I am to have them done by Wednesday, but one of them is a reprint of a Commentary I know pretty well already.   He was asking for you, and asked me again to do yon Ackermann for *The Witness*, which I will if I have time.

So you see it 's absurd of you to ask me to come to West Mains (and if you come here I won't speak to you till the day you ought to have come).

One thing more : that is, don't you go and believe what Willie Jeffrey tells you about me ; one night over here he would have made me believe I was not six hours from death, had he not drawn it quite so strong and tumbled into the ridiculous.   He will need to alter his tone before he passes, or he will kill all his patients with low spirits.

To his sister Mary

11 CASTLE STREET,
EDINBURGH, MONDAY [*January* 1861].

Marsh kindly sent me in your letter to her this morning, which is the immediate cause of my writing to you.   I am glad it was not to me, for I want one from you in answer to this.   Is he going to growl again ? you 'll say. Yes, he 's going to growl, unless there 's something in writing to you that necessitates that I interrupt the tone that is at present habitual.   Know firstly, that I have been, and still am, very unwell. . . . You won't be astonished if things look blackish to me under these circumstances.   But the worst of it is, I believe I could fight this illness off if I had anything to take an interest in ; but what can a man do who has no work ?   Now I know if I were perfect I would go visiting about among those people, who don't care a copper about either me or my visits, and be always lively and ready to preach, though it were but once in six weeks.   But to tell you the plain truth, Mary, I don't believe in what I hear ministers talking so glibly of—love to souls in the abstract. I never found myself loving a man's soul distinct from the rest of him, nor did I ever find myself loving men unless there were something to which I could distinctly refer the cause of love. Thus I could almost always find a feeling for the High Street people, pity for their so evident misery, and pity, as you know, is gate-keeper to love, and so on ; but what natural sentiment can be moved by the people I have to visit here ? There are a few sick, these I visit heartily ; a few aged, these also I like to see. But of the mass, what can you say ? Is it wicked to be uninterested in such work ?

And then, Mary, you (I think rightly, *in the general*) speak much of the *intention* of God in earthly events by which He deals with us : what then would you say about my case ? Do these two years and more waiting not show that I am seeking my work in the wrong direction, or why do they not show this, or *how* long would show this ? Possibly you may say, ' Wait till some evident call to some other work arises ' ; but then, of course, evident calls enough would soon arise were I to put myself in the way of them, *e.g.*, were I to go along to Clark the publisher and ask him for some work, or go out to Harvey of Merchiston and ask him for some ; whereas, so long as I keep myself back from such openings they are not a tenth part so likely to arise. But apart from growlery, let me give you a problem. I will give it you in the concrete, as being easier stated and easier apprehended. Is it right of me to wait and see whether I get a call or no, and let this decide whether I ought or ought not to take a charge ? To me it seems not (though it 's just what I 'm doing), and on this ground, because in fact we find that God has often suffered men to enter the Church who were not worthy—because, that is, the call of the people does not always represent the call of God.

I never seem to get one bit further on. I have the same humbling, heart-breaking surrender to make day after day. There is no gift of the Spirit in retention, or at least I seem to need to ask just as fervently and as dependently for His grace to-day as at first ; and it is no easier done. I cannot understand the Christian course that some people lay down.

Thursday.—So far, my dear Mary, I uttered myself on Monday, but I relented and thought it really too bad to send you this as a companion of your solitude. I send it now because I would not write it now, because it does not now express and me. I send it merely that you may know what I was on Monday, and that on Thursday I am not quite so deep ; for now I have work, a Harrow boy whom I used to have in his holidays, and two Commentaries to review. Both came unasked, so by one of your rules I accepted both.

Your letter that came this afternoon was very delicious to me, but really I can't undertake to answer it, for you see I am busy now ; but I will try and write soon to make up for this.

To his sister Marcia

11 CASTLE STREET,
EDINBURGH, FRIDAY [*January* 1861].

But I have a matter. Dr. Bonar [1] has been at me again, not for Naples but Sydney. He tells me what he told me before, that Dr. Mackay there wants a colleague, and that no placed minister here who is fit will go. He wants me to make up my mind in about *three weeks, when* at the next meeting of Committee, if I would go, he would appoint me officially, or offer it me officially, which is

---

[1] Rev. Dr. John Bonar, then Convener of the Colonial Committee of the Free Church of Scotland.

the same thing. The church is the finest building in Sydney, and the congregation one of the best in Australia, and the salary would be about £400. I am thinking more of this than of Naples; the climate tempts me, the medium quantity of work, and the good position. Sydney is the most settled town in Australia—about 100,000 inhabitants. Were it here, I would jump at such a situation. I need not mention the other side; you will see it quick enough.

To the Rev. J. C. Macphail

11 CASTLE STREET,
EDINBURGH, 15th January 1861.

I feel a good deal ashamed of myself never having acknowledged receipt of your second son. I hope he will be second to none; and though you and I must have very different views regarding the respective merits of the heads and tails of families, I think that *at present* you will be giving more of your worship to the younger than to his forerunner. It 's a fine thing a family, after all; fine, at least, for baccalaureate speculation and contemplation, if not for the parties more nearly involved in it. I have often admired how the elder serves the younger by the poundings and other discipline he inflicts, as well as by the fraternal love that brings the strong to the succour of the weak. You must not be surprized that I dwell with some prolixity on the things that come after matrimony, for I hear that it is almost certain that I will get a call to Birdhopecraig, *i.e.* that I will need to marry, as Adam in Eden was not more desolate than a minister without encumbrance at Birdhopecraig would be. Sydney woos me with a very ambiguous ardour, and while there are many advantages held out by it, they are all suspended on a risk;

for all that Dr. Bonar can do, it seems, is to recommend me strongly.   And I would not like to be ignominiously thrust forth from the gates of Sydney to seek employment in the width of Australia, being of the same opinion as my ancestors of all times that a bird(hopecraig) in the hand is worth two in the *bush*.   If you know any young woman able and willing to rule a household, of high principle and not insignificant stature, of steady spirits and healthy tone of mind, who has also the power of cracking a hard and thrice-brazen heart, and of putting new wine into an ill-used vessel, and generally of fulfilling the duties of wifedom (experience, however, is not requisite), you might have pity on one who anticipates the life of an eremite and tell me of her.

I must not omit in this domestic letter to mention that by a pretty coincidence my second-born was obtruded on the attention of the public in the same paper as yours.   You would see an article headed ' The Christian Element in Plato,' but I do not suppose you had so little to do as to tempt you for a moment to spend any time in trying to read it.

To his sister Mary

11 CASTLE STREET,
EDINBURGH, 15*th January* 1861.

I have just read your letter, and sit down to answer it under rather unpromising circumstances, my mouth filled with toothache, or wherever there is not toothache, with creosote.   But you are so wise and witty in what you say that I can't help sending my acknowledgments at least.   And first, I do feel your affection most sisterly and precious, and more and more pity the poor fellows who have not sisters.   True, in the Sydney movement, I would decide a good deal easier had I not two sisters to leave, and two to take with me ; but you are certainly worth the distraction of a month's indecision. I would come more promptly to a decision in the matter if Marsh were not determined to go with me, and as I could not and would not leave Andie here (unless she were with you), I do feel considerable hesitation in thus mutilating the family. However, I have no parents.

As to the situation itself, there would be nothing in the very smallest degree heroic in taking it, for it is very good, such as many a man would gladly accept. I have yesterday received the minutest information I expect to get from Walter Macleod, who knows the place well. He says that had he health he would go at once; the climate is the best, the city is settled and supplied with all the advantages we have here, even to public libraries and Philosophical Institutions, the congregation is a new one (four years old), formed by some of the most reputable men of the place. Almost every one I have asked has advised me to go, always, of course, with the reservation that it is very far away. A merchant may go for ten years and come back with a fortune ; a minister goes for life. The advice I get mostly resolves itself into what I am pretty well aware of already, that it 's a good situation, but very far away.

In reply to what you say about the respectables being really as necessitous as the poor, I would ask you to remember the way in which the poor are spoken of in the Bible (and do not spiritualise the meaning out of it), and to whom Christ preached most and with most hope. The well-to-do are well enough ; the poor know at least there is *something* they want, and are prepared to listen.

And as to ministers, there are three classes—those whom the Spirit enlightens and enlivens for their work, those who are in the ruts, *i.e.* who do their work mechanically, and the professionals, or those who view the souls of men, not, as you say, the men themselves, just as physicians view the bodies, who gad about delighting in cases, who eagerly instruct and warn, and especially rebuke, but who all the time don't know the *man*, don't care for the man, and would not help the man if they saw him drunk in a gutter.   They view him, in short, just as a case, or a patient, or a subject ; and they themselves pay for this by ceasing to be men, and becoming merely professional men—the fault of the age.

Now, my dear Mary, do mind how useful your letters are to me, and write often ; you will, of course, write immediately just now about this Sydney affair, which is, at least, an exercise.   I am much better in health, and don't quite like your laughing at H——.   I have taken his stuff, and am better, and this is just the sequence on which allopathy grounds its proof of efficiency.   I never perspire at night now.   It may be porter, it may be H——'s nitric acid, it may be visiting instead of sitting writing, it may be change of weather, it may be that old brick Nature quietly shaking herself up, and laughing in her sleeve at all the assistances we give her ; but allopathists are not thus discriminating and sceptical when you take their advice and get well.

To the Same

11 Castle Street,
Edinburgh, *2nd February* 1861.

You see you have induced me to do what is quite contrary to my principles, to answer a letter by return of post.   It is a great tribute, possibly the greatest ever paid, to your faculty of letter-writing.   Again I am forced to begin and correct your mistakes, not theological this time, I am glad to find, for I was just thinking I would need to send you a copy of Turretin, as I know George

could not spare his even for an hour out of his study.
You are far wrong in thinking that we speak of nothing
but Sydney. It is not a very common topic with us,
for it must remain *in statu quo* for a month. Bonar asked
me along the other day and told me his committee does
not meet till the end of this, or the beginning of next
month. Something may turn up in the meantime.
I rather hope it will. I like your letters on the subject
very much, and I should have answered George's. Did
I ? I have been in such a variety of employments lately
that I am a little not-a-Nephalist. (As you say, physic
to the dogs (so long as you can do without it) and porter
for me. I am getting fat on this last.) I have had a
good deal of visiting and some preaching lately : item,
I have written another article for *Good Words* on Monks,
a good deal more readable than the first. In this day's
Witness you will find a column on Plato by the same
penholder. No doubt you will find it very interesting,
particularly as you have ' read Plato,' or at least helped
me to translate a translation of him.

I greatly rejoice in our present establishment, and fear
often ' we shall never see the like again '—not much
responsibility, but as much work of a kind as I choose—
time at my own disposal, and an adequate comfort in
my fellow personages. A little of you would be quite
endurable, but I suppose your historian and your novelist
have more need of you, though I do not *see* this.

Marsh is out on some errand for Andie (which puts me
in mind to say that Bonar and I and all sensible people
think it would be wild for these two females to go *with*
me). John and Tom both think I should go—Smeaton
too. Marsh is going a second time (think of the young
woman's dissipation) to hear Hallé the pianist to-day
with Mr. Hogue and Mima.

Now write often so long as the letters can reach me for

a penny. Sometimes I take lazy and think I will just
stay here and potter on.

To S. R. Macphail

11 CASTLE STREET,
EDINBURGH, 13th August [? 1861].

You entertained me vastly by your account of the
awful Board, and possibly you expected to be entertained in return by an account of my rural adventures ;
but really these were so commonplace that it would have
cost me some elaborate thinking to put them in an
interesting form, and I had too much regard for my
holidays to crucify them by anything like thought. I
became as much of a vegetable as I could, only instead
of nightly dews I substituted porridge and cream and
fruit, which I conceived to be more adequate to the
well-being of my internal arrangements.

Have you heard whether you are through, feathers
and all, or have been pl-ck-d ? I have not as much
shadow of a doubt about your passing as one of your
feathers would cast ; but I know the state of dubiety
will be not altogether unpleasant to you. Talking of
passing, I am glad to say that the youth I had for a time
has passed fourth out of the two hundred. He ought
to be satisfied, and I dare say will ; but some people I
know would say, ' Fourth out of one year, that is about
fortieth of those who go out in ten years, about a
hundred and twentieth of those whom I must compete
with during my career,' and thus would reduce the
apparent honour to a very humbling state of affairs.

My effort to escape from Edinburgh has been again
unsuccessful, and now that I have failed eight times, I
begin to feel that I have a right to do a little in the
growling line when I choose, a kind of bank of despond-

ency with a large account to my credit, on which I may perhaps sometime hereafter be inclined to draw a little. For the present I hope to find more profitable employment.

Tell me all you know when you write. Will it be a long letter ? If it 's going to be *very* long, then restrict it to all you have *experienced* within the last fortnight, but don't be metaphysical, nor mathematical, but only Simoniacal. I hope to hear the Rev. William Miller on Sunday, as Lady Glenorchy is still open only to painters.

To his sister Marcia

11 CASTLE STREET,
EDINBURGH, THURSDAY [*22nd August* 1861].

I do think you might write a little oftener, or spare me a child or two, or Andie or something. I have had my festivities too, however ; for not only have I bowed to several people that I don't know (but who looked as if they too were men and brethren), but I have met and spoken to Mr. Crawford (of the Canal), and then on Tuesday evening I gave a great blow out and had all my friends to it (except Miss F——), *i.e.* William Miller. I asked Miller whom I could get to meet him, but he did not know any one except one fellow I don't know ; and though I was very much inclined to ask him, as you feel quite intimate with everybody when there is no crowd to keep you separate, I did not do it. I enjoyed Miller very much. We had a great deal of talk, an awful amount of tea, and some walk, and when I came home I felt inclined to go and call on him—but did not.

Yesterday I went further up the Canal than I have ever been. The evening no poet could describe, nor painter depict, and the little skiff was animate, occasionally giving a little yelp of delight. To-day the rain is falling as if it would make up for yesterday's beauty, and as there is a considerable balance on the rain side, I hope a good many days after this will be fine.

Mr. Davidson is getting no better; at least, as soon as he seems to be beginning to get on, back he goes again, as if there were some inexorable drill-sergeant before him, repeating ever the command ' As you were ! ' Tell Charles I read *Night Thoughts* aloud to myself and admire it vastly. Don't think there are five other poems as good in the language.

To S. R. Macphail

Write soon to 11 CASTLE STREET, EDINBURGH, 11*th September* 1861.

Your letter sticks in my unanswered corner, reproaching me with a bitterness that reminds me not unnaturally of its author, of whom, believe me, I have often other and more tender reminiscences. It 's late to-night, and I have been at my meeting (I did not meet an old friend that used sometimes to catch me), so you must not expect much epistolary effort. The truth is, I don't think you are so much a person to write to as to talk to. *I*, now, on the other hand, am first rate to write to, I should fancy, and the sprightliness of your letters convinces me I must be right in my conjecture ; and if I am not good at the answering side of the correspondence, you 'll own it 's something to be a good receiver. There 's very little in town here either to talk to or of. Your friends Miller and Innes are the main pillars of my friendly qualities just now. We had a pull together the other day, a great many crabs and a great deal of laughter. When I think of you it 's in connection with crabs of nature's own production. I picture you going along a rather bleak beach with a rather forlorn countenance, as if you had given up most things as vanities, and occasionally brightening over a shrimp or an anemone, and wishing you were as merry as the one or as beautiful as the other. Why don't you tell me more about yourself, that my fancy may have less to do ?   So in your next be sure you give me less of Phaethon and more of Simeon, or as you might express it, being mathematical, Phaethon minus, Simeon magus (is that spelt with a ' g ' or a ' j,' by the bye ?   I know you can answer).

The best articles in the *Encyclopædia* are not the articles, but the preliminary dissertations, which are by Dugald Stewart and other stalwart men.   I don't know the articles on Socrates or Plato, but should fancy them good from the authorship.

Do you not think of coming back in October ?   How about your teaching ?   And when is the bursary competition ?   And what of your Skye visit ?   Oh ! the barrenness of that last epistle.   Write articles for yourself, for so you will be able to judge not only of the things you write about, but what is of far more importance, of yourself, your defective way of thinking, and your faults of style (which also are really faults of thought, in the finer connections of thought), and, above all, Live.   If I had a couple of voices like Mr. Tennyson, one of them should be disencumbered of all other work and should be appointed to say to me with all its breath, ' Live ' : leave no faculty sleeping and a mere weight on the others, but be always all awake.   You see, Simeon, I take the liberty of lecturing myself through you, and instead of saying what might be disagreeable to myself, that I have been a sleeper, I say the next thing to it, that you *may* be one.   My paper tells me I 've said about enough and will, you see, scarcely leave me room to say that I am your ally . . .

To the Rev. J. C. Macphail

11 CASTLE STREET,
EDINBURGH, 13*th February* [1862].

This is not a Valentine, but a letter, born mainly of
two desires, the first being to thank very warmly Mrs.
Macphail for her refreshing letter, for which I feel quite
as grateful (and justly so) as she can feel for the little
book;[1] the second being to ask you to remember the little
book aforesaid, and do what you can, without going out
of your way, to promote its circulation.   I don't know
that it is the best book in the world, but it has external
neatness and a worth of its own inside.   And if you gave
away two copies of such a heinous volume as —— *for*
——, you should at least give *some* of this away to
counteract the evil effects of your former liberality.
Seriously, however, I would like if you would let your
bookseller know there is such a book in the world.   I
think you yourself will like it, especially the second part.

I have been very busy lately, as most of the reviews
in *The Week* have hitherto flowed from this quill ; besides
that, I have been beginning what, if it continues, will
prove very pleasant work, a series of translations of the
most interesting minor patristic remains.   I proposed
to Smeaton such a thing, and he at once said it would
do excellently for his *Review.*   He wants them annotated
also, which will cost a good deal more trouble, and
possibly when he sees them he may not think their
fitness so astounding.   These things and a sermon a
week and visiting hurry me rather more than I quite
like ; but now I look for a little more time, if not a great
deal more, as Mr. Davidson is going to try and take up
his work himself again.   How he may succeed is another
matter.

[1] The writer's first publication—the *Manual of Devotion*, translations
from Augustine.

O

Probationers are now to be circulated according to rule, and I am to be circulated to the synods of Orkney and Shetland, and those adjoining (which includes Aberdeen, so you may again have the felicity of seeing me, as you have more than once before seen me, in the rosy colours of a hopeful candidate). It is your old friend Robert Gordon who sits and distributes, and when he is to begin his solar work I don't know ; but if he sends me beyond the milky way somewhere, I fear I 'll prove a rebellious planet, and prove that the canon law is not so rigid as the law of gravitation. But for your sake I pause. I have a salutary idea (founded on I can't say what) that you are about the hardest worked man ; so adieu, and if you can write you will throw some saccharine into the somewhat souring life of . . .

To his sister Marcia

[MR. BRYANT'S, 12 ST. GEORGE'S SQ.]
CHELTENHAM, SATURDAY [*March* 1862].

As I will probably find no time to write again till Wednesday, I begin a despatch now. If I were just to express myself as I have been all day, you would just hear growl upon growl. Having nothing to do is bad enough, but when to that is added having no one to speak to, it is beyond my small powers of endurance. Besides, one or two things look as if I had some chance here, and that sits on me. I feel so unlike the place that I believe if they want me I will hear of something else.

I have read *Tom Brown* and *Ravenshoe*, both excellent, but I look in vain for *my* novel. *Tom Brown* has many points of approximation, but no author is bold enough to make his hero really weak : he only has some weak points which very rapidly strengthen. Novelists, however, are becoming wiser, and there is yet hope.

Here I am interrupted by Mr. Williams, the only person whose acquaintance I have made besides Mr. Bryant ; he had come to pay me, which he did by giving me £5. This pays my expenses, and leaves an irregular sum over and above. They won't be inclined to hear many candidates at that rate. I am the last, I hear. There are 130 members, so the stipend must be small. Would it not be better to hang on in Edinburgh (to which I feel a strong affection at present), as Innes has always advised ?   Would there be any room for you and Andie in a place like this ?   I fancy there would.   But why calculate, after all ?

The temperature here is that of the dog days at the Equator (which is Irish astronomy, but never mind).

To the Same

ANICK GRANGE,
HEXHAM, 12*th June* 1862.

Your letters came this morning and have three times over given me much delight ; not unmingled, as you may suppose, yet where affection is at the bottom the troubles that rise up from it are but as bubbles rising from a pearly bottom, which disappear and are at the worst transparent. You see I have not been reading *Gotthold* for nothing.

To-morrow afternoon I hope to be at Newcastle. I *wish* I knew where you two were to be, but it is some satisfaction to know that there is a place provided for you into which you will most certainly be brought. At times I could weep with you and help you to conjure up things as direful as Andie can have conceived in her bluest bilious attacks, and at other times I make you sympathize with me in that happy indifference to futurity which is now a more frequent mood with me than it used to be, and which, if it be unjustifiable while I regard other people, I hope will become habitual regarding my own lot. But Newcastle and you together are hard testers of Stoicism, and I feel sometimes my old New-castle feeling of being quite different from everybody else in it, separated from all and sundry by something or other, from the most by religion, from many by upbring-ing and sympathies. There is no Peg to hang my thoughts of you on, but when my stomach is right, and my appetite for work strong, I look forward with some of those ' mighty hopes that make us men,' and (again you are indebted to Alfred)

> ' . . tho' my lips may breathe adieu,
> I cannot think the thing farewell.'

I am, as usual here, in the prime of health, and cannot cease looking with admiration on the firm flesh and healthy springiness of my hands. I wish Tom was the same, but to-day he just dragged himself about with a weight and a heat and a lassitude I very well know. Gotthold has an Emblem on a weak stomach, but it deserves nothing but obloquy and medicine.

Polly and Sam are sold, so there is nothing here to ride but a pony whose achievements have earned it the name of Vixen. It was called Kate at first ; they might have added ' the curst.'

To the Same

6 WHARNCLIFFE PLACE,
NEWCASTLE, 19th June 1862.

Tom was in here on Monday, and stayed over night to be at Tuesday morning's market. He is dull and not well, and I was at my wit's end, when he himself proposed to go and see Mouat ; so we did, and (undreamt of luck)

Mouat was in ; so he gave him a pipe and was as easy and
talky as if he had known him for twenty years.   The talk
somehow or other got on character, so he told Tom all his
inside as if he were reading it off a book, occasionally
aiding or correcting himself by diving his fingers in among
his hair and feeling his bumps.   He put me into fits once
when he was saying I was ' combative ' and Tom invited
inspection of his bump on that matter.   Mouat laid his
fingers on, but before they were well on twitched his hand
away as if he had been stung, saying ' Oh, horrible ! '

I have been reading *Shirley* again and keep it now for
my dinner book.   It is much better than *Jane Eyre* every
way, and is a wonderful book, and to me most pleasant.

It is evening now, and as it cleared up I did my visits.
I think the people here have more horrible diseases than
elsewhere ; or else it is that they take more hold of me,
having no one to talk to at home and forget them.   I wish
I could get something more than a scarcely audible and
very resigned ' Yes, sir,' out of Mrs. Murray.[1]   I think she
is nice enough, but she might almost as well be dumb.

The people are all very cordial, and that helps me
greatly, and I dare say I am as much fitted for them
as any people.   There is a large number of truly good
people, and a good many thinking people, and few of
that rude, uncultivated kind ; there are some working-
people and a number of shopkeepers ; but they have a
native civility and hospitality about them that makes
it pleasant to work among them.

To the Same

6 WHARNCLIFFE PLACE,
NEWCASTLE, MONDAY [23rd *June* 1862].

This letter is merely interstitial (do you know him ?),
and therefore will be short.   I have just been to a

---

[1] His landlady.

7 o'clock meeting, come in and found a letter from Simeon, doleful a little, affectionate very. Yesterday I preached my Mission Sermons, but I hear the collection was very small—of course because the people don't know how to give, not because I don't know how to preach. I had a very pleasant half-hour with Mouat after evening service. He is really a most enjoyable person. There is a nice prayer-meeting after evening service, at which two of the people pray. Some have great gift that way, and in the Session there are men whose activity and willingness puts one to shame. But the town is really awful. At any time you can sink your spirits by walking thoughtfully along any street ; and some streets make you think whether you will or no. This week is Race Week, which means Pandemonium. I really think I would sooner have the choice of hell for company than many a gang going about here : the stupid, fierce, intractable, reckless beastliness is frightful. A solitary room is not the best place to bring such thoughts and impressions home to, but I am a somewhat stronger, or a somewhat more indifferent person than I used to be— which, I do not quite know.

PS.—*Gotthold's Emblems* is DELICIOUS. I am quite sorry I promised to give it to Katharine.

To the Same

6 WHARNCLIFFE PLACE,
NEWCASTLE, 26th *June* [1862].

It 's very queer to think of you at Torphichen Street ;[1] indeed I don't ; to me you still inhabit the back parlour at No. 11. I have ever returning compunctions on account of the break-up, and though I seem to have done right, I cannot perceive how it should be right to do

---

[1] The house of the Gibsons, who moved to Edinburgh about this time.

such a very disagreeable, unseemly, and blind kind of
thing.   And after all, it is but a poor consolation to say,
' It 's done now '—a settlement without a solution is apt
to be like a heavy dinner ; it goes down and settles for
a while, but continues to speak back in a most unseason-
able fashion.   This solitary and grave atmosphere is not
so good for writing sermons.   I have grand times for
study, but cannot make much way with writing.   Last
week my lecture was as cold as if I had no heart at all,
and this week I have been searching about for a text till
this morning, and am now nibbling away at the beginning.
You must not expect a long letter, therefore.

Would you send me a July *News of the Churches*,
and a *British and Foreign Review* IF *my Monks* are in it.
Would you ask Stevenson (in Maclaren's) if he thinks
he could get the first series of Robertson of Brighton's
sermons *second-hand*.   I feel the want of genius just now.
I can't light my own fire, and think he might do, but
I would not dream of getting it new—they may have
a library copy.

Since writing the foregoing, I have had a good evening's
work.   It really is a great matter to be able to sit down
as sure as mortal can be of anything that no one will
interrupt you.   *Your* presence was always rather a help
(except in the day-time), but I see now by contrast what
a great deal of time the socialities take up.   I believe if
I came back I would prohibit the whole fraternity,
sisterhood, and all the rest of them.

If there was such a thing as reading *In Memoriam* to
satiety I would be doing so, but there is not.   I feel very
comfortable among my printed friends.

To the Same

6 WHARNCLIFFE PLACE,
NEWCASTLE [1*st July* 1862].

This is Sunday evening, and it is so queer coming home to this desolation, even after being strengthened by my usual allowance of Mouat, that I must say a word to you as if you were here. I have been reading Calvin his *Institutes* on the Sunday question, and he has put me further wrong than I was before. He is far more lax than Dr. Arnold. This is the time of all others when I feel the want of you. I can't go and growl, I can't whistle, I am too tired to think, and there is not even a sofa to go and sleep on ; so if you ought not to be here, I wonder where the reason of things is. But you must not think I am dull, for I am not, only I may get accustomed to do without you, or in plain language, I may become a brute.

I wrote a sermon last week on the ' great salvation,' but did not warm once in the whole length of it, and so did not preach it, but took ' Consider Him,' and enjoyed it myself very much. There are such grand batches of men in the church, pew after pew together undisfigured by a single bonnet—it 's enough to make one halloo. Of course this is a carnal feeling, but it 's mine ; perhaps also it is stupid, for if you influence women you influence men, and it 's easier, I believe, to get at men thus. But there they are, and welcome certainly. In the gallery I doubt if there was a single female this morning.

Mouat is going to Edinburgh this week. I wish I was he, or I wish I was you, or rather I wish I was myself with you both. He wanted to know if I had anything for him to take, but I hadn't. Had I anything to bring ? ' No, unless you could bring me a sister or two.'

Mrs. Murray volunteered a remark last night (this is now time secular, or Monday morning, on which I *feel* far wickeder writing to you; indeed it won't do, and I must stop), to the effect that we might sing at worship; so sing we did, *Maggie* striking up, and Mrs. and the sons striking in. I knew they could do it, because the house has generally an air Scotch or other floating about in it.

Mind, you must get a hold of Mouat some evening; he has promised to call, but if there is any way by which you could make sure of him, it would be safer. Charles would like him, I think, though none of you will like him as much as I do; indeed I don't think anybody does. Most here seem to think well of him, but as for making an intimate of such an incoherent being, that's not what he is there for.

Now this is all mere introduction, but unfortunately I can say nothing of the subject proper of my letter till I hear from Mr. Wrightson of Caius College, Cambridge, who wants me to read Greek with him (and oh, dream of joy, he wants to read Sophocles). The only obstacle to his beginning at once was that he had engaged with the Rev. —— Weeks, curate of St. Paul's. He seems to think this nothing, and will probably come to me. If he does so I will need to ask you to send Andie's box in which I put my Grecians. When he asked my terms, remembrances of the fabulous fees of Oxford tutors crossed my mind for a moment, but I asked for about the fifth part, which you will be surprised to hear he at once accepted.

I got a letter from Laird of Dundee asking me to go and preach as first step towards being his missionary— to preach occasionally for him, and do other congregational work. Of course, unless this were a good deal more definite and promising, my present employment is better.

Wrightson has been here, and has abolished the temporary arrangement with Weeks (no pun), so please send my books. Markie will, I dare say, go along to the GOODS office of the North British, and all he needs to do is to tell them to call for the box. The goods place is down Calton St., the first gate on the right hand after passing under the arch which supports Waterloo Place. If he prefers jumping from Waterloo Place down, he will take less time to get to the place, but perhaps longer to get away.

To his sister Marcia

[6 WHARNCLIFFE PLACE,
NEWCASTLE, *July* 1862.]

I was ashamed of the letter I sent to Charles this morning, but sometimes one cannot write a letter. I would not mind had it been to you, because I think you have seen as far towards my backbone as most people—(except Mouat ? No). I am always writing you letters when I am out, and when I go to bed, and when I am sitting waiting for people ; and I go along grinning at schemes that never see beyond the narrow limits of my own brain, schemes for your future which have probably as much resemblance to the reality as the surface of the earth has to the interior. I like you well when I am with you, but when I am away I single you out.

(Here comes my box, 2s. Many thanks to Andie and Markie—how jolly the pets look. It goes against my grain to take them out, they are so snug—that box was not made for Andie. I kiss old Wunder's *Sophocles*—how suitable a gift from the trio.)

But I must really stop, or at least pause, for the wrangler is coming at 9.30 to-morrow morning, and his fashion of bringing written down all the questions that have occurred since we last met, and writing down all you say, is rather confounding, and tends to make one prepare with some caution.   However, he is not a ' terrible scholar ' otherwise.   He seeks to be a grammarian, and puts me some very useless queries about secondary and tertiary predicates ; but I think we 'll get on.

When are you to be done your teaching ?   And mind, you are not to go slap through to Hexham by that abominable new line.

Oh ! the happy, happy days of old.   Well, I have not the bitterness of reflecting that I was not sensible of my blessings when I had them, for I was happy and knew it.   Love to everybody.

To his sister Andrea

6 Wharncliffe Place,
Newcastle, Friday [? *July* 1862].

I had no sooner closed my letter to Marsh from a strong sense of duty, than my slippery conscience seemed quite to approve of my sitting down and writing to you. However, on reflection I thought sermon would be the right thing, so sermon it was ; but now it is 4.30, and I am going up to Mr. Miller's in a short time, so I may indulge for a wee bit.   Your letter is dated in a general way ' June,' and I think you must have been writing it all June to cram such heaps of news into it.   You should have been attached to a newspaper editor—I do not mean erotically, but only literarily.   All your news, too, is good news, which cannot always be said of your own or any other person's letters.   There is one omission, however, which I cannot overlook, but which I fear had you supplied I could no longer have said that all was good.   You say nothing of your health, and I suppose because you have none to speak of.

As you are interested in my squattation, I may tell you that opposite there is a row of houses, each of which is divided into two, having a front door each, the one leading into the house on the ground, the other opening on a stair which leads aloft.   They strike me as being gems for the baccalaureate life, but they seem to be inhabited by young mechanics a year married, whose wives can do a bit of work, and who have a lassie to clean the step, dig the garden (*N.B.* with a kitchen knife, not unfeminine), and rub the brass facings, also I presume attend to some of the internal arrangements.   I can't make out where there is any room to sleep or anything of that kind ; they seem all front and window curtains.   But I find myself growing jealous of the upstarts of two-and-twenty airing their wives of an evening at the open windows. If Solomon lived in a house like this one, I see the full propriety of his saying, ' Curse not the King, no, not in thy bed-chamber,' for the partitions are so thin that one is afraid to cough, sneeze, or whistle for fear of disturbing one's neighbour.

To S. R. Macphail

[NEWCASTLE, ? 1862.]

This place would do you good, Simonides.   It 's the wickedest of the wicked, boisterously scoffing, and might convince you that if there be any means of counteracting or destroying the works of the devil, a life spent in the use and application of such means is not spent in vain.

I wish you were here to get a good talk.   It 's no use beginning to say a few things when there is such lots to say.   This is the grandest place to study.   I have had *one* caller since I came—a lady who would scarcely sit down.   Whenever I choose not to visit I can live in solitude and silence ; but men are better than books.   I

like the people very well, though they are the very anti-
podes of my Edinburgh friends, and am becoming more
and more content to jog on, remembering that I am not
called upon to redress everything and interfere everywhere, and that it's no use getting out of temper or
sitting down to moan over what you can't help, while
there is something that you can help.   Such is the philosophy native to a healthy stomach ; but when out of
sorts I am nigh to cursing.   Also in visiting I am becoming accustomed and reconciled to my own flatness, and
to feel it less, on the consideration that people won't
expect to find perfection in me ; and that if I do what
I can, though it be a dull, mediocre business, I do all I
was intended to do.

   But I must stop, and let you have a turn ; and let it
appear on my horizon speedily.   Reflect that I am alone,
and give me lots of news—any Aberdeen tidings you
may have, and tell me about your work.   I love facts
dearly.   Laugh and grow fat, beware of a bad stomach
and the insidious approach of dyspepsia, read your Greek
Testament, take notes distinct and easily referred to of
all you read, from placards on the walls to the mystic
letters engraved on your own spirit, be on good terms
with as many people as you can, and nail your colours
to the mast, as becomes a British bulldog ; and finally,
excuse the insolence, reciprocate the affection, and accept
of the best wishes of . . .

To his sister Marcia

6 WHARNCLIFFE PLACE,
NEWCASTLE, 10th July [1862].

   I feel as if my letter this time should be an answer to
that article of ——, seeing as how I have written
you twice since receiving yours on Tuesday.   —— comes
nearer the thing than most of them ; but I wonder he

did not see and say more when he had got the length of
discovering that ' The Man ' must be the great foundation of the orator.   That 's precisely and emphatically
the kink.   And here 's the man.   To me a great deal of
his advice is useless, though to some others it may be
profitable.   For me to mellow my tone and call my
hearers ' My DEAR friends ' would be hypocritical ; and
for similar reasons a good deal of what he says is not
to be done.   Another good deal I discharge on the ground
that I think it a mistake to expect that preaching is
always to be oratory.   You don't think so, so don't say
you do.   The man you most admire as a preacher is
about least an orator.   I believe that the power of my
preaching, if any, will not be oratorical power ; and some
day I may write an essay to show that there are other
powers of words than oratory, but I am not going to write
more now.   If you want to see where I am and would
be, think of the influence of books.

All yesterday afternoon I spent at a funeral.   It was
a publican's, and from 2 (which was the hour) till 3.30, I
had to sit with a lot of fellows in the tap-room drinking
ale, eating cheese and bread, and smoking long pipes.
Then when they came into the room where the coffin was,
they got wine and whisky and gin.   Fancy being asked
to conduct the worship of these men, three of them at
least being drunk, and all of them stinking of liquor !
The whole process cost me three hours.   In Edinburgh
it rarely exceeds one, and commonly is within forty
minutes.   I felt much inclined to say something, but
confined my rebuke to reading the end of 4th and beginning of 5th Thessalonians to them in the cemetery
chapel.   They dress you up, too, most disagreeably in
long black scarfs.

Smeaton has cut out all yon funny stories about the
monks, which I thought the cream, and which really

were. They were the realities, and would have lodged in a reader more than anything I have said. Do you think his edition is to be commended ?

To-morrow morning, and no letter, and the wrangler will be here *tout de suite*, so I must hurry to a close.   The sky is still leaden, though the sun occasionally breaks through.   Had it been a fine day, I intended to go down to Tynemouth and get a pull.   For want of company, you must understand, I ask myself to dinner once a week at some place, often at a very comfortable eating-house that I 've discovered, and for want of a drawing-room of my own I frequent the first-class waiting-room at the railway, where there is always a glorious fire, and a grand sofa, and every means for enjoying a wait, if you can.   So I am much a gainer at the public expense.

To J. C. Stewart

6 WHARNCLIFFE PLACE,
NEWCASTLE, 13*th August* [1862].

I embrace you for your letter.   I am glad now I wrote none of those times I resolved to do so, for so delicious a sense of your kindness in writing first possesses me, that I would not for a good deal be robbed of it.   I have far too many sermons wrung from me perforce to be in any mood for sermonizing when I may epistolize.   You seem to think you have only to tap me, and I 'll run you off a forenoon and afternoon diet of two hours each.   I swallow all your ' mocking ' and ' mourning,' and anything else that is yours with appetite, for in all I get you whom I know, and I have so often used you as a safety-valve that I am relieved to find you grumbling a little too sometimes.   There is little need just now of your advice to me to keep up my spirits, for I have got into a way of tumbling on which, if known and understood, might be found inconsistent with a ministerial profession.

However, I hope I 'll tumble into the right bit some day, and know that it is the right bit ; but I dare say I have missed many good things already through my indecision and want of knowing my own mind, or want of having any mind to know. You do seem to think very little of this world as an institootion, but I rather like to see you seeing to the back of things, knowing that slowly one so learns the aptitude of God's remedy, and learns (ever ? at last, far off) to accept the bad of everything here plus the good provided as its cure, and to be content therewith.

Talking of men, are you aware that Innes begins now to rise in his profession by going into the Glasgow firm of Couper & Mackenzie ? He leaves Edinburgh on the first of October, and henceforth puts his pen behind his ear. He is a fine fellow that ; at home and charitable among his fellows, expecting much in others, but content when he finds only a little ; intelligent to mark faults, but wise to make large allowances. Aitchison must be in a marvellous condition of stamina if he has taken on £400's worth of setting up.

And now of women. Of the sex generally as represented here, I may say that they have free, roving eyes, healthy complexions, wholesome mouths, springy figures, without a deal of beauty, and rather lacking culture. Would make better brides than mothers, better sweethearts than brides. For the men here I have some respect. You can know them easily ; they are frank, intelligent, sensible and cordial. But everybody is busy, and I see little of anybody, and some days don't speak a word. For health this is not a bad place—early hours and wholesome food—but the world seems to have got ill just now, judging from the confused, out-of-sorts state of the weather. But, man, I wish you were here to talk it all over ; it seems such a poor affair writing you. I

have just as much to say now as when I began, and would
have, I suppose, though I wrote you eightpence worth
by the book-post.   Ought you not to visit Durham ?

Now I must shut up and go to bed.   Do you mind the
midnight walks we used to have when left in charge of
our respective abodes ?   I would almost smoke with you
just now if you were here.

Do write soon again like a good soul, and believe that
whatever you write is acceptable and delightful to . . .

To his sister Marcia

[6 WHARNCLIFFE PLACE,
NEWCASTLE-ON-TYNE ? *August* 1862.]

I had a very pleasant evening with Mouat on Thursday.   We told stories, a new thing for us.   Peter did
not, except one of his own experience the day before :
he had slipped on a piece of orange peel, and went down
on his back ; women screamed, and men ran to pick him
up, but he achieved that himself, when a small ragged
boy, looking up at a taller neighbour with a grave, im-
perturbed, inquiring gaze, says, ' What would be his
fancy for that, now ? '

Monday morning.—Last night I had a short but very
interesting walk and talk with ——.   I fear, poor chap,
his spiritual experience is of the queerest, and that the
gravity of his character (the underlying gravity) is
owing somewhat to this.   He sees more deeply into
these matters and talks more largely and freely on them
than any one I know here, and yet he won't become
a member.   He was in his boyhood tremendously
grounded in orthodox theology, and has the idea of
man's inability so firmly in his mind that he won't
believe he can believe.   (I think myself he has believed,
but he says No, and that he can't.)   And then it 's so
useless speaking to him, for he knows everything far

P

better than I do. No wonder he never opens out to ——, who thinks the whole thing is just cut and dry, made like a railway, so that if you go into one end of a tunnel on the rails, you come out all right at the other. I beg his pardon.

I saw Widow Eltringham last week ; she is able now with much pain to walk from her bed to the window, where she finds the air *so* sweet ! I wish you saw it— she is just on the top of a lot of black chimneys, in a neighbourhood I think the worst for rickety houses, dirty brick, heaps of slag, and dingy wharf, I ever saw. As we were sitting the bell began to toll, so she said, ' Aye, there 's another got away,' as if we were all here in a kind of prison.

The more I know this town the more wicked and immoral it seems. To walk along the street on Sunday is as effectual a mode of sickening the spirit as could be devised. The talk you hear is coarse, and full of cursing ; loud laughing and singing and whistling meet you on the main streets, and if you go behind scenes, as I had to do yesterday, it gets worse and worse. When I was sitting trying to instruct a man about the Lord's Supper (in his own house, or room), the door suddenly burst open, and a drunk man and woman fell in. This was the climax of a din fit to bring down the sky. Fancy a man trying to live godly there. It is awful to feel that the mass, the bulk of the population, are wholly regardless of religion—never think of it. And what to do ?

To S. R. Macphail

6 WHARNCLIFFE PLACE,
NEWCASTLE, 19*th August* [1862].

I have no doubt you are as well aware as I am that it is a long time since I received your last, but you may not be aware that since that period I have had almost no time. Part of it I have been wandering over the face of the earth, and part have been nailed to this same desk, but at other compositions than this. Marcia has had to go to Marseilles to nurse our sister-in-law there, who is seriously ill, and not liking to cast the unprotected female (who feels her unprotection as much as if she were 17) to the tender mercies of the city which even ' its own poets ' have named ' stoney-hearted stepmother,' I went with her at about an hour's warning, and saw her safely through those interminable streets and never-ceasing processions of omnibuses. I have seen London before, but it is just as overwhelming to me as ever ; a place to think of, when you can get up to that over the first prostration.

I saw the Exhibition, too, but many will have told you, or tried to tell you, about it, for it too passes wonder. You feel that, wonder as you may, you cannot wonder enough. As sometimes in a bright and glorious summer day (I don't speak, as you see, from *this* summer's experience) you long for a friend to help you to enjoy— according to that of our friend of *The Christian Year*,

> ' Of the bright things of earth and air
> How little can the heart embrace ! '

—*so* (apodosis here beginneth) in the Exhibition you long for twenty unsophisticated persons to help you at wondering, or for ten of the *nil admirari* kind, to see them floored at last.

Talking of apodoseis, I never cease to thank you for Clyde. I read it much (false knave, saying I would not read one of my own, though I did yours), and consult it almost daily ; *ecce signum* (or something like it), I touch it at this moment, without moving my hand, touch it with the end of my quill, and it's a short quill, often mended at the one end, often bitten and sorely unbefeathered (what's the German for that, pupil of the Commentator on Job ?) at the other.

Speaking of my right-hand friends, what do you mean by all that in your letter about *In Memoriam* ? At first I thought you were in love, then I thought you were in hatred with all and everything, and finally I concluded you were an ' unaccountable muskin.' This decision you will not deny is a safe one ; but if your dream has an interpretation, pray send it, for none is more ready to receive the wailings of *one* student than this desolate and afflicted parson at Newcastle. Think not, O Simeon, that though my ears are dinned the day long with steam-hammers, they cannot detect the fine vibrations which the whisper of affection excites ; think not that though the calluses which were rowed into in good and pleasant company are slowly and reluctantly disappearing from my hands, my heart is growing dull or callous to the titillation of the most delicate sympathies. (If it is this style you want, just say the word and you will have folios ; tap me, and I flow.)

There is one plain question, however, which, I suppose, you want me to answer, whereas you should have answered it for yourself. Of course, *In Memoriam* is not as it would have been had it been written at the side of the object loved. First and most plainly, our love is called into *expression* by bereavement, and expression reacts on the sentiment, deciding, confirming, and maturing it. Moreover, we have always something to regret about an object removed, as to our neglect or want of entire appreciation of it. This makes us anxious to say the most ; this reveals points before missed. Further, and perhaps nearest what you mean, we instinctively believe that the separate state is an *advance* on this, and therefore ascribe perfection to those who are in it (perfection according to their own character) ; we think of them as fully enlightened, and freed therefore from many little foibles, free also from the necessary

taint of flesh, this flesh at least.   Finally (at least on
my present horizon), there is a sacredness of mystery,
an *aw*ful reverence, which, while it does not increase love
in the passion of it, nor in the delight of familiarity,
exalts, purifies, and perfects it.   These items evolve for
yourself, and tell me by return of post, or as speedily
thereafter as convenient, if you are satisfied ; and if
you don't write immediately, I 'll think I have offended
you, and that you are never going to speak to me again.

I miss greatly our walks and talks, our rows and rows.
All were stimulating, and were such things as we of earth
grow by from day to day.   When am I to see you again ?
What are you doing ?   Write me fully.   Assure yourself,
if you need, that all you are concerned about interests me.

There is nothing here to tell you about.   My pupil
has worked himself into bed.   The weather is extraordinary—every day bad, and yet every day different.
There is a frightful lack of good company in this town ;
nobody that knows the things you know, and cares for
what pleases you.   However, it 's a discipline.   What
of that letter from your brother ?   Has he addressed
it wrong ?   Put another goad into him.   Now, Simeon,
I 'll be wroth if you don't tell me all you know about
yourself immediately.   I have been reading very variously
lately, mostly Calvin, also Macaulay.   Do you know, it
strikes me we are not brought up as we might be, and
that unless we open our own eyes no one will do it for us.

This is sapient, is not it ?   But I must go or the people
who ought to be visited won't.   *Believe* me, therefore,
your very affectionate and truly solicitous . . .

SIMEON R. MACPHAIL, Esq.

> Maximus in posse,
> in actu non nihil.
> δεινὸς πολὺ φρονεῖν
> σπουδαῖος μανθάνειν τε καὶ δρᾶν.

To his sister Marcia

6 WHARNCLIFFE PLACE,
29th August 1862.

Sandeman was here the other day on his way from London, and spent the day with me. He told me about it,[1] and told me good news as well, that he has at last got a call. However, I don't know what the Mrs. Hogue school of comforters would say to it, for it 's about the wretchedest little place in the Church, scarcely a hundred people ; and this call for Sandeman, a man that might be nobody would like to say what, after four weary years of probation. He, of course, however, continues to me the comfort which has not been true in his case, and is certain that in a few months some very desirable place will fall to my lot : *nous verrons*, as they say in Marseilles.

Here is a girl of about 16 come and planted herself plumb opposite the window, and gazing right in. I tried to stare her out, but that was vain. They often do it here, and seem to think writing sermons or letters is a kind of public exhibition ; and I may add, gratuitous. Perhaps she is my good angel, though, and tells me to stop ; so I will, for the present.

They give you threepenny organ performances here in the Town Hall on Thursday evenings. Last night I had an hour of it. It is rather loud, but a Sonata Pathétique of Beethoven's was grand. He is different from the rest of them, tho' the rest be Haydn, Handel, Verdi and Bach. It was strange to see the people coming in just to listen for an hour. There was no dress, no performers but one organist, who sat with his back to the audience throughout ; music mere.

[1] The death of a friend.

To the Same

6 WHARNCLIFFE PLACE,
NEWCASTLE, WEDNESDAY [*5th September* 1862].

The unluck of our family has been much upon my
mind lately—how Papa never seemed to get his due, how
Tom was so long kicked about, and John yet, and Anne
might have expected easier times than she has had. Why
is it ? Why are you not a princess ? Of course you will
say it is better as it is, but it 's not the remote cause I
speak of, but the near, the secondary.

Do you know, it only struck me the other day for the
first time that you and I might really have to live sepa-
rately. Though all our plans lately have been for
this, yet it never entered my imaginative noddle that
such a thing could be a reality ; and when one does realise
it, I can't say the sensation is by any means pleasant.
I hope, at all events, our lots won't be very distant.
If people could only be patriarchal, and dwell together
in tents, and if, in short, Eve had not eaten that apple,
and we were all floating about in happiness and sunshine
like bees among flowers !

You must excuse havering, for what can one say
from this place ? All is as monotonous as the ticking
of a clock. Do write often and long ; it seems months
since your last came. Mind, I am quite a Sir Having
Greedy in this. It 's a queer fourpence worth this, but
I don't grudge sending it, for many a fellow pays three-
pence morning and evening for his cigar or his pint of
beer, whereas I have not even had my threepenny organ
entertainment this week.

I agree with you about wrestling in prayer, and for
my own part feel it best to say simply what I desire, and
calmly to leave these my desires before Him who *can*
if He will. Nothing has given me anything resembling

the peace of God more than this, when it suddenly surrounds you as sunlight that God's knowledge takes up every fraction of your case, and that His love has already been preparing its best result. And in looking at you, it always seems to me so distinctly evident that Christ loves you, that I never have any fear about you. I know it is easier for me to see this than for yourself. But if there is one thing I can be said to know, it is that you are cared for ; and if I were not persuaded of this I would be at present supremely miserable.

What *my* trials are to be I don't know, but I sometimes fear that for all this sunny course I will be getting storm, and for easy living, day after day of distress, anxiety or suffering ; but I am glad to say this is wrong, and that one may always hope high and expect much.

PS.—I wish a letter could send you lasting strength, but you must believe that is nearer you than Newcastle, so look up, and you 'll pull through.

To S. R. Macphail

6 WHARNCLIFFE PLACE,
NEWCASTLE, 10*th September* [1862].

I am sorry to confess that I begin a letter to you just now rather because I know that this is my only time for three weeks to come than because at this moment I am very favourably situate and disposed for writing you. However, many thanks for your last, with its heathenish admixtures. Your picture of your view of Inspiration is not hopeful, but I trust that at last you also ' will beat your music out,' and. . . .[1] You don't need to be told that the truth which has cost us no such misery in the

---

[1] Parts of the letter are torn away, which accounts for the omissions. Further, it is unfinished at the end of the one sheet which has survived.

attaining is little worth.   You won't come, I hope, to
Mr. Sterling's (Carlyle's friend's) position, who said of
Dr. Henderson's book that H.'s conclusion seemed much
equivalent to ' Mark was probably inspired because he
was an acquaintance of Peter, and because Dr. Henderson
would be reviled by other Dissenters if he doubted it.'
Why did you not send some of your problems ?   I don't
profess to be good at a puzzle, and specially disclaim
infallibility on the point of Inspiration, but I like to
hear the griefs of a friend, and to hear what puzzles a
serious . . .

Your letter was very welcome, even unusually so, for
I was busy and unwell at the time, a compound state in
which I hate to be, but still find myself—an awful deal
of pottering about to be done ; and after trudging the
streets till your feet are bruised, and your spirit *do.*,
you come home, and just as you are sitting down, up
into your memory rises with a spasm the one thing
omitted that dashes all your day's work.   Indeed
nothing suits me better than the verse you send, ' οὐδὲ
μακάριος οὐδείς.'

. . . I wish now I had spent *more* than I did upon it.
I now see that what I maintained, and what Cunningham
approved, was mere infallibility.   I am at present in
the midst of a subject which is costing me as much
difficulty—Infant Baptism.   It is irritating to see the
sublime way men like —— reiterate arguments for the
thousandth time in utter contempt of objections and
difficulties, and go on comfortably and complacently
saying all manner of pretty things for the ladies, and
breaking forth into pious ejaculations, without once
coming near to the point at issue.

To his sister Marcia

6 WHARNCLIFFE PLACE,
NEWCASTLE, 11*th September* 1862.

I have one piece of news for you.   I heard yesterday
from a minister who has come to the other Presbyterian
church here, that Rainy said that *I* (do you understand ?
I) am the man for the High Church.   This produced at
once two thoughts within me ; the first that it would be
a nice thing to tell you, and the second that it 's nice to
think one is considered by Rainy.   Further I cannot say
this affects me much, nor will.   However, this morning
I have a letter from Maxwell asking if I would come and
preach in Walter Smith's, Free Roxburgh, in Edinburgh,
as it will be vacant in a week or two.   Of course I won't
refuse, though it be just to go through another course of
uncomfortable suspense and botheration, ending in a
more thoroughly fixed opinion that nobody will have me.
But I often feel as if there were not much more work in
me.   I can't make out my inside at all.

I had a nice letter from Stewart.   He is a true friend,
than which nothing is better.   His letters are long, but
I like his talk better.   There is a great deal in having
known a person long, and having them connected with
years whose griefs were lighter and whose joys were
more plentiful than these.   Do you know these lines of
S. T. C. ?

'A grief without a pang, void, dark, and drear,
        A stifled, drowsy, unimpassioned grief,
        Which finds no natural outlet, no relief,
            In word, or sigh, or tear.'

And do you remember his lines on Chatterton, beginning :

'O what a wonder seems the fear of death,
        Seeing how gladly we all sink to sleep,
        Babes, Children, Youths, and Men,
        Night following night for threescore years and ten !'

It's a lovely morsel. What a strange, unearthly kind of being he was : surely he lived as much in some other world as in this. On the other side there I wrote these verses for you, which perhaps you know already, but if you have not them by heart, you won't think them a bore. There are a lot more, but I send only those you want at present. To me they seem exquisitely beautiful in their simplicity. What hosts of beautiful things have been said, and good feelings felt ; plenty of salt if it was only well at hand.

> ' In the hour of my distresse,
> When temptations me oppresse,
> And when I my sins confesse,
>> Sweet Spirit, comfort me.
>
> When I lie within my bed,
> Sick at heart and sick in head,
> And with doubts discomforted,
>> Sweet Spirit, comfort me.
>
> When the house doth sigh and weep,
> And the world is drowned in sleep,
> Yet mine eyes the watch do keep,
>> Sweet Spirit, comfort me.'

Now I must shut up. I am alive, as you see, and if it's any comfort for you to know that I love you now as then, and hope to love you then as now, be assured of this. I feel the want of somebody to speak about you to. Mr. —— sometimes asks for you, but not in a way that invites much fulness of utterance in answer. May better times be at hand, and may contentment and patience lead us to them.

To the Same

6 WHARNCLIFFE PLACE,
NEWCASTLE, 23rd *September* [1862].
TUESDAY, 8.55.

I have been living fast since you went away, *running* away from thinking about my loneliness, and to-day I have done it to some purpose, having visited eleven families since 2.30. After a visitation like this I always feel as if I had done *something*—what, it might not be easy to say. However, my legs have been going pretty continuously, *aussi* my tongue, and so I deserve a small holiday. Yesterday I was not so successful in the tea line as I expected. I visited two or three houses where I had been asked to come *any* night (' Now *any* night '), but in which there was no invitation. At length it was getting late, and I was driven to the fashionables, and I thought by the savoury smell of baking in Mrs. Wood's that I had hit upon the hour to a nicety ; but, alas ! I had to leave as hungry as ever, and only got to Wilcke's eating-house as my inside was fairly rebelling. There I had a substantial and comfortable tea with butter and bread, *quantum suff.*, and the newspapers, for 5d.

No letters since you left. Kindest love to the household. Tell Tom to read *Hypatia* first, for I feel kind of queer without it. When you are not to be had, my books make my home. Bourrienne he may keep *sine die* ; it has not become mine yet, though it 's paid for.

By the way, one main reason why I write is to ask you if I might get for Andie a history of Illuminating which I see here on a stall, price 25s. It would be a possession for her life, full of lovely letters and borders and all that, a quarto, like a vol. of Scott's Commentary, or Liddell and Scott's Lexicon cut in two. What do you think ? It is cheap as a book, and it would be a real treasure to her and help her through the winter. Please say. I am not rich just at this moment, but the money would just go somewhere else and no more be seen.

To S. R. Macphail

6 WHARNCLIFFE PLACE,
NEWCASTLE, 15th October [1862].

I have just received your doleful epistle, and do not intend to answer it now, as I have not time; only I want to touch your hand, and also to tell you that it is not my fault that you have not heard from me, for I certainly wrote to you in time to catch you before leaving Macduff. If you want *two* letters for your one I decidedly object.

I am not sorry for you—at least only partially ; yours is so much better a state than what I myself commonly enjoy.   To be an earnest seeker is the one road to finding, and to be dissatisfied with what you have been, the beginning of better things.   I am not good at unravelling other people's doubts ; I don't know if any one is.   We should be left, I think, like chickens to break their own shells, or there may be danger of premature birth.   A grub is a very ugly circumstance, but it's the slow, disagreeable, unlikely antecedent to a butterfly ; and any one who tried to boil or otherwise evolve more rapidly the butterfly out of it, would probably find he had better have stood by and held his hands off.   However, one thing that seems to stagger you is very evidently just what saves us all, that is, the keen feeling of our helpless plunging.   Your faith is often, you say, quickened by a fall.   Of course it is ; there is nothing so good for one's faith (not for its *confidence*, but for its reality of grasp) as to fall over head and ears into sin ; just as nothing will make a prude take hold of your arm decently but a slippery road, and a felt incapacity on her part of keeping her feet.   I need not say to you, for I speak to one of the liveliest of consciences, that ' faith and a good

conscience' prosper or are shipwrecked together ; yet
the above is also true, because sin confessed and be-
wailed is the companion of a good conscience. But
am I speaking in the line of your difficulties, or only of
my own ? The conclusion of the whole matter is that
we plainly enough need to be saved, and God has given
us a Saviour, One who through all kinds of entanglement,
doubt, vice, waywardness, obstinacy, and every seed of
the devil, will show Himself the Author and *Finisher* of
our faith.

'Darkness and light are both alike to Thee.'

Do you use the Lord's Prayer ? Some days when all
else has been thick darkness with me, these words, 'My
Father which art in Heaven,' have shot through to the
Eternal light, and carried my soul to the presence of Him
who is ' OVER ALL *God blessed for evermore.*'

But, Simon, I must not write, for this is prayer-
meeting day, and I have to digest Cain. Thanks for all
your news. Never expect any news from this place, nor
ever suppose you know what stagnation is till you have
lived alone in Newcastle. In Edinburgh there are lots
who can sympathise and think with you, if only you can
find them—'Some soul you can ever find who can respond to all your agony '; but here, unless you talk of
iron and lead, coal or alkali, you are alone. I wish you
could come and see the public works here, the most
wonderful applications of steam to the working of tools
and machinery of all kinds. You seem just to have to
touch a few handles and observe, and a locomotive is
the result. When will we get these handles into studies
and oratories, or are they there already, if only we get
the hand to use them ?

Kindest love to your brother. He has not written,
and does not intend. Is his preaching for Dykes pre-

paratory to his call to the High Church, and mine to the East ? [1] I think I 'd have cheek to take anything that offered. What kind of views do you think you would have if you were four years licensed, four and a half from College, and no prospect of settled life ? This, however, you will never be. Macphails were always prosperous—ἀεὶ εὐτυχεῖς ; and may they continue to be so, especially in the person of Simeon Ross of that ilk, is the hope of . . .

To J. C. Stewart

6 WHARNCLIFFE PLACE,
NEWCASTLE, 15th October [1862].

I don't need the interference of anything but my own conscience to make me aware that I have treated you shamefully by not more speedily replying to your last. Mind, my conscience has been telling me dismal stories ; item, my affection has conjured up your image in my dreams, and so pleasant is it to meet you even in so shadowy a form, that if I was persuaded that you would continue to appear if I continued *not* to write, I doubt if you would hear from me at all. But last night you began to assume a very distant manner, and fearing you had some cause, I determined to break silence.

What did you think of Gladstone's speech here ? Do you believe in him ? Partly, I suppose. He seemed to believe in the Tyne and its shipping and chimneys—so much smoke can't be all smoke.

By the bye, you are good at an advice. Would you advise me to publish ? It 's a set of Lectures on the Lord's Prayer, which some of my *admirers* want to see in print. Maclaren is prepared to take the risk, and give me some share if it goes away. What do you think ? People don't like young men that publish, etc. — a

---

[1] The Rev. J. C. Macphail's church in Aberdeen.

number of objections will occur. I think you heard one
of the sermons, only they would need to be recast for
the gullible public, or called ' Paternoster ' or something,
to make them go down. I must settle about this immediately, so if you can let me know at once what you
think, I 'll be your most obliged.

I hear —— is to get £1000 p. an. ; is that true ? If
so, I would like to see you with the same ; money is not
everything, but it is something. Is your charge George
any nearer earning his bread yet ? I sometimes rather
envy you your conduct towards him. I am not good
enough to envy you the *doing* of all you do for him, but
the having done it. To have done something, to be able
to see that you have not lived altogether in vain, goes
far to reconcile one to life.

I must not forget to tell you that I made my first
appearance as a platform speaker on Monday night,
without seeing any reason to depart from the conclusion
you and I long ago came to, that whatever I was qualified
to shine in, it was not in that sphere. The planet Mercury
must have been in conjunction with the sign of the paper-
makers when I was born. This sentence being rather
Tennysonian, I may state that it means, *Anglice* and
vernacularly, that I like to read my public speeches.

To S. R. Macphail

NEWCASTLE,
SATURDAY [? *November* 1862].

BELOVED SIMEON,—Your letter has lain on my conscience ever since I got it. You must not go and write such
pathetic ones again, or you will seduce me into an undue
amount of correspondence. I am not going to write you
a letter to-day, only I want you to go and see Marcia,
who is in town at Torphichen. She is going to the
Fordyces at Brucklay, so she may be interesting in your

eyes as a probable inhabitant of Aberdeen and hearer of your brother. If that last-named person preaches such sermons as he has, I hear, been doing in Candlish's, he will be riven from his dear congregation to the greedy South.

I am to be in town on Friday, I hope, to preach in Walter Smith's. I suppose it's a poor place, and that I won't get it, but one must fall in with the order of things.

I have been extra busy for a fortnight preparing my Lord's Prayer sermons for publication. I don't think I ever in my life accomplished more MS. in a fortnight. Of course my ordinary work would not stop till I got through.

I wish you were here ; you may imagine how queer it is having no one to talk theology or even literature with. There are some half-dozen, I hear, in this place who read, but I have not fallen in with them. Now with hopes of seeing you, and much gladness of the pericardiac and diaphragmal regions at the thought, believe me . . .

To his sister Marcia

6 WHARNCLIFFE PLACE,
NEWCASTLE, 24th *November* [1862].

Your note came this morning, being the second effort of the postman on my behalf since I returned. The other contribution was from Innes, kind and unselfish as usual, offering to review my vol. as soon as it appears. Of course I accepted promptly an offer which will go far to give the thing a good start.

I am glad you are to get on, though your note is very sober, and you are a frightful distance away. R——and you should speak French always ; do you ? They ought to have a Parisian accent, and it is lovely, beats Aberdeen. I am getting fonder and fonder of the Morayshire voices of this household, and have added to my ideal woman a musical voice, not your plaintive way women have of reading the Bible to you or speaking to you when you are ill, but something with cadences and clearness, as if it came from a well-formed and clean mouth, and between pretty teeth. But one cannot separate voices from the associations of districts and events, etc.

Last night I preached from ' The Lord hath done great things for us, whereof we are glad,' a queer text for me, you will think, and so did I, and wished as I read it that people would take texts instead of sermons and feed on them ; they would have a chance thus of getting at their meaning and fulness, and not take hold of mere skeletons, that sermons give them. I need not say where I was after sermon when I tell you it was 12.40 when I got here. This is not late either for the house I came from or for this, for as yet I have had no evidence that Mrs. Murray ever goes to bed at all.

Of course, Tom will give me the money whenever I ask for it, but I intend to draw a lot from the Bank, for I am penniless, and there are 1,000 calls here, and what is the use of money ? Only, women should, ought to hoard, for the curse of labour was not upon them.

To the Same

6 WHARNCLIFFE PLACE,
WEDNESDAY [3rd December 1862].

This will not, I fear, prove long, but I am to be off on Friday morning to Liverpool (108 Stanhope Street ; let me see that in your handwriting pretty frequently) for ten days, and till then I 'll be in a hurry, for I have work cut out. I want to write an article on Colenso before I go.

I think you must be in my old bedroom at Brucklay.

It was just at the top of the main staircase, looking towards the gardens, with a turret.

All the proof [1] has now been through my hands, so it depends on the binders how soon the first of the ' *opera* ' shall appear, as a few strokes of a steam-press will soon throw off 750 impressions.   Some bits I am greatly disgusted with, and have often repented of publishing, yet I think on the whole it is best.   Mouat will buy some, and Maxwell, and Innes, and you, won't you ?

To J. C. Stewart

LIVERPOOL,
9th December 1862.

Excuse this paper, for I am in a foreign country, and write under various disadvantages.   Were you ever in Liverpool ?   It is certainly worth seeing, and I am not yet thoroughly tired of being sent to places for no better end than to see them.   I will be glad to have been here, though I never hear more of the vacancy on account of which I have come.   The docks, goods stations, bond-houses, sailors, merchants, and *horses* are astounding.   Item, there are some fine streets of dwelling-houses, but the English don't seem to understand the art of dwelling.   They can furnish well, and I suppose by an effort can build well too, but the bulk of the houses have no comfort in them—loose window-sashes, boxes which it were an abuse of the word to call *rooms*, and instead of lobbies, narrow passages which a housemaid with decent crinoline entirely occupies and blockades.   Said housemaids, however, are better than the Scotch, speak prettily, civilly, and smile when they ask you if you will dine at one or two.   I wish I (and moreover you) had the art of taking life so pleasantly that smiles come up

----

[1] Of *The Prayer that Teaches to Pray.*

to the face like perpetual bubbles to the surface of a
stream, without meeting one care or one bitter thought
to scatter them or obstruct their rise.   They must surely
be shallow ?

The church here is a very fine one ; has an exquisite
organ ; organist gets £80, and seems to be worth it.
The congregation is small, and look rather ashamed of
themselves in a building seated for 1150.   (Of course if
I came, that would soon be altered !)   I fear this will
be my bane here.   I might have a wee bit of chance if
the church was full, but of course they are wise to be
on the look out for a thoroughly popular person who
would fill their building.   I do resent the desire of con-
gregations to be moved and pleased.   I used to think
they desired this *in order to* instruction ; now I don't
believe it.   Men ' who can split the ears of the ground-
lings ; who, for the most part, are capable of nothing
but inexplicable dumb-shows and noise,' are the men
to get churches.   But don't say that I think so, for I 'd
be set down as a soured and disappointed person, which
I am very far indeed from being.   Only I wish, ardently,
that people really did desire instruction at church, and
not pleasant excitement and entertainment ; or that our
halls openly recognised the state of matters and appointed
a teacher of rhetoric of a noisy and gesticulating order
to the best endowed chair in the hall, so that young men
might know from the first what they were going to do,
and what would be required of them.

I came here in company with a score of Irish drovers,
who very fervently devoted Garibaldi to the region of
the Shades as we came through the long tunnel of England's backbone.   Howling, smoking, cursing, and chaffing the guards and one another were their main *diver-
tissements*, from which it was not disagreeable to be
shot.

I began to write to you partly because I have a cold in my head, and am rather miserable. I find I must stop for the same reason ; the flow is not through my pen.

To his sister Marcia

LIVERPOOL,
THURSDAY [11th *December* 1862].

Why have I not a letter this morning ? I just set myself down without a book or thoughts, in the full persuasion that in five minutes I would be filled with the most pleasing imaginations called up by your hand of write, and lo ! it was a dream. I am beginning to wish I was well back at Wharncliffe Place, though I have been getting on nicely here. I have met one or two nice people enough, but no Mouats. One man has been very kind coming and taking me with him in the evenings ; only he makes me smoke too much. Last night he spent 5s. on me, and took me to a concert which was all done by Germans in aid of Lancashire—mostly residents here. I was never in a finer hall, and never heard better amateur singers. It grew slightly wearisome, and we left before the end. The large Concert Hall here is magnificent, outside and in. Hamlet has, however, been my chief entertainment and friend since I came here—Mouat's nice little copy. I have read and re-read it, and spoken it aloud and acted it, and through all admired and wondered at it. I would like to see it acted by Mrs. Siddons and the Kembles, but not by any one second-rate. Now I think I must stop, for I have no more news, and objective truth is the only kind worth having. I have spent more than £1 on books since I came here. Is not that profane, in Lancashire ? I feel somewhat like a robber, but I will save more than £1 on my travelling expenses by going 3rd class. But I think I have left my conscience at Newcastle ; at least I have seen no evidence of its presence here, and only hope I may find it ' at home ' when I return.   I have been doing much in speculation lately, under the influence of the book Clark gave me.   It does one good to follow men like Leibnitz and Newton ; only I wish I had them here to ask them some questions.   Perhaps they have forgotten what they wrote while under the moon.

I have a note from Carstairs Douglas, the Chinese missionary, asking me to go out to the mandarins, but really I do not see my way to that.   I don't know one quality I have suiting me to be a missionary—not one. I have some that *may* help me at home.

At this juncture a note comes in from Dr. John Bonar asking me to preach in the Free High.   Sure it is nonsense, is it not ?   I don't know what to say.   Of course, it is useless going to preach for the mere *éclat* of the thing, and yet can I honestly give myself out as a candidate to succeed Rainy and preach to the Professors ?   I think not.   I would rather adhere to my plan for the East Church.   But write at once, my Daniel, to Wharncliffe, and direct me.   Now don't just get off, but really advise.

I wonder if the state of separate spirits is an active one, after all.   Of course, they cannot have material products of their working to show, but are there fruits of spiritual activity which would, if we could see them, astound us as much as these Liverpool docks or the electric telegraph ?   We are a benighted generation.

To the Same

LIVERPOOL,
Sunday Evening [14*th December* 1862].

It is almost Monday, and most of your Sabbatarians are in bed, and if they were not, I doubt if many of them would be employing themselves much better than this.

Certainly none of them have the opportunity of acknow-
ledging such jolly letters as I have to acknowledge.   You
are an awful deal to me.   To-night I think of you, my
Kadijah, with appreciation, for though I have preached
my *very* best here, and never had for four consecutive
services such freedom and pleasure in prayer, the people
evidently don't seem to see it, and to-night there was
a mere handful.   This is my usual fate, but what annoys
me is that the people should have brought me here after
my telling them distinctly that I was not a popular
preacher.   Then if I go to the High Church, it will be
' Oh ! he 's very good, but we want an older man.'   And
yet they ask me to go, as if I had no work where I am, and
was just a shuttlecock to be knocked from one end of
reaction to the other.   (That 's into them all.)

Well, I know I don't deserve to preach, I mean comparatively with other men ; so if I am shut out, a better
man will be let in ; and though this life is *most* disagreeable in many things, still it is in many ways good.
This little visit I have seen much, and enjoyed a good
deal, and perhaps done something.

This is Wednesday morning, in Peter's parlour.[1]   I
have written to Rainy telling him I do not see my way
to leave this for the sake of a quite temporary engagement.   Of course, if they like to ask me to go for one
day as a candidate, I will.   South Shields is fixed, and
not with me.   Liverpool I told you the state of, and
Roxburgh Place I expect to hear no more of ; so ' As you
were ! ' is again the word.   I don't think I will go again
to a vacancy, unless an Edinburgh one.   I am so convinced of the utter uselessness of it.   Peter wants me
to change my whole style of preaching ; but I see plainly
enough that if I am to succeed, I must use what would

---

[1] This paragraph was added to the letter in Newcastle on the day after
the next letter was written.

be, in me at least, clap-trap ; and I won't.   I will
never say ' Oh ! ' unless my *normal* state of feeling is at
that height.

But I dare say you have had enough of this from . . .

To the Same

Mr. Mouat's Parlour,
Newcastle, Tuesday [16th December 1862].

I have a long letter written to you, but it lies in the
North-Eastern Rwy. Station . . .

I found also on reaching home that it was not as
a candidate but as supply that I am wanted for the
Free High, so I am this morning in a mess.   Peter last
night thought I should not go, but, like Mamma, advised
that we should sleep a night upon it (which he began to
do by keeping me from sleep till near two).   I can't see
what I should do.   There is a letter also from Dr. Mackintosh asking me to go there, but I am not going.   You
might say what you think about this.   It would be work
for probably six months.   They would get more good
from my sermons than any other congregation, but I
do not want to be in Edinburgh.   It has done me much
harm, and I am getting clean of some of it here.   But
again, and what at this *moment* almost decides me to
go, is that I would be much more likely to get work there
than here of a permanent kind.   Of Liverpool I expect
to hear no more.

To the Same

6 Wharncliffe Place,
Newcastle, Tuesday [23rd December 1862].

I preach my last here on Sunday evening, having
agreed to go to the High till they get suited.   At Roxburgh my chance is perhaps slightly bettered by my
second preachment, but my Irish competitor has still
the heels of me, I fear.

Wednesday, P.P., *i.e.* not plum-pudding, but *post prandium.* Last night we had our Congregational soirée, and I took leave of the people.   To-morrow I shall have to preach, and on Sunday evening.   I am very sorry to leave this place, and some of the people I would gladly take with me.   Peter came yesterday to ask me to dine on New-Year's Day with him ; which I do.   He also said he was very sorry I was going away ; which I believe.   Where are you to eat goose ?

I am done living on 15s. now (though it did very well for a time, and with strict economy never got any less) ; I have got my money, so if you want some, command me to any amount not exceeding—— [1]

I went to see if Mrs. Archibald could take me in, and was dismayed at the forlorn, dingy, cold aspect of the room.   It won't be the same.   However, it 's better than another place.   She wishes 14s.   Is that too much, coal and gas included ?

To his sister Marcia

11 CASTLE STREET,
EDINBURGH, *9th January* [1863].

Here I am once more, but here you are not.   It is a little dismal, no piano, and no one to sit thereat.   I have made the room pretty comfortable, sticking up Kingsley on one side where Newton used to be, and St. Nicholas' steeple where Milton once was suspended.

The John Knox people gave me £13 odds, and the young men gave me an inkstand, valued about £3, 10s.   It was very good of them, but I wish I might spend the money on trousers—they want me to keep it, and put it in something more permanent than bags commonly are.   It was very sad coming away.   Peter was quite touching ;

[1] *Sic.*

the last night I was with him till late, and he was in an
uncommonly delightful mood, just tempting you to kiss
him ; and after sitting talking fast, he saw me more than
a mile to home, saying often that he was very sorry, and
that he would miss me very much, and I saying the same,
and both of us with truth.   I was very sorry to leave the
Murrays too.   Mrs. M. and Maggie both shed tears,
which I did not ; but I think I was a great deal sorrier
to part with them than they with me.   Mrs. Maclintock
also used the onion, and gave me a pretty travelling
dressing-case.   So I left, feeling about the meanest,
most ungrateful and selfish of unconvicted rascals.

To the Same

11 CASTLE STREET,
[*January* 1863].

Of all people in the world you certainly write the nicest
letters, and of all the letters you ever wrote your last
has always a way of being the best yet.   But I think
you are sly, for I very often get your letter, I notice, just
after I have despatched one to you, and yet I invariably
feel inclined on getting yours to sit down and have a
regular holiday of writing to you.   This present is
Saturday, and I am reading over ' Ephesus ' and ' In your
patience ' to make my debut in the Free High to-morrow.
I have no defined feelings on the subject to communicate,
only I don't think this place agrees with me.   There
must be something quite different in the air, for I have,
this second day of my stay, my old feeling in the head
and the old taste in my nose that I have nowhere else.
It may be in the beefsteak, and not in the air ; and I
think I will introduce as much of Mrs. Murray's cooking
here as I can.   She almost never gave me steak.   I am

still very much from home here, and pine for my little
room in the smoke with the Morayshire maid warbling
and stepping through the house.

I have a very great deal to tell you, but am somewhat
pushed for time.   First of all, Innes heard me on Sunday,
and came in the evening and had tea.   He was very
kind and friendly, and blew me up about my delivery
to a frightful pitch, sealing all by telling me, and dog-
gedly maintaining, that my manner is colder than Rainy's.
This, of course, I have not yet taken in, and tried
to show that 'worse than Rainy' was an impossibility,
but he held to his position, and told me many unpleasant
truths.   I think he has been trying to persuade the High
Church people to take me, which I sincerely trust they will
not do.   I don't think this is laziness, but I will do what
I am driven to.   They will surely not be so daft after all
as to think of me.   It was queer preaching to Rainy.
He wears a light-coloured topcoat, and sits beside his
wife in the afternoons, to show he is not altogether a
cleric now.   He and Bannerman came into the vestry
and greeted me.

After tea I went to bid Maggie Stewart good-bye, who
is now away to Durham, though not at all strong.
Giles and I had a dirge in the streets on the misery of
women working and families breaking up.

To the Same

11 CASTLE STREET,
SATURDAY [? 17th *January* 1863].

To-day I am taking Sally to the back gallery at Hallé's.
It's all I can afford ; I think she will like it.   I wish
you and Mima were to be with us.   Of Simeon I have
seen a good deal.   I go up to hear Rainy often, and meet
him there, and he comes across frequently.   But I

always think visitors are looking for you, and I only feel half at home. There is no one else to come but J. C. Stewart, who has not come, and Willie Jeffrey, who sent me Hanna's book the other day, but has not been himself. I visited him and took tea with him. Peter has a width and depth and power of taking you into his width and depth, that none of them have. I so wish you knew him. I like him all the more because he minds me of Stewart.

Some day there will be plenty love in us and freedom to emit it, and persons to bestow it on. Meanwhile there is the more difficult, if not the higher way, which I have scarcely heart to commend to others, having so little heart to follow it myself.

Poor creature that you are, do you suppose other people find they can cast off evil habits as they do old clothes ? I could tell you on the spot, without reflection, of ten things I have been trying to give up for almost twice as many years, and here I am still.

If you can get a hold of Worsley's *Odyssey*, you will find a very correct representation of Homer.

To A. Taylor Innes

11 CASTLE STREET,
EDINBURGH, *19th January* [1863].

Your notice [1] has at length appeared, and is certainly worth waiting for, only I fear the discerning few may see more of the friend than the critic in it. However, the public is ' gullible,' and I believe your recommendation will help on the book and its author considerably. People do, for the most part, require to be told what to think of what they read, and I trust they will in this instance follow your guidance. I have sent a paper to Mrs.

---

[1] Of *The Prayer that Teaches to Pray*, just published.

Maclagan, Aberdeen, being sure that she will like to see it. What you have said is far, far more valuable than all the other notices put together; indeed, to tell you the truth, it almost persuaded myself that the book was a worthy one.

I have been hearing Rainy for the last week, and intend to hear all he has got to say on the Alexandrian teachers. It is the fittest subject for him that I can think of in Church History, and he is doing it well. You may imagine how he revels in that philosophico-theological region which they occupied, and how his humour and his profanity find ample room to disport themselves abundantly. He is marvellously wise. He can't possibly have read these men themselves, and yet when listening to him you cannot but feel that he has not only read them, but pondered and lived among them. A slightly better arrangement would, I think, make them more useful. He has great command of words, though not of sentences and paragraphs. Many of his phrases are most memorable. The fellows are lost in admiration, and all the more lost when he plunges into a mist of abstractions.[1]

I am, as I need scarcely say, much hurried just now, but will write you soon again. Meanwhile believe me, your very much indebted . . .

To his sister Marcia

11 CASTLE STREET,
EDINBURGH, 22nd January [1863].

I have been at the prayer-meeting. Rainy was not there, nor Walter Hately, so after appealing to the ladies

---

[1] A later letter to the same, not printed, says: 'Dr. Rainy is doing admirably, and giving the nicest little shines at his house to which students have ever been invited. They think him as good a host as a professor.'

to start the tune, and waiting in silence for the sticks to begin, I had to weigh anchor myself and launch at random into a ditty. This with a bad sore throat, and a stupefying cold in the head, was a nice commencement ; but it's wonderful how things get done and come to an end.

I am wonderful, as I told you ; dine at 4 and tea at 8.30; but I am not getting into my work at all, and wish more earnestly than ever that I were settled. I think there must be some curse on me—at all events, there is something about this city that irritates and depresses me as nothing else does ; and it is very unpleasant to feel corrupt to the bottom of the heart, ' from scalp to sole one slough and crust of sin,' and unfit for the society of your kind.

I have been at Rainy's lecture just now. It was on Origen, and the best I have heard from him ; indeed it could not be better. I never heard him quite in the same style before, either preaching or lecturing, and did not think he could do it so well. It was biographical, you know, but very rich—fat biography. He is a wonderful man. He is often very witty in his class, and says many very ready things, much to the point.

I understand Roxburgh Church is to be settled on Monday evening. I shall scarcely believe it if I am fixed upon. But if I am not, I think I will be done with vacancies. However, Ulysses was ten years in finding his way back from Troy to Ithaca ; but even he ate his great heart.

To the Same

11 CASTLE STREET,
26th January 1863.

Tuesday.—I have been to one of the Roxburgh Place elders and heard once more my doom. Murphy, a de-

clamatory Irishman, has got it.   I feel this more than
I have felt any of my numerous rejections.   I had *every*
chance.   Murphy did not preach a second time ; I did.
My book had just been lauded in a paper which some of
them at least would see ; the Lady Glenorchy people
came in force to hear me ; and then being in the High
Church, I feel now as if I had really been considered and
rejected, which I never felt before.   I feel, too, a strong
inclination to be wicked on the subject.   To be told so
repeatedly that you are not fit for the work does go to
a personal belief in that fact.   And to be thrown back
so often from particular spheres of the work, does tend
very strongly to throw me off the work altogether.   It
is very difficult to keep in quite a good humour with the
world, when a score of times in succession it tells you that
you have mistaken your place in it.   One cannot just begin
again as freshly as before.   And now here is the future ;
by being in the High Church, I 'll no doubt be asked to
go to, say, four vacancies.   These vacancies it will, I
suppose, be my duty to go to, and these vacancies, after
an interval of ten months, during which a host of others
are heard, will in succession reject me.   I dare say most
people would have taken the telling I have got and
given up long ago.   The worst of it is, there is nothing
else to do.   I am too old now to go in for anything.

Now please don't be going to answer this.   I have been
as wicked as man can be ever since I left Newcastle, and
see little prospect of being otherwise here.

To the Rev. J. C. Macphail

11 CASTLE STREET,
27th January 1863.

I received this morning from Marcia a copy of *The
Free Press* containing a notice of my volume.   Whether

this was penned by yourself or not, it is due to you that it appears, and I send you my warmest thanks. Of course the flattery runs a deal too high, but I am well aware that the ears of the public have been rendered so callous by hearing the praises of authors bawled constantly into them, that unless any new intimation be sounded loud indeed, it has no chance of being heard.

Moreover, I have to-day received a dose of the other thing which will keep the flattery from doing me harm. I have heard that I have been once more rejected. This time I had every chance that man could have. It was in Roxburgh Church here, where Walter Smith was, and the Lady Glenorchy people came in force to hear me, and in many other respects I thought I had a chance ; and having been defeated where I am best known and most appreciated, I cannot expect anything else else-where. I never felt the *least* cast down by any of my former defeats, but I do by this, or at least my pride is hurt. To be told so repeatedly as I have been that you are unfit for your work, works in you a belief to the like effect. But you had no probation, and cannot under-stand what nearly five years of it is.

Simeon is keeping at his work well, and winning golden opinions from his Professors. He worships Rainy. I have heard Rainy several times since I came to town, and his lectures could not be much, if at all, better. One he gave the other day on Origen I never heard equalled.

To his sister Marcia

11 CASTLE STREET,
THURSDAY, 29*th January* [1863].

Here is Thursday morning, and no letter from you. Are you ill ? Or what is the matter ? You must not expect anything from me. I am empty ; and when I

turn a voice of pitiful entreaty to my brain to do something, it just echoes, like the dear old song of the dear old
girl ——, ' No, no, no, no, no, no ! ' I think I never
felt so utterly and hopelessly stupid in my life as I have
done since coming here.   I just sit like a lump of slain
sheep, and hold a book before me, and sometimes for
variety's sake take up a position before a sheet of paper
with a pen in my hand, and having spent two hours in
this position, I lay down the pen and put away the paper
as clean as it came out of the mill.   Then I sit down by the
fire and think, or dream rather, that these are the best
years of my life that are passing ; and then I wonder if
it 's not time to go out to Rainy's Lecture, and it isn't,
not for long yet, and so I sigh and gaze about, and take
up the first book that comes to hand, and so go round
again.   And nobody by any chance comes in to break
this.   I thought I had some acquaintances, if not friends,
in this old city, but if so, they don't know my address.
I liked the long forenoons at Newcastle, made short by
an abundant amount of work to be put into them, and the
long evenings when I never expected anybody to come
in ; but here it is different, in this old room that used to be
such a real home, the best, as I thought, in Europe.

And then, as the crown of all, there is never a ground
for grumbling, and that stave of old Latin comes up
and up, and won't be put down, ' *Sit miser, qui miser
esse potest* '—Let him be wretched who can—which is the
sum of the whole business, there being in all bad weather
a sun behind, running his usual course, who comes out
after all the clouds have spent themselves and are for
ever past.

Thursday afternoon.—I found at this point that I was
in a sermonizing vein, so I took out my three sheets, and
began a sermon on ' Rejoice in the Lord always,' and
actually wrote two pages.

R

Simeon wants to introduce me to a friend of John Gibb's, a fellow Whyte, a student; so I intend giving a young supper some night.

Do you read all I say? Because I just write away more for the utterance of myself than the entertainment of you.

To his sister Andrea

11 CASTLE STREET,
2nd February 1863.

I am ashamed of always writing to you in a hurry, when I have such jolly letters from you to answer, but almost all I do nowadays is done *currente calamo*. Many thanks for your poem, which is, I think, the best yet. I have read it to two judges, Simeon Macphail, who has great sympathy with modern poetry, and Stewart, who has a riper judgment, and both were much pleased. Stewart especially, who thinks also that you write a beautiful hand. Here, I think, he is mistaken; you *could* write well, but you don't write so well as you could.

I don't think you need torment yourself about —— —— not writing to you. I suppose she writes to no one. Also don't try to make more of that friendship than it really is. You were never suited to be heart and heart friends; circumstances threw you together, and you liked one another, but you are not pledged to an ardent, consuming, confidential attachment on that account. You can be good friends without that; you can have fond memories of schooldays, and be glad to see one another again, without dying of love. I would never dream of expecting Davie Hogue to unbosom himself to me, or to shed tears if I said I was going to New Spain, or to write to me if I was there. Nevertheless, he is a very nice fellow, and though I knew Peter

Mouat better in ten minutes (and he me) than I would
know Davie Hogue in as many years, I do not on that
account stimulate him to more ardent love. As much
evil, in my opinion, is done by over as by under culti-
vation of one's friends.

Here endeth the lesson
on Friendship.

To his sister Marcia

11 CASTLE STREET,
2nd February 1863.

Yesterday Rainy came into the vestry between sermons,
and had a long talk about his work, which he greatly
likes. I wanted to let him know how thoroughly he
was appreciated, but could not get it out. Item, he asked
me to meet a lot of students on Thursday night. Item,
I walked down with him in the afternoon, and he whistled
a profane melody on Princes Street, which is of a piece
with his grey trousers, light greatcoat, and half-tipsy,
rollicking gait, about which the little world here is talking.
He is almost as good a listener as a preacher. He thinks
my manner improved.

To the Same

11 CASTLE STREET,
THURSDAY [? *5th February* 1863].

I was wrought up to a pitch of expectation this morning
which I knew could not be disappointed, but I could

scarcely expect such a treat as came. I do wish you would write oftener, and that you had nothing else to do but write letters to everybody all round to set them on their legs again and do them good.

By the way, if John Gibb is in low spirits, tell him with the kind regards of one who has tried it, to write a sermon on ' Rejoice in the Lord alway : and again I say, Rejoice.' specially the latter clause. I am just home from Rainy's —a nice party enough—only I had an hour with Stewart before, which was some nicer. I admire Rainy, however, in every capacity. To-night he introduced the students to the ladies one by one, and just was a host in himself, or a host in his company rather. Only I don't, no, I don't understand him. There were two girls I think I could have got on with ; fortunately I did not get near them. One was very good-looking. The rest of the company was the ordinary thing. A lot of songs, the whole of which multiplied by five nights would not weigh up one from lips I know of, and have touched with mine —no, a song needs a woman behind it. On making this kind of examination of the evening, I think I must have been asleep most of it, and in a kind of molluscous state, and I think I am that always now, whether for want of you, or Innes, or Peter (chou !), I don't know, but I am much a vegetable.

Are you aware that yesterday evening there was one of the most appalling storms that ever visited this town ? The wind was a tempest, the hail *hissed* through the air, the lightning blazed and darted, and the thunder rolled, till a lot of people thought the last day had come, and I dare say every one would feel the helplessness of man in presence of the Elements. Might not people see how they are restrained ? What is to prevent them increasing their fury a little, say doubling it, and sending every earthly thing to smithereens or shivereens ? Your infidel shoemaker would say it is necessity, that things must be that way or they would not be at all ?   There must be something in leather conducive to scepticism ; but I almost wish I was he, to get your visits.   If you lend him your book, you 'll get it back smelling of leather —not Russia.

To the Same

11 CASTLE STREET,
16th *February* 1863.

A letter a week from you is doubtless a very good and acceptable thing, but it is a very poor substitute for your company.   I gnash my teeth pretty frequently just now ; and find that for me there is no society but yours.   And when I am obliged to write a sermon a week again, I don't know wherever it is to come from, if you are not back again to put some life into me. Now I am mere beef—bad beef—I do nothing, I think nothing, I feel nothing, but wickednesses.

But to change the subject, do you know that Rainy is a Doctor—conferred by Glasgow University ?   I am not proud of it ; if it had been Edinburgh it might have been tolerable, but Dr. Rainy is no more than, if so much as, Rev. Robert Rainy.

I had an offer on Friday of the sub-editorship of *The Friend of India*, £400 per an., with board and lodging, which is fair remuneration.   It came through your old ally Constable, but I declined—perhaps foolishly.   I never know.   It would be a good deal more than Rainy is getting now, or than I could ever hope to get here by literary work, and really the prospects of a self-denying, poor and ecclesiastical life seem all rapidly departing from me.

Tuesday afternoon.—Your letter has come, for which many, many thanks ; but more and longer ; mind, I live mainly on them.   You can't imagine how few people I speak to.   To-day, for instance, not a soul but Beshie.

I have been considering that situation more since Sunday, and being in a wicked mood, and wholly out of sympathy with Church, Free Church, matters, I feel a little drawn to it.

To the Same

11 CASTLE STREET,
23rd February [1863].

I am happy to say that this week I have a real reason for being brief in my epistolary efforts, for Guthrie of the *Review* has sent me two big volumes of Dr. Cunningham's to notice.   If it turns out any way decent I will send it to you, also a notice of William Miller's book, if I am not ashamed of it when I see it in print.   It is a great refreshment to get something to do that must be done this week.

Yesterday there was a first-rate congregation, by far the best I have seen in the church since I came, and Rainy was pleased to say he was greatly interested in the 'Seven Churches.'   But when the 'Seven Churches' are done, can you aid me to a subject ?   Please say.   I think of the Parables.   But I know these won't turn out to be so exalting a subject as the Seven.

How could you go and say that it is not your absence makes me queer ?   No youth of my kind should live alone—it 's more trying than people think, and few are so alone as I am, for my business during the day does not bring me into contact with anybody.   Sally looks up often to ask what ' Black Monday ' or ' the Sophy ' was, or what is the difference between a comedy and a farce,

or such queer, useless questions as schoolmasters develope
school-girls' wits with.

If you want something to say to ——, you may
tell her I am reading Trench's sermons and am disappointed, after the account she gave me of them.   They
are orthodox, in good taste, and practical.

To the Same

Of work I have done next to none this week, and had
to have recourse to a novel, choosing vol. 1 of *The Vir-
ginians,* vol. 2 of which I hope to peruse.   He is a great
artist, is Mr. Thackeray—introduces Johnson, Richardson,
Washington, Wolfe, and a lot of swells of the period, so
that really it is a ' useful book.'   But he likes the bad
side of the world too much ; and I always feel as if he
were wishing us to say, ' How this man knows the world ' ;
whereas I am not sure that he does.   One thing he fails
to do—to mingle the good and evil as they are in life.
He paints his character and writes, ' here is a blackguard,'
and tries to paint another, and says, ' here is a good, respectable person,' but he cannot show us that place we
all live in, and where the good and evil are run through
one another—the good man having in him and often
letting out of him the qualities of the evil one, and
vice versâ.

To the Same

I would like nothing better than to be able to send you
yesterday [1] as it was to me, but I know it is impossible.

---

[1] The marriage-day of Albert Edward, Prince of Wales.

No one has ever seen anything like it, and I much fear that no one will be able to describe it. But to begin at the beginning, I should tell what I had beyond the public. In the morning Simeon took breakfast with me at 7.15, and we at once adjourned to Torphichen Street and got Sall and Mary, and had one of the very best pulls up the Canal. This is my first on the Canal this year. It was a very cold morning, snow on the hills, and blue and purple on M. and Sally's faces, but they were in too great a state of delight to mind. Sim and I were of course not blue, to say the least of it, for we went to Slateford and back with our cargo within the hour. We got back to Torphichen Street, and left for the Review at 9.15. The crowd was tremendous—Charles thought above, and I under 100,000, and a man I consulted thought 1,000,000, that is to say, the biggest number he had ever had to make use of. It was very cold standing, though Charles was jolly. We were glad to get back to T. St. and get something inside, then four tunes from Sall, and then here to dress for the Andersons, which being accomplished, Simeon went along with me almost to the door.

At 7 we sallied forth. You know the illuminations were mainly confined to George and Princes Streets and the High Street, so these were just *packed* with people ; and had not the arrangements been beyond all praise, it would just have been mess and row. The Scots Greys stood with their horses, and when needful walked in among the crowd, and divided the mass moving one way from the mass moving the other, so there was not the slightest approach to riot or accident. The conversation of the crowd was one exclamation of wonder and delight. To give you any idea of the effect of the Castle is impossible. If you can fancy the rock covered with lights, and lights at every porthole and along every buttress, throwing out every point in the wall against the black night, and then row upon row of lights across the sheep-park, and all through the gardens, straggling sometimes like the camp fires of a great army, and then the whole old town brilliant with shining devices, and the scene all changed every minute with a red or green light thrown *over the whole* by a chemical preparation, you may have some idea of the thing ; but really it seems just like a dream ; nothing in the *Arabian Nights* is half up to it.   I never saw buildings so used before.   Sir W. Scott's monument was covered in all its outline with lamps, and so was St. George's (which, perhaps, was finer than any other building), with lamps in beautiful lines down the dome, so that the whole form of the building was brought clear out.   Then most astonishing fireworks were being discharged the whole evening from the Salisbury Crags, and a bonfire on Arthur's Seat.   St. Andrew Square must have had about 3000 lamps in it of all colours, and in all designs, festooned all round the gardens, and skilful use made of the column in the centre.

Well, we walked from 7 till 10 in this, and I suppose will all remember those hours as long as we live.   We had all to follow one line of march laid out by the authorities, and the people seemed so astounded that the mass just went docilely on.

To the Same

11 CASTLE STREET,
FRIDAY, 13*th March* [1863].

Many thanks for your little note yesterday, if it does not mean that I am to have none to-morrow, which surely it cannot.   I wish you were well, and here.   I don't know whether it is foolish or not, but I feel inclined to tell you in every letter what a different world this is to me because you are in it, and how different a life I lead. But I suppose I must not enter at length on such a subject in case of offending those fine feelings of yours. So I will give you the news since Wednesday morning, on which forenoon I wrote a lump of sermon, then went to Rainy's and met John Gibb.

I could get on with him, I think ; indeed I count him a friend already, for yesterday morning he came up at ten to go along to see ——, whom he does not know. We did so, and he took the same impression of —— as I have always done. He said he felt at once in the presence of a perfect stranger. He is a man preoccupied, or indeed a man who is away somewhere else, and has merely a representative in your presence, with powers to say things about the weather and facts in general, but no authority to make revelations of character.

On leaving ——, it seemed to strike us that we might do worse than go to the Exhibition, where I had not yet been. So we went round by Frederick Street and got his catalogue. We saw the pictures, and made our remarks. He does not instruct one so much as Innes in art matters, but said many nice little things, and true always, and lenient.

I have read Colenso's second part, which is a very dangerous book, a popular and wholly one-sided exposition of the leading difficulties which have hitherto been handled only in scientific introductions. (Are you aware that John Gibb is one of the most erudite of young men on Biblical subjects ? I so wish he were here to read with.) It was William Fordyce who very kindly lent me Colenso, he having it out of a circulating library. I think our views of inspiration will be greatly altered in future years. Indeed mine are very different from those I received from Gaussen twelve years ago.

If you want a book, I think you would like Max Müller's lectures on language, selecting bits, you know, as you thought fit.   But Shakspere is the best book— a wholesomeness and truth about it, which makes you more than you were before, a something like Peter Mouat.

To A. Taylor Innes

11 CASTLE STREET,
EDINBURGH, 14th March 1863.

I was a good deal ' taken amidships ' when I found you had been here, but am almost glad now, since I have got a letter out of you.   A friend of yours has been here for a week, John Gibb, to wit, with whom I also have struck up a friendship.   He has been in Heidelberg finishing himself, and is now in a mission in connection with J. C. Macphail's congregation.   He is one of the best-read students I have met, an intelligent and lenient critic of men and things, a good deal chastened by bodily weakness and acute pain, and possessed of a faculty of clear and independent thinking.   On exegetical matters he certainly has gathered an unusual amount of information, and gone through an unusual amount of thinking.

I am profoundly lazy since I came here, have written four sermons which I cannot preach, and feel as if there was not another possible sermon in existence.

I suppose you have not seen Colenso's second part. It shows much greater critical aptitude than the former, though there are no new results.   He brings forward in a popular form the usual signs of a later date than Moses which are to be found pretty largely in the Pentateuch.

To the Rev. J. C. Macphail

11 CASTLE STREET,
EDINBURGH, 16*th March* 1863.

Since receiving your last letter I have had many intentions of writing to you, and these have been kept alive
by the constant solicitations of Simeon, and finally
quickened into this present by the visit of John Gibb and
his sister.   Is it too late to thank you for your letter ?
If not, accept of my gratitude, and also please consider
my request that you would write soon again.   I can even
give you a subject, for I see by the papers that the
situation you long ago spoke to me of is now more desirable than ever—to wit, assistantship in Trinity.   I do
wish now to be settled.   I fear I am but wasting my time
at present, for I have a stock of sermons that lies between
me and my work, and forms a kind of padding through
which the ordinary *stimuli* do not penetrate.   Also this
half-work is sickening me of the whole affair, not that
I am not as sensible as ever I was (or more so) of the
reality and use of the work of a minister, but simply that
being so long kept from this, I am tempted to turn to other
things as *my* work.   I know that were I settled, all this
would vanish in a week, so if you think still that Trinity
would be a suitable place for me, I should feel obliged
by your at least keeping me in remembrance, as I am
sure you do.

I am *very* glad to have made John Gibb's acquaintance,
and wish he were here that it might grow to friendship.
I don't know that I have met with a man of his age who
has studied Exegesis so thoroughly, or has a larger stock
of information on certain subjects in Theology.   He has
also an unusual number of carefully formed opinions, and
held in such a state as to admit of accretion and growth.
Also from his leniency and truth of criticism on men

and things, and from his healthy spirit, he is a most agreeable companion. I felt very sorry that I am doomed to scramble on here alone, and that he should carry away out of my reach so much fresh thinking and so much ripe judgment. If he were here, I would use him till I got all out of him that would pump.

To A. Taylor Innes

11 CASTLE STREET,
23rd March 1863.

I duly received your very delightful letter, and thereafter its mysterious little appendix or satellite. Your remorse I vehemently resent, especially if it threatens, as it seems to do, fruits meet for remorse in the shape of any alteration in the style of your letters.

As to your remonstrance about my preaching, I am very sensible both of your kindness and justice in making it. I am trying to preach the gospel *simpliciter* more frequently, but find it so much easier to arrest attention by the declaration of new truth than by the illustration and close enforcement of old, that I am (through the weakness of the flesh) always going astray from the grand centre. Sometimes, too, one can preach the gospel more effectually by preaching the law, such law and fulfilment of law as the gospel requires, and as nothing but gospel can supply.

Your old friend Miss Johnson I have been to, seen, and been conquered by. She put me in mind of your father the moment I saw her. She worships a lawyer in Glasgow with nearly as much devotion as a professor in Edinburgh ; and imparted with much feeling and some prolixity the sorrows she has recently sustained by bereavement—her golden age is past. I hope to see her frequently.

By the bye, should I tell you that I am reading *Tom Jones* just now ?   I am greatly delighted with the wisdom, humour and freshness of it, and a good deal disgusted with the looseness of it.   But he is surely superior in penetration and in humour to all who have taken in hand to write novels since.

To his sister Marcia

[11 CASTLE STREET,
EDINBURGH, ? *March* 1863.]

Your last was delicious, of course, as your cuffs used to be sweeter than anybody else's kisses.   About writing to you, there is no question of the selfishness of that amusement, for I feel inclined to write to you at all times, when I weary of sermonizing, when I come home to this empty no-home on a Sunday after preaching, when I am too tired to read, when I am glad or sad, at all times it is (or would be if I followed my impulse) my relief.   If I am lenient (in saying which I hope you are true, for I should like to be lenient), I owe it to you ; having had such a specimen of humanity for my constant study has redeemed me from taking low views of my kind, whereas if I had been from day to day nagged and fretted, Diogenes would have been a Moses compared to me. (By the bye, about the hymns, I did not, of course, mark many, because I had not time to read many, and some were too good to mark, such as ' Jerusalem, my happy home,' which might sing in heaven ; it is perfect.)

I sometimes wonder I don't fall in love with some of the multitudes of young ladies I meet nowadays (about thirty a week), for I am quite in a position just now to do so—half-idle, solitary, etc.   I suppose the reason is I am slow of apprehending the female character, and also considerably selfish and leathern about the heart ; but to have lost the capacity of really losing one's heart to another is a very miserable loss. Shall I become sentimental, as the next best thing, or shall I continue to comfort myself with those incomparable male friends of mine ?   I have a friend as lenient and, if not as true, more penetrating than John Gibb ; and I think that a good man, a man, is perhaps, as you seem to be willing to admit, the better creature of the two ; only I don't believe this, nor desire to believe it, and certainly for general purposes women are as good.

Thursday.—Yesterday I wrote all day, and went to Dr. Duncan's in the evening. The Rabbi nailed me most of the night, and translated Bohemian to me and gave me a photograph of Ian Hus, who was ' *epalen* ' or burnt for the word of God. There has been truth in the world.

T—— is to go into an office for a while, then to learn farming, and finally (so *l'homme propose*) to be set up by his uncle in a farm. How easy life comes to some people, but how it must limit their souls and minds to be chucked into a rut at the beginning and run on in the same to the end. This is what comforts me about you, when I have not the higher faith, that you are worth while developing even by severe measures, and that you are a grander person than you would otherwise have been ; also your influence is a rare one and ought not to be nailed down to one spot. Only this, as you will see, is superficial philosophy.

I have this day finished my ' Coats of Skins,' and hope people may find gospel in it. Really I don't know what they want, unless that I should say at the end of each paragraph, ' Now this is gospel.' Also I have seen Miss Johnson, and your worship of Rainy is a trifle to hers. What a pity you were not rheumatic and old, and then you might have had him once a fortnight all to yourself—think of it! She was very affectionate, I suppose as I was both Innes' and Rainy's successor. She has all the photographs of Dr. Cunningham (wears one in a locket) and of Rainy that have been published.

Now I must put on the hash for the prayer-meeting, so good-bye.

To the Same

11 CASTLE STREET,
MONDAY [*March* 1863].

You seem to be quite unaware of the amount of suffering you have inflicted upon me. At 3 o'clock on Saturday I was hurrying home an hour sooner than usual, expecting what no other person in the city could expect, and it struck me as I was coming along Princes Street how horrible it would be if I had not a Saturday letter, and how odd even if it failed me once. Alas! I was to experience the oddness; no ring set my heart in a thrill; I waited till 3.45, and then asked Mrs. A. if the postman had not been here. No, he had not. I received my Saturday guests with a blanker expression than usual. We had cracks, but they were dullish, and when they went away I waited till eight, but still no letter. Then I thought you must have been took, and I went to Queen Street glum, and of course they would think it was because the High Church people had called Dykes and not M. D., which it wasn't.

Anne is mostly in bed just now, and of course can't write to you, but we are always talking about you. I go along often for my walk to see her; indeed it is the only place I have to go to. I can't understand how I know so few people. When Simeon goes, I'll have nobody to walk with by day. Stewart is only visible at night, of course; he generally comes up on Sunday evening, and is nice, very—very—very.

To the Same

11 CASTLE STREET,
EDINBURGH, *2nd April* [1863].

I did not write sooner, because I had nothing to say, neither to you nor anybody else. I am not yet out of the mud, but am better, and have some disposition to work. How thankful you should be that a piece of unfeeling and unthinking mechanism called a clock orders you to your work without appeal, and saves you from your own reasons for delay and indolence. I could tell you a number of things you should be thankful for, but take for granted you know them better yourself. For your letters I am thankul, and hope to have a revival of my sense of gratitude on Saturday ; mind your Saturday letter is the thing in my week I count upon. This present week has nothing particular to separate it from its neighbours.

The weather here has been magnificent for some days, and the town has been half daft with Palmerston. I did not see him.

There is a select preacher wanted in Madras : should I go ? There 's an editor wanted for *The B. & F. Evangelical Review* : should I apply ? You know I 'll be *twenty-nine* in a week. Our family will soon be away and the young Gibsons playing their parts, and then it will be their turn—if the world lasts as long.

To the Same

11 CASTLE STREET,
MONDAY [*6th April* 1863].

Many thanks for your Saturday letter, which, however, was too historical. Your best letters are your growlers, I suppose because there is most of yourself in them. This is only to answer your query about the Preacher ;

S

of course I sympathise deeply with the class, and gladly do what I can to further your benevolence towards any member of it. I would say give him Baxter's *Saint's Rest*, for that has been meat drink and tobacco, reading writing and arithmetic, wife and family, and a great deal more and also a great deal less, I am happy to say, to me ever since you gave it me. It 's the book that is never done, and has something to say to you in all moods and on every page, only I know it is disagreeable to give the same book twice—almost (might not I say ?) as disagreeable as to receive the same book twice—so I don't recommend Baxter at all. Of the three you speak of, there is a danger about two of them—a lot of preachers have Bacon's *Thoughts*, and some preachers' sisters have *The Book of Praise* (but of course *all* preachers are not lucky enough to have sisters). Tauler again is, I believe, very dear. I don't, of course, know how much you would be inclined to give to the Preacher. Judging from myself, I might venture to suggest cheaper books which would suit his taste. Thackeray's *Four Georges*, Goulburn's *Personal Religion*, etc., etc. There is a book advertised by Wertheim, Mackintosh and Hunt, *Illustrative Gatherings for Preachers and Teachers*, but it will likely be rubbish. But your Preacher will be very well off if he gets what your judgment approves. For myself, my own birthday is this week, and I also am of very decided literary tastes, and as my birthday falls on Saturday, I expect a letter from you with at least a page for every year of my life, so see and don't disappoint me. (If your heart is set upon Bacon, you know it is a dirty old scuffy thing I have, and has not a quarter in it, I suppose, which the new one has.)

To the Same

11 CASTLE STREET,
EDINBURGH, *9th April* 1863.

I was thinking I would be twenty-nine quite soon enough, but a parcel from Maclaren came in this morning, and greets me as if I had already reached that point. I was wondering how I could possibly thank you rightly for your last letter, and now I am altogether gravelled, and must just ask you to use the same charity in supposing me grateful, as you have already displayed in giving me cause for gratitude. But are both the books for me ? If so, I am very much a deceiver, for Goulburn is, I find, almost as much as Tauler would have been. Tauler was published for 16s., but now sells for 6s. 6d., which I did not know when I wrote to you, but I think Goulburn will be quite as useful, though not so handsome, and Thackeray is a book to read always. I never weary of his *Humorists*, and I am fond of history. I suppose your presents will be the only ones I shall get, but they are enough to make this 29th a memorable birthday. I am getting old.

I am not a great deal better in body, and none in spirit. I feel as if that book of Goulburn's were my last chance, but where Baxter fails I don't know who may succeed. I am utterly wretched at the prayer-meetings, or rather not so much wretched as dead—just beef. I think it is partly, perhaps mainly, the want of you—only I was not so bad at Newcastle—but then the Murrays were friendly and came in to prayers, and Peter was there to chide me and make me do my best.

I never feel dismal now as I used, which is either better or worse, and I am getting a little work done, but not much in the way of sermon-writing.

To the Same

11 CASTLE STREET,
TUESDAY [14*th April* 1863].

It is worth while having a birthday, after all : yon is
the jolliest letter yet, I think. Many, many thanks.
Nothing else came to me, except two pots of jam and
three stalks of rhubarb from Anne. I preferred your
letter, but did not object to the rhubarb. I suppose
the jam will go back to Torphichen St. in instalments,
i.e. in little stomachs, two or three of which come to
me to tea on Saturday evenings always. Simeon generally comes to meet them, and is much a favourite.

Rainy's great mental excellence, I think, is the scientific
cast of him. Everything takes shape before him, and
arranges itself ; he sees not only the thing he looks at,
but its connection with all other things, and especially
with its principles.

I'm glad you like Mr. Gibb.[1] Simeon tells me he
built a third of the New College, so it's no wonder he
should wish to trace some good to it. I never spoke to
him except from the pulpit.

I have read all the *Georges*, and about 200 pages of
Goulburn. It is very English, not what I had heard it
was, but useful, perspicuous and practical, warm but not
extravagant. I am always reading Macaulay ; he is all
excellence, the best historian.

I have a new friend, a man Whyte, who is always at
me to marry and establish a barracks for students. He,
poor chap, is supremely miserable in lodgings alone, and
maintains that he is going to the dogs—a locality which
certainly has a bye way from solitary apartments of
single gents. I have not just taken a house, neither a

---

[1] Father of the writer's friend, Professor John Gibb.

wife, but if you hear of anything of the sort, you 'll know the author of it.

Simeon has just come in and made me a gift of Tauler, so all things are well ordered.

Tuesday afternoon.—I have been all day expecting one of the most disagreeable duties, and lo! it has become almost a pleasure. I am, you know, seeing young communicants just now, and yesterday Mrs. —— called to say that her daughter was coming to-day, so I have been waiting for a stiff, coquettish, vain miss, and have been agreeably disappointed by rather an interesting conversation with a girl, young to be sure, and good-looking and swellish, but still not very affected, and I think really in earnest. She has her difficulties, and told them more plainly than I expected, certainly. I must be old-looking to be treated in so fatherly a manner, but it 's a horribly difficult and dangerous business, this ; one may be deceived by a word.

To the Same

11 CASTLE STREET,
16th April 1863.

I am much in your debt for your words of good counsel, though if I were captiously inclined, I might say that it is quite as difficult to say ' If Thou wilt, Thou canst make me clean,' as it is to make oneself clean, or just about it. Especially if, as people say, when you say ' If Thou wilt, Thou canst,' you are firmly to believe that it is intended you shall be made clean.

This (Thursday) morning I am quite well, partly, I think, owing to Simeon taking me for a farewell pull on the Canal. We went sixteen miles—to Ratho and back, and enjoyed it much. The banks were all budding and warm and bright, and to be right into the country does

one an amazing deal of good, if the wind is west and the
sun out.   I then went and dined with Simeon, so it was
quite a holiday.

I am intending to buy a great lot of dear books :—

Stier's *Words of Christ* .	.	.	£3 0 0
Smith's Dictionary	.	.	5 0 0
Pressensé's *Histoire*	.	.	1 4 0
Bruder's Concordance .	.	.	1 10 0
Origen's Works .	.	.	3 10 0
Bingham's *Antiquities* .	.	.	2 0 0

£16 4 0

and a great many more ; only, as I have at present no
money and no habitation, I am going to wait a little.

Now I have nothing more to say.   It is about nine
months since I was visited by an idea of any kind, and
if you can believe it, I am no more stupid in my letters
than in my sermons—only I have sense enough remaining
not to preach them.   But it's all your fault going and
leaving a fellow to his own resources.

Stewart has taken to golfing lately.   It supplies him
with endless jokes at his own expense, and with some
blisters.

I find a strong tendency to begin all my letters to you
with thanks, and to end them with apology, but this
must be mere habit, and it's stupid to fall into a form,
so I will end with a command instead (which is quite
new)—write often and long, historically if you like,
to . . .

To the Same

11 CASTLE STREET,
22nd April 1863.

It was very kind of you to write so soon again, and
such a jolly little epistle.   I was in great need of it when

it came in.   Yet I have got a great deal of work done
these three days—not so much as Sir J. Stephen used
to do any morning before breakfast, but then he was a
genius, or at least was talented ;   item, he must have
got up very early.   I have written what is to be represented by seven or eight pages of *The B. and F. Review*,
and I hope to finish the article soon.   It is on Clement,
my old friend.   I will be sorry when there is no plausible
excuse for handling him ; but, by the bye, you have
never seen him.   I got him at Liverpool, and he is my
handsomest book.   What a lot of stuff I might have laid
up these five years had I known what to work at ; but
I am no further on yet, and have just as much idea as
the Queen has of what I should choose as my department.

Speaking of Rainy, Mr. Martin said a good thing about
him—that he laid himself alongside of you.   (*N.B.*—
Mr. Martin henceforth is a nice man.)

Tell Mrs. Urquhart that her book-mark, which perhaps
she has forgotten all about, ' Der zufriedene ist nie arm,'
lies on the surface of my desk always, and does me good
sometimes.

I send you a note of the Dr.'s ; if his lectures are
written like that, I trust he won't make me his literary
executor.   There is nothing in the note, but I thought
you might like to touch what he had touched, and to
think the things that had passed through his mind.   Is
not it considerate of me ?

How hard it is to believe we have an eternity in front,
yet we are in but ' a day ' for many things, and while
repose and dignified calm are good, hurry and diligence
are also necessary.   What I wanted to know, and what
you don't answer, is—Must a man when he prays believe
that he will certainly get what he asks for ?   Some
verses of the Bible seem to say so, but where (then)
' shall He find faith on the earth ' ?

To the Same

[11 CASTLE STREET,
EDINBURGH, 26*th April* 1863.]

This is Sunday evening at 8.30—just home from the
evening service, trembling with tiredness, and if I don't
write to you I 'll do horrible thoughts. You don't know
what or how many a devil lodges within this person that
goes by the title of the Revd. This has not been a
pleasant day to me—the first thing I had to do before
breakfast was to go and find supply for to-night, which
I had no sooner succeeded in doing (after spending
Saturday almost wholly in the same occupation), than
the beadle came and sent me off to find supply for to-
morrow, which I only succeeded in doing at 6.15 this
evening.

Rainy was in one of his finest moods to-day, and I was
wishing that you had been taking notes. At the table
service he broke down. I don't know whether he intended to stop when he did, but at ' poor lost sinners '
his voice wavered, and he had just enough left to go
through the forms. After the first table I went and lay
at the foot of Anne's bed (a favourite place of mine now),
and read her your yesterday's letter—it 's the first I have
read to anybody, but as it was purely historical and *so*
nice, I thought I might give her the benefit of it. She
is better a little to-day. Charles gave her on Friday,
for a birthday present, *Counsels of an Invalid*, by George
Wilson. Anne *has* a very fine face.

What a marvellous power of expression Rainy has !
It must be nice to have a mind like his.

I could not help thinking, this evening at Church, of
the old times when we used to go, a seatful of us, with
Mamma, on the *Sacrament Sunday* nights—how very kind
she was to us, and with all her cares and difficulties how

well she managed ; and yet all that might be so pleasant
in my reminiscences of her is remorseful—is all material
for remorse.   I almost wish she had heard me preaching
regularly in the High.   It would have pleased her greatly,
I believe.   I suppose I may say to you that when I stand
by her grave (which I almost never do), I have a feeling
of home that I have nowhere else in the world.   I never
knew what a mother was till I had not one, and I have
known it more since you went away—to have one that
will be happier than yourself at all your success, and
more cast down than yourself at all failure, and yet help
you through it ; this is what very much makes life worth
living.   I know that a *man* has no right to feel lonely, even
though it be ' *Athanasius contra orbem*,' but a man does
—does a woman, one woman in particular ?   Isn't it so
hard to believe that this world is not far more worth
than Eternity ?   So hard to wish to get through these few
years *to* that life where God shall give us the desires of
our hearts ?   I am sometimes afraid to think of what
must be done yet in me if I am ever to be right.   O
Marsh, you 've no conception what I am, what a deal of
tanning I must come through if I am ever to be leather
at all.   Everything turns to abomination in me, things
that ought to set me right put me all wrong, and as I told
you before, it 's the longer the worse.

Tuesday morning, and not much time to write.   Yesterday I rose early and sewed my brace for half an hour
(Mary coming in to do out the room while I was so occupied was taken, and was carried out in fits.   She still asks
for you periodically), then had a capital read at Clement
till Church—heard a nice, peculiar, Episcopalian kind of
man, came home and went into Clement again, and did
as much as I sometimes do in a week ; then after dinner
Whyte came and then Charles, and we talked till eleven.
We *discussed* a good deal, and profitably.   Before

Charles came, Whyte told me something about my preaching that makes me fear more than ever I did that I shall never get a call. Do you not think it would be more prudent at once to commit myself to something else—Whyte's 'barracks for students,' or a boys' school —Wanted a few nice youths from 16 to 22, no vicious or disagreeable need apply ? I have long known that I am past going to vacancies : if I do get anything it will be accidental. It is mainly pride, and a good deal of vanity, that has spoilt me. I did not set myself at first to the task of learning to preach, and now I can't humble myself so far as to begin at the beginning again, even though I know I am at the beginning yet. It is easy to say, Do your work for to-day, and let to-morrow's evil be accounted for by to-morrow ; but have I got my right work for to-day ? I have, I think, lived too much (at least sometimes I think so) on the Providence principle —merely escaping the trouble of deciding for myself, and leading a lazy, good-for-nothing life. Now this is all your fault, so write immediately to ask pardon.

To the Same

11 Castle Street,
Edinburgh, Tuesday [*April* 1863].

I am not intending to write you a letter, but it would be impossible to go on with my work without saying 'Thank you' for your jolly epistle. I was scarcely expecting it either, for though I am always hoping to get something from you, I generally prepare myself for disappointment. When Mary told me, however, there was 2d. to pay, I hesitated a good deal about taking it in, but being ashamed to appear stingy before her, I surrendered the amount. I wish cordials of the kind could be had for twopences any day ; what mints I

would spend. All its news is delicious. Mind, I like
your histories when they are about yourself ; it 's only
when they are about people who were great-great-grand-
uncles of the Conqueror's, or something of that kind,
that I feel just the slightest shade of insipidity in the
detail. When you are yourself the author, too, it is
more palatable than when you give a digest (though
surely it was generally an expansion you used to give)
of something you have read.

But all this is introductory to H——. You will
know far, far better than I what to say, both because
you know the girl, know the church, and have more
wisdom and truth to guide you. But if she had asked
me, and you were not by to refer her to, I might say
firstly, and in the first place, that it is no proof at all
that a thing is right and proper that it is adapted to
some dispositions, and that though 400 men and boys
came daily and behaved devoutly, that is no proof, for
anything like a proof, that the service does them good.
It proves only that it is attractive and impressive. If
this did not convince her, as most likely it would not,
then I would ask her to apply her proof impartially,
and she would find that services the very opposite of
All Saints' were equally evinced to be ' very true and
very commendatory,' *e.g.* the New York prayer-meetings,
where cabmen and coalheavers, clerks and littérateurs,
pour out their souls before God. But you see the difficulty
with her will be that decorous solemnity is the test of
sincerity in worship, which it is not ; a thousand things
besides true religious feeling make men decorous and
solemn. Granting, as I hope is the case, that her 200
are true worshippers, the question still remains, would
they not be wiser worshippers to worship without all
that ceremonial ? Surely she would not say that it is
the ceremonial which is the real source and spring of

worship ; and if only an aid, then it may be questioned whether there may not be a better, whether if these worshippers (who have the real spirit of worship) were transferred to another church of less august ceremonial, they would not worship better.

Another thing, which I would not, however, say to her, but which is certainly true—people will do a great deal more for the sake of proving some dear opinion than for God's sake, and many of these persons who seem devout because they are truly worshipping, are probably only apparently and decorously devout because they have pledged themselves to the opinion that a High Church Ceremonial is the fittest worship, and mean to show by their demeanour that it is so. Rather I would grant to her that in the Puseyite Church much is to be commended, such as opening daily, but that in every Church there is something commendable, and that each practice and each doctrine must be judged by itself, and not adopted because it is contiguous to something good, or rejected because it is bound up with something bad.

Is —— —— as High Church as she used to be ? I fancy not, for I think she is a girl whose romance and latitudinarianism (what a long word to use about a girl !) were *real* and not affected, and will therefore develop to womanly sense.

To the Same

11 CASTLE STREET,
30th April 1863.

Always write nonsense if that was a fair description of your last. I was scarcely expecting so long and delicious an epistle yesterday, and don't know how to give you an idea of how much I enjoyed it. I quoted it largely to Stewart, with whom I had a walk in the

evening, and put the happy woman question to him.   Do
you think men are happier ?   I am writing this week
(having finished Clement) on the woman that had the
issue of blood—a remarkably fine subject, but I can't
preach, and people are telling me so more freely.   What
a horrible twelve years those must have been to the poor
creature.   I hope it may do me some good writing about
her.

Friday, 1.15.—I have been writing lecture for four
hours and have, I need scarcely tell you, written four
pages, *i.e.* half my matter.   It is not perfect (need I add ?),
but it is just what I suppose I must make up my mind
to as my ordinary performance.   I find the narrative
full of instruction, and full of harmony, one bit with the
other—two features which always do appear in the Bible
when you look a little closely.   I wish I had John Gibb's
exegetical knowledge.   I am sorry to hear every one
who knows him speaking so despondingly of his health.
Malta may be the place for him.   Dick Stothert's first
charge was soldiers in Barbados, do you mind ?   No,
it was Bermuda.

What I feel about women more than their unhappiness
—though after all I dare say it is the same—they have
no suggestion in them.   You always set me a-thinking
and make my work come kind of natural, but I don't
find any other do so—but then I know almost none.
I dare say —— thinks and sets others thinking, but
don't know her sufficiently.   Some people have a few
favourite thoughts which they suggest to all comers,
but what I like in woman, or man, is a continuous thinking
which hits on new things, and lives always in a stream
by your side.

End of Disquisition of Suggestiveness.

I have no gossip.   I have been just where I am, *i.e.*
at my desk almost all week, and save the interruption

of a beadle and the other things I 've told you, nothing has passed over my consciousness.

To his sister Andrea

[11 Castle Street,
Edinburgh,] 6th May [1863].

You ask me what I am doing.   What else do you suppose than writing sermons ?   I have got one a week done for the last week or two, and am adopting a much lighter style, against which my soul revolts.   So instead of writing one page a day as of old, I now write six, that is, almost a whole sermon.   I need not characterise the quality ; but the people like them, the noodles.

To his sister Marcia

11 Castle Street,
Tuesday [May 1863].

Is John Gibb to be here any time, or is he just going through ?   I fraternise considerably with his friend Whyte, a fine, honest, doctrinal, outspoken, hearty fellow, that knows what he is himself, and does not require others to be much better, though he thinks they are.

I am thinking of doing the Syrophenician woman this week, if I can.   I liked the other woman vastly.

To S. R. Macphail

11 Castle Street,
Edinburgh, 12th May [1863].

As your first letter ended with a promise of a very speedy successor, I did not expect that successor to be so long in coming, nor did I expect it to begin with reproaches for my silence—a silence, of course, wholly due to regard for your feelings, and a not unaccountable desire to let you perform what you had promised. But no doubt man's (and especially my) most considerate actions will continue to be misunderstood—at least, so long as there are people like you in the world, and so long as people think evil themselves they will ascribe evil to others. Many thanks for your letter, however, with all its calumnious prefaces.

I have such lots to say to you, I don't know what to deliver first ; my utterance is like the exit of a crowded theatre, where every one is pressing to the street and where there is a general jam and block up.

To begin with what is nearest and freshest, I am just restored by a sleep from the effect of Whyte's talk last evening. My brother-in-law and he are mutually friendly, and so I had them up last night. Mr. Gibson left at 10, but Whyte stayed till past the witching hour. You know what kind of talk it would be—your name emerging sometimes—Aberdeen stories—moans about the inner man—dubious prospects—comments on preaching and uncharitable speeches about preachers ; more gaiety than happiness and more amusement than profit perhaps, but yet such an evening as one likes to spend and as is remembered. You are certainly complimentary in saying that a good book is as good company as a good friend. I am not brought to that depth of depravity yet ; perhaps when I am I may cease to consume my own smoke. I don't suppose you have anything worse inside than your neighbours. No doubt, one is tempted to overflow to a receptive person, and it does relieve one ; but is not the stronger nature made by bearing our own burdens, and like Prometheus, speaking comfort to the Daughters of Ocean while our own heart is being gnawed away ? The things one is tempted to communicate are generally

those which it is better to keep to oneself, but so long
as one sticks to an indefinite moan or growl it does no
harm either to growler or listener. I have an uncon-
querable aversion, however, to be either party at a
confession. If it goes deep into our real condition it
leaves one too much at the mercy of the party confessed
to.

Do you understand me now ?   If I see a man miserable
I am ready to do all I can to cheer him, without asking
him what particular sin he is reaping the wages of.   This
may expand into a philosophy.

There have been no rows since you left.   The week
the weather was so fine I had scarcely time to eat, and I
have still lots to do, and I miss you coming in to make
a fellow somewhat more lively.   But many thanks for
Whyte. I think we 'll get on well. I like him for his
honesty, his intelligence, his goodness, and his real
happiness of spirit.   He has sorrows, but they don't cut
very deep, as how could they in a fair-haired Scandinavian
like him ?

John Gibb you have little chance of seeing now, unless
you go to Malta.   He left last Friday, and did not pause
here, whereat I was some disappointed. I hope Malta
may set him up, and that permanently, though he strikes
me as being too good for earth and too well-prepared for
Heaven to have much more to do here.

To his sister Marcia

11 Castle Street,
14th May 1863.

Beenie is presenting a very superb illuminated Psalter
to Prof. Miller for all he has done for her. It cost origin-
ally £16, but is now £4, 4s., and is magnificently executed
—a folio it is. I told her I thought it was too good to

give him, and that she should make him understand it
was for future as well as past services, and that when
any of the family had him they should say ' See Psalm
xvii,' or ' That is page 26 '; but she thinks it is little
enough for all the pain he has given her.

I am writing this week on the lunatic boy (after the
transfiguration), but fear to come to ' All things are
possible to him that believeth.'   It is really a difficulty.

In looking back on your life, one feature of it is
evident—that the things you have had to do have been
difficult things, such as not every one was fit for ; and
that does make up, in some measure, for being cut out
of a good many things you would like to have had.   And
I believe that to your own mind it will altogether make
up.   What the use of me is I don't know.   I seem to
exist wholly for myself, and not even for myself, for I
am not becoming anything.   But sometimes Joel ii. 25 [1]
is good and credible.

Now the more I write the duller I 'll make you, so I
must stop.   I am reading Boswell still, and delight in it
much.   Sam. was a very huge man and a true, reminding
me often of Dr. Chalmers.   He had the same big, abstract
way of thinking and speaking.   I am also doing duty
on Buchanan's *Ten Years' Conflict*, which is for me very
hard work, but enlightening on some points, though
I know that had I been brought up an Erastian, an
Erastian I would have remained.

I wish you were here to talk to.   Whyte moans so
about his loneliness that he makes me think more of
mine ; and it 's only by not thinking I can get on nowadays, by a blind rather than a faithful taking the day as
it is, and having no to-morrow.   Whyte is a very high
Calvinist, and a lover of the Puritans, and would talk
doctrine for a year on end.

---

[1] ' And I will restore to you the years that the locust hath eaten,' etc.

T

To the Same

[11 CASTLE STREET,
EDINBURGH, ? *May* 1863.]

Have only time to say Look here, Peter, the identical, flesh and blood, unchangeable, sometimes felt too nice and elevating and sustaining to be the friend of a mortal, for to know him and be with him is to be above the sad and level vale of mortality, the ready, keen, generous, true Peter HAS *been* here ; I saw him but as you see a fish flash past in a stream, one crack, one rove on the streets, he smoking and shivering, and it is over. However, I feel set up.

To the Same

11 CASTLE STREET,
19*th May* [1863].

I would not write you to-night, only I think you may be expecting to hear about us all. Your letter [1] was the most moving thing I have read for long. I don't know how I shall ever meet the youths. I do feel for them, and doubly since hearing from you. I trust that by this time the sharpness at least of the pain is past, though it will seem a strangely different world to them all for a time. I hope you are none the worse of the past week. It will do you no harm in the end, all this. So Solomon said, and so I have seen in you in past times.

Do you mind in *The Christian Year* the hymn beginning ' When brothers part for manhood's race ' ?

> ' Even round the deathbed of the good
>   Such dear remembrances will hover,
> And haunt us with no vexing mood
>   When all the cares of earth are over.'

[1] Announcing the death of Mrs. Fordyce.

I was reading in one of the Puritans (you mind Goodwin) on Sunday, and came upon this : ' Death parts two old friends (body and soul), but it joins two better friends, the Soul and Christ.'

Now don't think me horrid for not sending you nicer letters. I can do nothing that requires feeling nowadays, and am almost afraid to write to you lest I communicate to you any part of myself. I sometimes think I would almost go through all that you have gone through if the end were that I should be like you. Excuse me saying this kind of thing, for I dare not say it to your face, and I cannot say it to anybody but yourself ; for what would make others envious of you and despisers of me as an extravagant and wild lover will not, I believe, either make you worse or make you think worse of . . .

To the Same

11 CASTLE STREET,
21*st May* 1863.

To-day has been the opening of the Assemblies. I went with Charles, Markie, Annie and Charlie, to see the Commissioner : item, I saw a lovely girl in the crowd, and have been dull ever since. Before eleven (when they came), I had read and written a review of a pious little weak book ; after coming home I began a big, stupid one by ——, and to-morrow hope to begin a great production of Cunningham's just published. This is all along of Guthrie of *The Daily Review*, who sent me the three. You may suppose I am not sorry to have something to keep me from the Assembly, but I am a Free (if any) Churchman now, and may perhaps develope into a zealous Ecclesiastic, though I think some other developments are more likely.

I am living more alone than ever I did in my life, and expect to find myself growing a shell some morning. I

wish I could fall in love or get a frightful deal to do.   It
is not easy to live without an object, but I suppose there
is a path of good works from every point where one finds
himself.   I think I might get on if some one would give
me reality in exchange for selfishness.   I could make up
any amount of the latter article of any quality fit for
ordinary use and below anything refined.

But again I must remind you that this which I show
to you is not me as I appear to the little world that sees
me here.   You are my only smoke consumer.

I spent three hours at the Assembly seeking for a man
to preach for me, and could not get one.   I offered to
go to the country for anybody, but nobody would, so I 'm
sold.   However, I saw John Macphail, who looks well,
but is very far from it, being, he says, forbidden to preach.
I expect he will come up.   I like him much ; there is
something singular about him, different from any other
man I ever met.

Whyte thinks I would have little chance of getting
the East Church, but he thinks I have very little chance
of anything, unless I study for ten years and go in for
some chair.

To S. R. Macphail

11 CASTLE STREET,
29th May 1863.

This here city is an ecclesiastical Vanity Fair just now ;
the world comes out strong in the Church this week ;
applause, dinners, humbug, and religious flirtations are
rife.   I have been in the thick of it, and have missed
you in the corridor and students' gallery.   —— has been
to be found in the last-mentioned locality any time from
11 A.M. to 11.30 P.M. this last ten days ; he must be filled
with *popularis aura* to a prodigious extent by this
time.   I hope he'll go to the country, or explode,

before he comes within my range.   I have had much pleasant meeting with old friends, among whom not least your brother John.   I have been unwontedly busy this week ; 3 vols. (one of them Cunningham's Discussions) came from *The Daily Review* to me, and they have occupied me, and I have asked about a hundred men to preach.   When are you going to Aberdeen, or are you there ?   And where are your wits ?   Are they sojourning in the clouds trying to find an inspiration theory, or groping among the monks of the Middle Ages ?   Expound yourself to me, when you write.

Davidson is looking very fresh after his appointment, and a union with the U.P.'s is inevitable ; so you and I and John Gibb will go to Kamtchatka, or the moon, or somewhere, and teach the people the gospel, Greek, and the arts, and make for ourselves good degrees. There is no chance henceforth for the like of me, you know, and what I say to myself I say also to you : If you want a church, begin and read aloud, and practise speaking at every opportunity, and cultivate your popular gifts if you have any, and if you have not, create, buy, or steal them ; above all, have your heart a movable and feeling heart, and neither stone nor leather as some people's I could name are.

To A. Taylor Innes

11 Castle Street,
Edinburgh [*May* 1863].

The Assembly being now gone with its wind, we here are like a pinched india-rubber ball.   I have not time to enter on a discussion of all its follies, but your visit remains as the salt of it, and I could stand a monthly Assembly, much as I detest the genus, if you were a member.   Everybody has gone to his own place, and said places I do not envy this coming Sunday. Think of the odd performances that will be gone through in the pulpits of the land after this dissipation. I am writing a sermon myself, but feel a kind of surprise as I see line after line growing under my pen, being conscious of no preceding thought. It 's wonderful how mere dead flesh can sermonize.

To his Sister Marcia

11 CASTLE STREET,
2nd June 1863.

My Assembly mood came to a climax on Tuesday and Wednesday, and I really could not write to you. I knew that if I did write I should only vex you, and you have plenty burdens of your own to bear. So excuse me, and think that the omission of my letter is greater kindness than the writing of it would have been. I feel wicked for having been too wicked to write, but not wicked in not writing. I have great capacity of being miserable, and have not been so fully aware of this for some time. People in the general must surely do a tremendous amount of blasphemy, don't you think ? I would often like to go about cursing, and then get somebody to tear in pieces ; but I am a little better than I once was in this latter particular. I am not so envious, I think, as you have known me ; it comes back upon me, but rather as an old memory than as a present habit ; but I am worse in the matter of murmuring, my circumstances are more between God and myself than they used to be, and it is sometimes more than I can do to accept what is allotted me, though it is very much better than my desert— but it is easier for a person to endure what is not his desert than what is, of course. The example of a young Swiss pastor, who was just going to be married, and was caught by the authorities and sent for six years to the galleys, has been useful to me, and may be so, I think, to others.

Anne is very much better, and I go along *fréquemment* and give her an airing. It is very nice, only it is quite different from half an hour with you. We would need to be melted down and soldered together in some common trouble before we would be intimate. I could step into Anne's heart and confide to her; but you know, or perhaps you don't, that one is not tempted to do this with many people, or perhaps it is that I, having you, am not prone to make other confidants. Then you are more suggestive and life-giving than Anne. If ever I marry, it is 'wanted a suggestive woman' that shall be my advertisement. Did you ever know a girl like yourself at all? a moody creature that sat with her elbows on her knees at night, *combing* her hair, or would read a book all evening and not speak to you, or would thump you till blue, or play herself out at the piano, or cut off her right hand if she could thereby help you, or do any of those disagreeable things that women do? If you know of any such tell me of her. What a range of women there is—from the narrow, housekeeping, strongly-prejudiced, routine, bitter, peevish, sharp, weak woman to *the* woman, unselfish, warm, liberal, happy, patient, intelligent, wise.

'What life is to come to' with you I know, that is, I know good will be the end of it; what it is to come to with me, I don't know. If I am allowed much longer to be my own employer, and to find I am of no use on earth, etc., etc., I shall break up and disperse to some unknown regions. To be destined to receive daily the compassion and condolence of those who think I have mistaken my road and have need to retrace the steps I have been making for the best years of my life, tends to make me bitter and savage. In your life I see what

I would call misfortune, and what I would have altered, but a better spent life I do not know ; and I can believe in the case of another that things which do appear are not exact representations of the things which are not seen. In your answer pray do not say anything about me ; it's a subject I am sick of at present, but I will tell you when to recur to it.

Week after week I have forgotten to tell you that —— and —— have agreed to accept in company the fortune of this life, and one more is added to my list of instances which prompt the induction that a man may have any woman he wants : there are exceptions, but this is the rule. I had thought her a girl who would get somebody a good deal more *compos mentis* than —— ; but I don't know women.

Now I must stop. Pray excuse this doleful epistle. I have not time to rewrite it, so you must take it as it is.

To A. Taylor Innes

11 CASTLE STREET,
TUESDAY [*June* 1863].

Excuse me bothering you about a matter of mine, but you know I have no one here to advise, or at least no one whose advice I have counted worth seeking. The matter is Carlile's congregation at Bombay. I have reason to believe that when the Commission is sent empowering a party here to engage a pastor, I will have the offer ; at least, this is so likely that it is expedient for me to make up my mind whether I would go or not. I do not know any more about the congregation than that there are some good and some wealthy people. But what would you advise ? If I spoke my mind, I would say I was unutterably weary of the kind of life I have been leading for five years, and there is little prospect

For your invitation I am also much obliged, and shall probably avail myself of it sometime.

I think you need not trouble yourself asking Stevenson or G. Carlile, as I have, or shall have, access to Dr. M. Mitchell and Carlile, whose accounts I fancy will be trustworthy. I do not like to apply to them just yet, as the matter is still unofficial, and it is disagreeable to be talked about ; also you remember one of the wisest sayings of Tacitus, ' *Haud semper errat fama, aliquando et eligit*,' and I do not wish that the Committee be influenced by popular talk, still less that I myself be influenced by it. The party commissioned consists of Charles Brown, Carlile, Hanna, Dr. Candlish and, I think, Dr. M. Mitchell. It was Brown who told me, but merely as a friend, that he thought it likely that when the Commission is sent from Bombay (it is not expected till the end of July), I shall be at once offered it. He had Dr. Candlish's opinion before he did this ; at the same time he said it was by no means a pledge (Dr. John Bonar, too, is one of the Commission), and of course things may happen to alter their plans.

Brown told me so much about the congregation as made me clear on this at least, that if it were at home and offered to me, I should at once accept. It is not numerous, but I don't like numbers. It is intelligent, wealthy enough to make its minister comfortable, and the city is likely to increase even more than it has been doing within the last few years ; indeed, considering its position, is it altogether unlikely that the government should be transferred to it ? Departments of the government (postal, *e.g.*) must be carried on there.

On the other hand, I might, by hanging on here, get something (but I might not) in my profession. I could always get work as a probationer, but that is demoralising. I can scarcely write for the High Church just now, so how could I have spirit to write for any other place a year or two or three or more hence ? So that I should be necessitated to seek other work : that other work I have only the vaguest idea of. I might set up a coaching establishment—I don't mean in the manner of Isaac Scott or Croall, but to guide youths. My father had to do that all his life, and I like the work, or don't dislike it. I never trusted to literature as a means of livelihood, though something suitable *might* turn up, but this is so improbable that it would be folly to count upon it.

These are my prospects so far as I have any, and as you see, they are vague, and in so far as not vague are poor. Yet what inclines me to stick to the uncertainties and difficulties at home rather than take this good certainty abroad is very deeply rooted in my nature, though it has never grown into any definite plan (which I am ashamed of, so much so, that had I not written to you about Bombay, I would have written asking you to talk over this with me, for you always ask me what I am doing and intending, and I have never anything to answer to either). I always feel, rightly or wrongly, that I could be and do more at home than abroad. I have some faculty of studying, and no other faculty I know of. What use this might be to me abroad is problematical ; indeed, I think that this one faculty would be sweated out of me, and I would become a wet glove ; yet study at home is an uncertain thing too—one may study all one's days and never get opportunity of using what one has acquired. Moreover, I do not know how far it is justifiable to refuse present work in the *hope* of getting something more congenial (I cannot say the *expectation* of getting something), nor can I calculate on finding employment at home which would afford me time for study. *If* I had a country place I *might* do something in this way, but then I might never get such a place ;

and if I did I might just as likely fritter away my time.

So you see it is more an unjustifiable feeling than anything else that keeps me at home. I think I would not hesitate to refuse any offer abroad or even good things at home for the next six years, if I had a decided bias to a particular branch of theological study. I would most willingly (with occasional grumbling, of course, yet on the whole stoically or Christianly) accept hard lines for six years more if I saw a subject on which I could spend six years—but I don't. Church History, Exegesis (and almost Systematic), are equally agreeable to me, and a fellow of this kind does nothing. I think I am best suited for Exegesis, but have not done more at it than anything else. If a man were to come and say, ' There is a thing that must be investigated ; it will take ten years to do, but being done, Scripture will be better understood,' I would jump at that and give up all idea of pastoral work, if I could keep life in, and a narrow margin of comforts. But things are not done in this way in our world : the invention of one man does not apply to the plodding power of another, and so——

If you have read thus far you know as much as I do about my ideas of the future ; or at least you see that my ideas are so vague that they will not bear expression.

If you think, as I believe, that your advice now would be most serviceable, please write to . . .

To his sister Marcia

11 CASTLE STREET,
10th June 1863.

When I sit down to write to you at a promiscuous time, I feel like a person standing in a bath in doubt whether to turn on ' hot ' or ' cold,' for I can flow at either the tap of growl or gladness ; but when I sit down under the in-

302 EARLY LETTERS OF MARCUS DODS [1863

fluence of your letter, to growl seems wicked, foolish, and
specially inappropriate. There is a delight in receiving
a letter, of a different kind from, if not equal in intensity
with, meeting a person face to face and seeing him day
by day, and moreover in a letter you get the essence
of the week all bunched up. But no, that is not true,
for a person only writes as he would talk at the same
moment. You say nothing about coming here in this
letter, that is to say, you say nothing in this letter about
coming here.

I am writing this week on ' A sower went forth to sow,'
and think of making it 9 vols. folio, as I do not well see
how any smaller amount of exposition will get below the
surface, only ' *ars longa, vita brevis*.' Item, I bought a
copy of *The Rambler* yesterday—only 3s., so don't be
alarmed—and am enjoying it. Also, do you know some
verses beginning :

> ' He spake of love, such love as spirits feel
>> In worlds whose course is equable and pure,
> No fears to beat away, no strife to heal,
>> The past unsighed for and the future sure.'

It has been ringing in my head, as ' I 'd choose to be a
daisy ' used to, and won't go away, so my *dernier ressort*
is to send it to you. If you would like some more, say so.
I always feel inclined to make the last word ' pure ' ;
but ' sure ' includes ' pure,' or is a deception. What are
you reading, or do you spend all your time in writing
to me ? A much better way.

Thursday morning.—I enclose a letter of his usual
kind from Innes. It does one good to see a fellow so
interested in another's affairs. I am not asking anybody else's advice. Innes really considers and thinks
to conclusions about you, which you can scarcely
depend on others doing. Mouat would, and I hope to

see him soon, as he is expected here in two or three
weeks. I have been writing a long epistle to Innes, so
you must get less.

In Boswell (this morning in bed—I get the girl to
knock early, and read before I get up) I came to this,
which I instantly applied to hours of which you are
cognisant :

> ' I prized the hours that went by
>   Beyond all that had pleased me before,
>   But now they are gone—and I sigh,
>   And I grieve that I prized them no more.'

That is Tennyson gone back to the eighteenth century.
It is from Shenstone ; if I thought there was much as
natural in him I would read him. But I am becoming too
quotative and loquacious generally. Outside is worse
than ever to-day. I am to take the deluge to-night, as an
appropriate subject, only nobody can possibly be at the
meeting if *this* continues, but then *this* cannot possibly
continue, neither, I see, can *this*, so good-bye.

To the Same

[11 CASTLE STREET,
EDINBURGH, ? 15*th June* 1863.]

On Saturday evening I went to dinner with Mr. Aitken
(tea merchant, Lady Glenorchy's), and met Dr. John
Brown and Harvey the artist. Dr. B. very nice, full
of tenderness and good stories, very grave, however, and
his mirth does not dispel the pervading solemnity of his
look and thinking—an edifying person to know. I
would enjoy very much frequent dinners, and I do not
know that it would waste time, really ; you get so much
stimulus by meeting better men than yourself—by meeting any men you at least get away from self.

There has been strong East wind here for some days and much rain, and consequently I am all out of sorts; rheumatism in the back of my head, and my stomach sticking all about my brain; the comfort is a lot of people are much the same, so one is not noticed. I wonder what is East wind at Bombay—doubtless something. Mr. Macphail sent me a note saying that he had asked the Trinity people, Aberdeen, who want a colleague for their minister, to give me a hearing; that is the place, you know, he destined for me long ago.

To the Same

11 CASTLE STREET,
17*th June* 1863.

This is Wednesday evening, a fact of which I inform you because I know that to you, as to all women, a date which merely indicates the proportion of the month which is past, can scarcely be called a date, if a date be a thing to go upon and help one to realise the events then occurring. It may be a more effectual temporal foundation for your understanding of my state of mind if I tell you that I have just received your widely written half-sheet. I am not to be done by any such thing; you are either very ill indeed, or you are culpably lazy. I believe the former, and if I do not get a letter at once assuring me that you are better, I will send my doctor to you, and it will take all your salary to pay him. I cannot blame you for being unwell if the weather with you has been at all like what we have had—East wind and thick drizzle, occasionally diversified by torrents of rain. I am nearly at the last stage of desperation; all my little stock of expedients ' have been used and used in vain ' (that is a quotation from several sermons) (chiefly unpublished), and here I am on Wednesday evening, as I have already observed, and without so much as an introduction schemed for my sermon. Where time goes I have been as unable as most other lazy people to discover, but wherever it goes must be a very big place. I would give a very great deal to be obliged to work hard at something on which I could spend all that is in me, but I have given myself a most irregular education ; and now there are things in me which have no right to be there, and which ought not to be encouraged.

Thursday.—You must be very ill, because I dreamt about you, and with a singular exactness, because you were in that thick, cream-coloured shawl, in which I think I only once saw you, and you wanted to cut me— why, you did not explain to my satisfaction. You were looking miserable. I find Johnson has a *Rambler* on the unhappiness of women.

Friday morning.—I was miserable all yesterday, sitting here scratching a burning head to get something to make a sermon of. In the evening I had the satisfaction of seeing *one* page as the fruit of a day's labour— and this is life : then came your mocking envelope, and this morning I expect another day like yesterday. I back an East wind against all creation for making a man sick in body and soul, for bringing him to the lowest stage in existence.

What puzzles me about prayer is, it seems so much instituted for the mere purpose of trying one's faith, with no reality beneath it, for you cannot believe that your prayer *moves* God to do so and so, and then one's own experience goes for nothing here, so far as I can see. For years a man may pray for a thing earnestly, regularly, submissively, Christianly, and yet not get it ; is that man to be expected to put as much confidence in prayer at the end of the years as at first ?   But it 's all a mystery.

Whyte is away to the country. He has been very

U

nice for walks.   Now there is not a soul to walk with.

Now I must stop, for nothing but poison can come out of me to-day.   If I don't get a fizzer from you to-morrow, I 'll run away and go down somewhere.

To the Same

11 CASTLE STREET,
25th June 1863.

I am glad to hear you have a medical adviser, though I don't agree with her in believing that the world takes Gregory habitually.   If I could physic the material globe, and these filthy, bilious-looking, hot clouds, and clear the atmosphere somewhat, all of us would be better, if not well.   With me, I have spent all my vital energy during the past weeks in striving to keep alive.   I have succeeded, but that is all ; it now takes all my time to keep myself going from day to day, and soon I shall scarcely find time for that, and fall behind out of the course of things.   I am taking a number of walks with Charles, and come in utterly done and sick of all things. His spirits overwhelm me quite, and I cannot keep pace with him.

To-day I could write to you ' *de profundis* ' : about prayer and everything else I am utterly at a loss.   Of course what you say is true, but no answer at all to what I asked you ;   *a* prayer may remain unanswered, but if all prayer remains unanswered, and the man just is where he was, or lower, what is salvation ?   No one could convince me that I am not worse, morally worse, to-day than I was years ago.   I know that I am.   Of course an orthodox preacher, one of your men that say such con-soling things and seem to live with the eternal verities, would find you a solution ; but how can a man possibly

believe in salvation if he has given himself to the Saviour,
and is not one whit the better for it ?   I do things now
that I could not have done once ; and it is useless to go
on playing with words, soothing your soul with pretty
sentences, if there is no change to be made in one's soul.
Of course you will say it is my fault I am not better ;
and no doubt it is my fault, my sin ; but why did I give
myself to Another but to be saved from my sin ?   If I
could save myself, the thing were quickly accomplished.
What may one expect ?   If I am receiving all that I
have a right to expect, then salvation is something quite
different from what I have been used to hear.   If there
were nothing more to go upon than my own experience,
I would certainly do very differently from what I am
now doing.   But there are the external evidences, they
remain, and Christ's life and death must mean something
for us, though I very much fear that if it is ever to mean
anything for me, it must be after a total wreck and
dissolution of all my moral nature.

And what improvement do you see on many, on any ?
They get into better circumstances, and find it easy to
live morally.   They like to be finely moved by the
feelings that are Christian ; but is there anything more,
and if not, what is this ?   Put them into other circumstances, and what will they be ?   I don't think I would
care a turn of a straw what my circumstances were if I
was right myself.   Of course, how can a man care for
what affects him if he is always rightly affected ?   But
to find yourself drifting into mere ruin is not delectable.
However, it must assume a practical shape with me
soon, as ever since I came here I have been getting worse,
and have not much lower to go ; and then I must give up,
which for a time, at least, would be an infinite relief.

In short, if I were to preach this week on my own
feelings, my text would be ' I doubt, therefore do I

speak,' and certainly could not be ' I believe, therefore
do I speak.' But Andie is coming on Saturday, and
the weather will change, and so I may get back again.
Really, if men do not despise themselves, laugh at
themselves, and cast utter scorn on themselves, they
must have strong faith. Now don't go and answer this,
but treat me with the confidence I treat you, and tell
me when you are wretched, if you ever are ; it 's not
good to pretend you are all right, if you are not. I have
to do that so uniformly, and to go and pray with sick
people when I could eat them, and express sentiments
for the congregation which I don't feel, that I am getting
into a most ambiguous position.

By way of counteraction to my poison, I send you
the remains of yon verses. By the bye, did you get
Browning ? I want to be thanked. I kept it for a day
and read some and marked a few good things. Excuse.

> ' He spake of love, such love as Spirits feel
> In worlds whose course is equable and pure ;
> No fears to beat away—no strife to heal—
> The past unsighed for, and the future sure ;
> Spake of heroic arts in graver mood
> Revived, with finer harmony pursued ;

> ' Of all that is most beauteous—imaged there
> In happier beauty ; more pellucid streams,
> An ampler aether, a diviner air,
> And fields invested with purpureal gleams ;
> Climes which the sun, who sheds the brightest day
> Earth knows, is all unworthy to survey.'

> ' He that lacks time to mourn lacks time to mend.
> Eternity mourns that. 'Tis an ill cure
> For life's worst ills, to have no time to feel them.

> Where sorrow 's held intrusive and turned out,
> There wisdom will not enter, nor true power,
> Nor aught that dignifies humanity.'

Friday, and no time to say more.   I have to prepare a book of Homer and write the bulk of a lecture before three, and it is now past ten, so good-bye.

PS.—Don't suppose I am dismal.

To the Same

11 CASTLE STREET,
EDINBURGH, MONDAY [29th June 1863].

I called on a sick lady whom I have only once before seen, and on coming away she gave me an envelope, remarking that young ministers always need books.   I, thinking that it would be a $\frac{1}{2}$ guinea or £1, said 'Thank you ' and pocketed it.   On opening I found £5.   You will want to know her name, and you will think it 's the right name for the right woman—Miss Wright.   She must be rich, but I felt rather nasty when I found how much it was.   So what book am I to buy ?

To the Same

11 CASTLE STREET,
EDINBURGH, 2nd July 1863.

Andie is sitting opposite me cutting up for me a book which a kind friend has given to all the Preachers to help them through their sorrows.   She is interspersing the switching sound of the paper-knife with groans from a twitching in her side.   But she dined, or did not dine, with Anne to-day, and then went up and found me at the prayer-meeting ;   though she was very tired on coming in, she has talked herself into spirits.   You know, whatever I am doing she just goes on and asks me questions, which are not always answered with that promptness which should characterise intercourse with a lady. She is trying to discover how I live on £100 a year, having tried a little ago to discover how I spent £100 ; this latter she found easy of solution. It is very pleasant having her.

Nothing of great pith or moment has been said or done here this week since I wrote you. Andie has been down learning sewing-machine from Nell, and I have been writing on the Parable of the Mustard Seed.

I have run myself very short for time this week, mainly by reading Foster's new thing on the improvement of time. You did not know he was publishing still, did you ? This volume is inferior to none of its predecessors. Tell me how you like Browning. He would form a good subject for criticism, would not he ?

To the Same

11 CASTLE STREET,
14th July 1863.

I have a great deal else to tell you, for Peter is here, and I could always fill sheets about him. On Friday evening I went to them,[1] and had more music and girls. Peter introduced me to a great lot of them, and gave me their characters, *ore rotundo*, as he stood before them— some fine creatures among them, others as usual. On Saturday morning I received an urgent note from him to go and help him to take charge of thirty-three young ladies to a picnic at Burntisland. I had refused the night before, but he put it so that I should have been a beast to refuse. We went in seven cabs (and returned from Granton in the evening in *ditto*, to the astonishment

---

[1] The Misses Mouat at this time kept a girls' school at Grange House, Edinburgh.

of the town), and got all right across, and to be brief,
I don't know when I enjoyed a day more.   Peter and
I had it all our own way, of course, and we got a boat
and a cargo of crinolines in, and pulled a long way,
and some of the girls helped, and we were all as happy
as kings, princesses in fairy tales, or lovers.   With any
other person than P. how different might it have been, but
all the girls seemed to share his frank, easy way, and not
once had I time to think of other things, or *reflect* on what
was going on.   After getting to Newington again we
had tea under the verandah, and sang hymns, then I
had family worship with them, and then they all trooped
away to roost, very happy, if as happy as I.   The queen
of the day was to me one of the girls whom P. exalts
to the rank of his ' wives,' who claimed a hereditary
friendship with me, being a grand-niece of ——, a pretty,
graceful girl, plays well, and Peter says is of very good
parts.   This I don't know, for she is so modest I never
could get a hold of her all day, and of course I could not
pay any attention to single females, for there was always
one of the thirty-three crinolines stuck on a rock, or
one sweet little boot jammed between two stones, or one
hungry little stomach wanting a sandwich made ; and,
of course, all had equal claim on us.

On Sunday I preached in the afternoon to —— in
Mr. Main's, and met her looking like all the Graces
rolled into one next morning.   She deigned to express a
favourable criticism, and so made me happy for the
day.

To A. Taylor Innes

11 CASTLE STREET,
,THURSDAY [? *July* 1863].

My sister and I were very much annoyed to find we
had missed you the other evening, and I might have

known you were coming, for you were in my thoughts oftener than usual on Tuesday, and I had an impression that you were on your road home. Andie could afford us only an unsatisfactory account of your travels, but I hope some day to have them from your own lips. I wish I could have been with you.

What Laidlaw says about Bannockburn is rather disconcerting to a candidate. If, however, it be the case that to please one party is to displease the other, the only way will be to please neither, and in that, I think, I shall have a chance to be as successful as most.

The Bombay business is ' up a tree.' Charles Brown received from Dr. Begbie such an account of my internal arrangements as at once decided him to seek for a man whose health would be more likely to suit the climate. If it interests you to know how far your advice had weight, I may say (what any of my friends here could prove if necessary) that I was rapidly making up my mind to go. Now my only prospect is at Aberdeen. I am going to supply James Macphail's pulpit the last two Sundays of August, in order to give the Trinity people an opportunity of hearing me in that delicate way which seems to suit the fine sensibilities of F.C. preachers. If this also becomes smoke I will write, as a last effort, a lecture on the man at the Pool of Bethesda, who was always anticipated by some more fortunate patient. He, however, had thirty-eight disappointments, I only twenty-one as yet ; but I do not feel at all disposed to make the analogy more perfect, and fear if I sit longer by the pool I 'll begin and throw mud at the angel, which must not be.

Excuse more now, but believe that if you have any sentiments, reflections, ideas, or experiences, that you want to get quit of, no one will receive them with more hearty welcome than . . .

To the Same

11 CASTLE STREET,
EDINBURGH, 5th August 1863.

Your letter almost made up for missing your call, and I should have answered it sooner, had I not wished to be able to tell you of my Bannockburn attempt. I was there last Sunday, though had I given way to my first sensations on Saturday night, I should have left it without preaching. I felt the wrong man in the wrong place altogether, or rather the wrong man in the right place, for it is a first-rate thing for somebody, and I do not quite understand Laidlaw leaving it for anything short of a city charge. But you know the place better than I do. I *did* not much worse than my usual, read very little, and emphasized with my hand at least three times, doing violence to my own nature and I fear also to the sense, taste, and instincts of my audience. They attended tolerably, but that hostile, critical, exclusive look of a congregation of weavers makes me præter-naturally cold, and imparts a measure of insolence to the petulant tone in which I usually preach. Of course I came from Church with the feeling of a man who has sawn his own branch off a tree, mixed with a desire to be at Cornwall, or Thurso, or Vienna. I consoled myself, or progressed from stolid indifference to triumphant callousness and a sublime fatalism, by reading Foster's Life, especially the letter in which he resigns his Downend charge after his charge had resigned him, did my best to get into Laidlaw's slippers—if I could not manage to stand in his shoes—and sauntered about the garden to give the lieges an idea of my Sabbatarian principles.

Speaking of Sabbatarian views leads me to the other matter. All that I know about Hetherington's berth is that my name was mentioned by some members of the

College Committee — Smeaton, Candlish, and James Bonar—but ——, with the usual meddling of a clever, influential, and ignorant woman, has so widely circulated a report that I am a benighted Anti-Sabbatarian, that I fear it may very considerably damage me. She has no doubt found a zealous helper in this good work in ——, who goes through the world with results not unlike those which follow the progress of a fox with his tail on fire through a field of ripe barley. Dr. M. Mitchell (who is now out of the way) is the only other person mentioned *here*, but if you think your uncle would be well suited for the place you will do a service by pushing his claims. I do not know that I would ever make a good or passable systematic. If you find it in your way or out of your way to do me a good turn, I know I need not press you to do it ; and being wholly unable to say (in this case) whether you ought to push my name forward or no, I am the more glad to be able to be quite confident that whatever you do will bear equal mark of wisdom and affection. I feel at present quite unfit to take any other such situation as my present : all power of writing sermons has forsaken me, and fits of indolence and fits of reading seize me by turns.

Write soon, whether you have anything to say or not. There is nobody in town, and I doubt if anybody will turn up on Sunday to be preached to by . . .

To S. R. Macphail

11 CASTLE STREET,
11th *August* 1863.

MY DEAR SIMONIDES,—As I have no intention of being up at three o'clock to-morrow morning (as all the sporting world will be, of which you will be apprised duly by the pop-popping all day around you, I suppose), I need not pretend to be full of bustle to-day. Moreover,

I am in another circumstance prompting me to write to you. I have just come from the Canal, the first time I have been since the farewell we had. I went to-day with Gregor (my Homeric youth) and Annie, my niece, and as it is a lovely day we had great fun, and talked much—much of you among other *things*. Everything was superb, except the rowing, which was always careless and often execrable. This holiday is no exception to my ordinary life at present, for my sisters are both with me just now, and so we are jollifying a good deal, though there is no one in town to jollify with. One day we were at Dalkeith, which is very pretty, and where we have very good friends. Another day Annie and I and Mr. Gibson and Whyte went to see the Channel Fleet, and thereafter bathed (Annie being commanded to a distance). So that as you may imagine, I am doing about as much as you seem to be, only that I have been devouring these magnificent volumes which Cunningham has left us. Whatever else you do, Simon, you should master him, Calvin, and as much of Turretin as possible, and let those rubbishing Broad Churchmen go to the wall, along with all unenlightened theologues (falsely so called). Homer I am greatly enjoying with Gregor, who is a good talker, better indeed at episodical digressions and irrelevancies than at thorough grind, but he is honest and has a fine nature.

I am sorry you are wroth at yourself ; only I am too much convinced that a man's nature will have its way, or at least that he is for himself the only physician, to begin and advise or even lecture you. Work, hard, necessary and constant, is what stands, I believe, between many men and perpetual misery. Patience also for the young. It is good for a man that he bear the yoke in his youth. And what need of hurry with Eternity before us ? Time enough to develope all that is in us, and

become and do as much as we are fit for.   What I am
to become or do the next winter, I have not the ghost
of an idea yet, but I did my best at Bannockburn, and
will do *ditto* at Aberdeen, but I suppose there will be
no one in Aberdeen to hear me.   So your advice must
go for nothing.   I should like to have seen your brother.

Whyte is becoming quite an ecclesiastical Mercury,
preaching like any licentiate of us all.   Your Tauler is a
continual good and a joy to me.

To his sister Marcia

[11 CASTLE STREET,
EDINBURGH,] WEDNESDAY [*August* 1863].

After you left I left the station too, following you in
thought as far as Gogar and then reaching this desolate
room.   It 's no use now sitting on the end of the sofa—
there is nothing at the other end but a tidy.   I looked
at the image on the chimney-piece, but there 's not much
in that, so I had recourse to Cunningham as usual, and
think I 'll read him till I become him—but what a dreadful thing that would be.   Last night I had a sublime
grind, my first winter evening with all the honours, no
intruders, no head, no frivolous conversation interjected
from the sofa, no seductive strains from the piano, no
amorous imaginings, but cold, rapid grind, and to bed
with a tolerable conscience : to-day *do. do.*   At eight
o'clock last night I did interrupt in order to consider the
geography and population of Buchan, and hope to hear
some certain intelligence of that quarter at an early
date.   Don't be down, there is positively no profit in
that ; this is wisdom !

I have made an offer to Maclaren for a book, but he is
going to consult some people first.   If he agrees, I will
go in at once (' go into retreat ' is the technical for it),
and get a month's work done, I hope.   It is my old scheme

of an introduction to the books of the New Testament for the use of governesses and other imbeciles. Now I must not be wasting time writing to the like of you. Are your eyes scratched out yet ? If so, send for me and I'll read you this. You know that no news can transpire in a town like this, so good-bye, and write, write, write amain to . . .

To the Same

11 CASTLE STREET,
1st September 1863.

Had Stewart and I not been men of consummate discretion and prudence, this letter might have been otherwise dated,[1] but yesterday morning S. came into my room with his tr-s-rs on and his braces hanging down disconsolately behind in that fashion which suggests that their bearer has no intention of dressing, nor indeed of doing anything else that day. Half asleep as I was (it was just 6 o'clock), I saw something was wrong, and did not take long to find out, for no sooner did I sit up in bed than I heard that heavy, continuous plash by which rain intimates the reverse of the braces, and that *it* means to be up and at it all day. Well, we got up, and eat our breakfast, doing our part, and hoping the weather might take second thoughts and let us out. However, though we watched the sky throughout the whole morning (proving what Stewart repeated as his best *bon mot* about twice in the half-hour, that ' it's a grand thing getting up in the morning—gives you such a command of the day ! ' This jest you will be satisfied was a good one, when I tell you that when we parted last night it was not the least threadbare, but both had

---

[1] *i.e.* from Aberdeen, where the writer had been preaching for two Sundays, occupying the house of the Rev. J. C. Macphail in the absence of the latter and his wife.

great satisfaction in repeating it when saying good-bye)—
well, the day, however, was not so to be done, but kept
command of us to an extent that would have been irritating to two less sweet tempers than those we wot of.
Of course, after breakfast at 6.30 there was a slight
difficulty in finding something to do which might be at
once interesting and useful. Several courses at once
suggested themselves to two fertile minds. Of course
we naturally proposed as a first measure to do something
for the beasts ; and that which seemed most likely to
conduce to their permanent satisfaction, was to put the
salt beasts into the fresh water, and the fresh ones into
salt lodgings. Then we thought of turning on all the
water-cocks (of which the house possesses a terrific
number) and gas-cocks, hanging the cat and the rabbits,
setting fire to the grate shavings, mixing seidlitz powders
in the aquaria, making the tower of Pisa *lean* a little more,
sweeping the mantelpiece (which is loaded with vases
and gimcrackerei) with the flower-glass of elegant
proportions in the drawing-room, and finally tying the
ancient and taciturn domestic, putting her spectacles
on and a pipe in her mouth. However, after weighing
the various paths, we adjourned to the washing-house
and smoked, which so promoted our comfort that S.
declared we were both ' a good deal more so.' On the
whole I never spent a merrier morning, and when we saw
it was useless to think of Braemar we went to the Bank
and got £22,000, which we found quite covered our
expenses on the homeward journey.

But I find that I have begun at the end. The beginning was that just as your letter (jolly) was opened,
we were sitting down as Mr. and Mrs. Macphail, and were
again sumptuously entertained. After dinner we followed
your advice, and went out the road past Willowbank to
Bridge of Dee, crossed the bridge, reading *all* the in-

scriptions, and taking imaginary jottings in our imaginary diaries of our imaginary tour, and up the other side of the river a lump, then back on this side right down to the harbour, then went and bought stockings, then home and tea.

Sunday I preached very comfortably in the East Church. Again I felt that no congregation puts me so on my mettle as that, and again I am at a loss to know why it should be so; the faces are intelligent, but not more so than in some congregations here. Good-bye, and believe what I do, that we have had as much fun in our disappointment as we could have had had it been fine.

To A. Taylor Innes

11 CASTLE STREET,
2nd September 1863.

Your letter with its not very welcome news has just come in, and found me, for our Aberdeen scheme met a watery grave. Stewart came to Aberdeen on Saturday, and I preached to him in the East Church on Sunday, and expected to start for Braemar and all the rest of it on Monday, but rose at 6 to see everything steeping, and a relentless rain busily doing its best to extinguish us. So like two wise tourists we came home again.

I am, or should be, greatly disappointed about Hetherington's, not because I think I could have done the work at all as well as your uncle, but because I think I could have learnt to do it passably, and because, while I have all along felt a natural incapacity for preaching, I have equally found a readiness and ease in teaching which made me hope I might not fall out of Church employment. I am much more fully aware than my friends how many years it would take to put me on a level with ordinarily instructed teachers; but if I had my work laid before me, and saw what I must acquire, I think it might be possible to get along without being hooted, or shelved as incompetent. At the same time I could not have expected the men who lead in the Free Church to know this or to weigh it, and think they have acted a very much wiser part in appointing your uncle : *ergo*, I am content.

Whether anything may come of Aberdeen or not I cannot say. I liked preaching there, and one Sunday I preached in Trinity (the church for whose behoof I went), but only know that the minister's wife thought I had a ' well-modulated voice ' ! If the people judge like the priestess, they may think my sermons were interesting.

I know nothing of Hugh Paterson, but the Renfield people will do Glasgow good if they get Kennedy.

De Sororibus

I feel quite sorry for you losing your sister for a whole year out of your life, but absence with frequent correspondence gives an oyster-like temperament (like mine) opportunity of uttering itself more warmly than it can allow itself to do when face to face, and in absence the strong and good points of a person remain clearly in view while the rest goes with the body to a distance, so that there are little gushes (spurts) of tenderness which ripen affection. If, however, you wish an essay on the subject you had better impose it on your sister as her first theme. My sister Andie has gone to her own place—Anick Grange, where the air is soft, the work easy, the people gay in *manner*, the surroundings of a physical kind tidy and regular, and all suited to her temperament. Marcia is still at Glenluce, chaffing me thence with epistles than which nothing could be more refreshing to an owl like your humble servant. She returns to Brucklay in about ten days.

To S. R. Macphail

11 CASTLE STREET,
EDINBURGH, 10*th September* [1863].

I greeted with great delight your letter to-day, but was rather saddened by its contents. If sincere friendship and real sympathy could do you good, you would be as cheery as any man of them all who have good stomachs, good consciences, and good surroundings. But here it strikes me that there is a friendship and sympathy of an infinitely higher style of reality and sincerity, which *does* lift to what it desires its object to reach, and give what it desires its object to possess.   The most that I can do when you growl to me is to send back an answering growl, and strange enough, the very evening before your letter came I had been treating your brother James (who spent a night with me on his way North) to a ferocious and altogether unpardonable measure of growlery.   The truth is, Simeon, I have had most serious difficulties lately, and of a kind, I believe, not altogether different from yours, though I know there is more of sin in my case, and more of misery in yours.   I have so continued in sin that I am very much at a loss to understand what it is a man may expect from a Saviour.   So long as I read the Bible it looks all beautiful, and I think I have found a ready-made Heaven.   I turn aside, and find in five minutes that I am as gross a sinner as I was twenty years ago.   This *must* be my fault.   I often say, without the prompting of a partner, ' Curse God and die,' often say ' Save me or damn me at once,' often blaspheme one way or other out of the bitterness of a heart that is ashamed to find itself weak and vile as ever ; but then I *know* all the while that this is mere folly, that whether I choose to partake of it or not, Christ did come to bring salvation, and has brought it.   Sometimes I can see well enough that I am altogether in a wrong state

X

of mind towards God, and therefore have fallen into sin. Sometimes I fall into sin after prayer, after doing all that seems best fitted to steel me against temptation; but in my saner moments, which are very, very few, I feel that my whole wretched case arises from my not yielding implicitly to God. I am just gradually getting to see what faith it is which attaches to the Saviour, gradually finding that it requires a man to give himself up to God, not petulantly *testing* His willingness to save, but believing that He will save, and this despite all the difficulties in the way.

If you say What is the use of saying this to a fellow who has heard nothing else since first he heard his mother's voice? I can only reply what I said before, that I am only meaning to tell you my own misery, not to bring you out of yours; and for my part, I believe it would be all right with me could my pride give way, and could I bring myself to *depend altogether* for everything upon God, for pardon, for renewing, for ordering my life. I find that I have been treating God in a very unworthy way, as if I had said ' I will see whether there is anything in this salvation or not; let me try it for a time,' or ' Let Him that calls Himself Saviour save me, it is His business '; but only very rarely and not as my habit have I yielded myself in the full persuasion that this good and holy God has unbounded love towards me and waits to deliver me from my sin.

That you have this difficulty, I do not know. Your reverence is much greater than mine, or than most people's, and that will help you; your conscience is tender, and that will help you; but from the make of your spirit, and from your physical temperament, you will have a long and often weary fight. But, Simeon, we have always the character of God to fall back on. He must be on our side against evil, against sin, and doubt, and misery. I hope one thing for you, that you may never be reckless as I have been, and been in the best of spirits when I should have been in dust and ashes ; and I hope you may not, as I have done, spend the best years of your life in mere howling, when I should have been by quiet confidence waiting for God and His Spirit.

What I say to myself is applicable to you, and all. Be persuaded that God will deliver you from sin, wait on Him, do not sink, do not scoff, do not suffer a shadow of doubt about it. I do not obey my own voice, but yet my past years say, if there is one verse of the Bible that is true it is about the waverer, ' Let not that man think that he will receive anything from the Lord.' Is it not, Simeon, the turning-point with us all when we can give God His place, believe in Him wholly ?

But enough : do write at once, and let me know how you get on ; and may God grant you a speedier deliverance than has been given to . . .

To the Same

11 CASTLE STREET,
FRIDAY [11th *September* 1863].

CARISSIME,—I have only a few minutes, but cannot help sending a line to see if my epistle found you, and to ask you again to write and let me know of your state. It is not true, as of the Philippians, that no man careth for your state. Don't take amiss anything I said last night. I am half dead, and can do little for myself and less than nothing for others at present. You ask where I am to be next winter. This you know as much as I do. I have not the remotest idea ; but partly in consequence of a thick skin, and partly in consequence of prevailing laziness, and partly in consequence of reading Foster's

Life, I am indifferent.   It will in the first instance be a relief to be clear of the High Church.   With my pupil I have got through twice the five last books of Homer, and with great pleasure, admiring more and more the old *vates*.   He has sent me to Milton, and the two together are not to be lightly thought of.   I wish you were here again to talk over all our old gods.   Really, I have not a soul to divulge, overflow, or spout to, except my pupil, who is an intelligent youth, and may be yet a light.   I bought a lovely Lucian the other day for 4s. ; would that you were here to go into him joint-stock.

' Now unto Him that *is* able to keep you from falling, and to present you faultless before the presence of His glory with exceeding joy ; to the only wise God our Saviour, be glory and majesty, dominion and power, both now and ever.   Amen.'

PS.—Make a point of mastering Cunningham's vols. before you leave College ; if necessary, make a vow.

To A. Taylor Innes

11 Castle Street,
Edinburgh, *16th September* [1863].

I fear you may think I have acted foolishly in refusing to preach in Renfield Church, and I myself fear I always hit upon the wrong thing, but in this case I do not see how I could have done otherwise than refuse your invitation, and I think that you will agree with me when I tell you that I am engaged to preach at Portobello on Sunday, that I have only been one day in the High Church for the last four weeks, and that I have at present three vacancies depending.   To have added a fourth, and thereby have left myself only two days for the High Church would, I think, have been unseemly, to say the least of it, some might say unjust.   It would have shown

an over-eagerness to grab at everything that is going.
If the people would like me to preach three or four weeks
hence, I have no objections ; only I do not wish to preach
as a candidate for the office of supplying their pulpit
until they get a minister ; nor would I preach only to
feed the curiosity of some of the people who may think
this a good opportunity for seeing all the kinds of
preachers that are going. You can easily understand
that at this stage I am very unwilling to go anywhere
where there is not a fair prospect of some benefit resulting ; it does me harm. I own I do not think it likely that
any of the three places I have been at just now will
come to anything ; but that is no reason why I should
look covetously at every vacancy in the Church. At
present concern for the future affords no stimulus, for
I have no such concern. To be always in a state of expectation makes one feel very weak and foolish, and possibly
makes one so.

Item, in the way of news, there is a giant exhibiting
here just now, which I tell you in order to tell you what
some man said of some other very little man, that he
was the smallest man he had ever seen *for nothing !*

Write please, and tell me if I am an ass in the Renfield business, and in any case believe me . . .

To his sister Marcia

11 CASTLE STREET,
TUESDAY [? 29*th September* 1863].

I had no intention of writing you to-night, but events
' over which I have no control ' compel me, however
reluctant. Your letter, which I have just devoured, is
possibly the inciting cause. But I have a matter of mine
to lay before you. Clark is translating a six-volume
book from the German by different hands, and wants me

to edit. He knows that I am deficient in German, as he has more than once offered me translation which, of course, I had to decline. He says that all he wants me to do is to give uniformity to the whole, and add notes so as to bring the book up to the present day (it is 15 years old). It is on the Gospels, critical, expository, apologetic. Now there is something to be said for and against this. For : I *know* of no other work after Sunday. This would force me to get up more German, and would also make me go very carefully over the Gospels, and would be work very much to my fancy. Against : it would be awkward if I got any of these places I am trying for, as I could scarcely do it and all the work one has entering a charge. I am not the most competent person, possibly not even so competent as Clark thinks me. And *this* has occurred to me (which is perhaps only superstition), that it has come to try me and see whether I will take to preaching or this kind of work. But of course I have no right to say or think that if I refuse this I shall get Bannockburn, or that I shall lose Bannockburn if I accept it. But what do you think ? Clark has sent me five German vols. along, so I must begin at once ; but I wish you would write a line to let me know what seems to you.

You see how prolix I can be when self is the subject, and you will immediately find how brief I can be on any other subject.

When I think of the future (I never do, but this offer of Clark's made me), I don't like it much. My present, too, is always so comfortable, the future seems cold in comparison. I should not like to drift into hand to mouth semi-literary life ; the prospect of a prime without a home, a wife, a position, is cheerless, but that seems to be the thing I am going to. But don't on any account suppose that I need your condolence, and a word in

season, or any of that kind of thing. What is to be is
to be, I suppose, and when taken in days, life can be
swallowed. Maclaren wants me to go on with the Introduction to the Gospels, but of course it need not be
out till next summer now, so there is plenty time for that.

To the Same

11 CASTLE STREET,
WEDNESDAY EVENING, 30*th September* [1863].

I have every reason to be in good spirits to-night, for
I have just finished reading your letter, and it is so nice
that it has shut out all that went before, and I feel
quite near to you. But oh! those real miles. Miss
Johnson (whom I was subject to to-day) thinks correspondence a fine change, but I threw such essence of
scepticism into my expression when she said so, that she
saw *that* would not work.

I am going to preach at Bannockburn a second time.
I am reconciled to the idea of it now. I could study
better there, though I fear my visiting of the people,
except the sick, would be constant weariness and vanity.

You have done well to hang my picture, thereby signi-
fying what you judge the proper fate of the man represented. I refuse to think of you in any situation, relation, or position which can at all draw forth affection
towards you ; 'tis but a vanity to attach oneself to anything, or, at least, to any person, here—so take your
dismissal.

I took a long stretch into the country on Monday,
and enjoyed it much, though alone, but subsequently
got wet and came home and read in Pascal : ' J'ai
souvent dit que tout le malheur des hommes vient de
ne pas savoir se tenir en repos dans une chambre.'

I dare say Chalmers is as good as anything else if you don't want to make much impression on the girl you speak ‚of ; it 's a good book ; but you know, I don't know the party. I am more and more of opinion that biography is the thing for young people ; no influence is like personal influence. (If any of your pupils have capacity for prose-poetry, Young's *Night Thoughts* might be good for a Sunday exercise.)

Maclaren has said nothing about my work, and I am doing nothing for it. I am reading theology carefully, but cannot write just now ; and as my oldest sermons are my best I see no reason why I should write, but that I can't is the best. Solitary life is conducive to very little good of any kind.

Now I must stop, for Miss Johnson is very anxious that I should write a sermon for her, and I think I will try ; but it is a text a lot of people would call heretical, ' Give all diligence to make your calling and election sure.'

To the Same

11 CASTLE STREET,
1st October 1863.

It seems to me I do little else than write to you nowadays. I wish one could make one's bread by any such pleasant occupation ; or rather I wish that all people were like you, and then all occupations would be pleasant.

Anent business, Anne is anxious to know if you have no intention of selling your piano and buying a mangle, or at least she thinks the first part of such a transaction would be advisable, as said instrument is reported to be going to pigs and whistles, especially whistles. So issue your orders—it certainly cannot be good for old bones to stand in a vault like yon nursery.

Clark sent me five fat, soft German vols. to begin

upon, and having begun I am delighted to find that the
German is about the simplest and the man the nicest I
have had to do with, so I shall, I think, just go in for it
neck or nothing.

I would like very much to go to Mary, only I think it
would be imprudent to be out of the way just now.
I suspect if I let another year pass, it will be all up with
me on the score of church-getting. Two or three people
lately have informed me that I intend to leave the
church and go—where ? And anything which might
be construed into a confirmation of that would do me
harm, so I had best stay where I am.

Charles and I are simply a critical society now ; we
see a good deal of one another, and all our talk is of
authors. He has a very felicitous utterance, but many
prejudices ; yet I don't know if I would trust any one's
judgment (thro' the piece) more readily than his—always
excepting yours, which is, so far as I know, infallible.
How I do wish we could live together ; I have not half
the judgment nor a tenth of anything else, alone, that
I have in your company. If ever a person had a good
genius, I have one in you.

To S. R. Macphail

11 Castle Street,
2nd October 1863.

Sunday eight days is my last in the Free High, and
then the wide world once more. The freedom is worth
the bother of seeking new work, *almost.*

Whyte was up last night for a long time. He is much
attached to you, and I listen not unwilling to your
praises. I think him improved by his preaching ; it
has sent him to the Bible, and a fellow's first fresh study
of the New Testament does him great good ; but how
soon do we cease to see the wonders in it.

Find time to write, if possible, before returning. I look forward with gusto to your first rush in upon me. I have a lot of new books for you to see, but the old ones hold their place. I am more and more glad that I have *In Memoriam*, and that I have it from you.

Now this is Friday, and I have not much time, so fare thee well.

To his sister Marcia

11 CASTLE STREET,
EDINBURGH, *3rd October* 1863.

I do not think I should have answered your letter at all, had I not been busy with illogical people of all kinds, and cannot refrain from a little delicate practice when it offers. Your letter presents so many points for criticism that it is difficult to say where you err most. First of all, you have mistaken the tone of my letter ; you seem to ascribe to me as an actual condition of mind what I expressed myself as only verging towards, and as possible in case certain fears should be realised. This is your $\pi\rho\hat{\omega}\tau\sigma\nu \ \psi\epsilon\hat{\upsilon}\delta\sigma s$, *i.e.* your fundamental whid. Again, you introduce, for the purpose of ameliorating this ideal condition, a principle which I have heard you express great contempt for, that, to wit, of comparing your own state with that of others. Two blacks don't make a white, neither do two whites make a black ; *ergo*, if J. and W. F. were both as white in the head as their father or Mont Blanc, that would not make me black. To say that they are old and still unsettled (unsettled forsooth, when they might have been their own paterfamiliases seven years ago) is not to bring me nearer a settlement, and perhaps if you were their sister you would hear some growling also from them. Neither did I mean, and I hope I did not say, that taking Clark's work would tie me to a literary career ; but only that some unthinking

persons might suppose that I was leaning more that
way than is the case.   It all resolves itself into this, that
living alone is mangey, and good for no Christian man ;
and a person who never did it can't conceive it.   I think
I stand it quite as well as most, though on reflection
I don't know any one who does it.   Students all seem
to go in couples, and for a man in business to come home
to a solitary room—why, that's a relief.   Conclusion,
I would like to get Bannockburn, and would growl for
a year if I got it.   I am very well as I am, and will, I
dare say, never be better off in my life.   Only vacancies
are wretched things—they disorder one more than hard
ham or tea at ——'s.

I should also tell you that Dr. Bruce has engaged me
to stand by him till his health is restored.   I had a long
talk with him this morning ; he is not allowed to preach
just now at all, but I dare say will soon be all right.
A very fine man he is, with all his peculiarities, and as
magnificent a head as ever I saw.

To A. Taylor Innes

11 CASTLE STREET,
3rd October 1863.

I have been for some days in expectation of hearing
from you, for I wished to write and let you know my
state.   But first of your inquiries.   Is there an appetite
for systematic theology in Glasgow to the extent in-
dicated by your desire to buy Turretin ?   I would like
much to be in your class.   If you wish a system of theology, there is certainly none so complete, none so satisfactory on each point, and so exhaustive of the whole
as Turretin.   For true blue, out and out, remorseless
Calvinism there is not his equal.   There are two editions
of him, an ancient but comfortable quarto, generally
about 28s., and a modern and rather naked octavo,

about 30s. or 32s., or more. But quarto is the size for systematics.

Alford would be far more useful than Bengel. He has most of what is good in Bengel and all the rest of them, with a fine tact of his own in interpretation, steered by accurate scholarship. He costs about £5 for the 4 vols. Of Bengel there are two editions, a very handsome 8vo, large, clear type on broad, clean pages, and a thin-paper, columned 4to ; a very nice book too. If you have Bengel alone you will miss a good deal of what is in the N.T., and often be at a loss. Alford gives you everything ; and if you can't work through a passage with him, there is something wrong either with you or the passage.

If you would allow me to add a suggestion, it would be that you should weigh the comparative merits of Cunningham and Turretin for a class or for yourself. Cunningham has the great advantage of being historical, a much easier method for attracting ordinary intellects and for holding in ordinary memories. You go over the same controversies in both. The difference in treatment is that in C. you have the way pointed out and the general outline of the thing, so that you really see the real state of matters and could floor any man who took the opposition. T. goes through the detail, handles text after text, argument after argument, besides showing you the state of the Question. Were I choosing a book for a class I would take Cunningham ; for myself I would have both.

Say which of all these you would like, and I shall be delighted to send them for you.

I fear I could not give the Renfield people a day, even though they should wish it, for Dr. Bruce wishes me to stand by him until he gets thoroughly better ; and as I can only help him one Sunday this month, it will

scarcely do to forsake him then also. He is a grand
old Scotch minister. I doubt none of our contemporaries
will grow up to a build like that ; that head grows upon
you—at least the front ; I should not like the back, or
the hair at the back, to grow upon me. His sister is
another of the same.

I go to Bannockburn the third Sabbath of this month.
Item, I have got a mass of work from Clark. He is
translating a book of Lange's (*Leben Jesu*) in six vols.,
and wishes me to revise and edit, so I am wading through
the soft, spongy pages, and see nothing beyond. I do
not know that I should have undertaken it ; it will too
manifestly expose my barrenness, besides that it will
prevent me sermonizing for some months to come.
Otherwise it will do me good. I am reading in connection
with this Renan's *Vie de Jésus*, which is certainly an
extraordinary fact. It is constructive ; and destructive
only in so far as it *ignores all* that has been said in support of the divinity of Christ, miracles, inspiration (of
even the meagrest order). He takes up the four writings,
finds that a Galilean peasant is the subject of them all,
and knows that from this person some great power has
proceeded, and recognising nothing beyond except what
history says, constructs a fifth gospel according to
Renan, which henceforth is to be the true one. Nothing,
he says, was further from the thoughts of Christ than
that he was the son of God in any other sense than all men
may and ought to be, etc., etc. It is worth *your* reading,
but not worth a place in a young ladies' boarding-school.

To-morrow I preach my farewell in the High, *i.e.* I give
them about the lowest of my old sermons, to which I have
been gradually reduced.

To his sister Marcia

11 CASTLE STREET,
8th October 1863.

I have had another episode with Miss Johnson. She
has given me money to buy Cunningham's vols., and as
I had them already, has written a loving inscription on
them. She also mourned over my hair lying on my fore-
head, and finally got a comb 'which had combed Dr.
Cunningham's hair' (I believe she would lend it him
that she might gather a lock of his hair), and combed me
till my head was sore. She is a funny but affectionate
soul.

Rainy very kindly came into the vestry on Sunday,
and said a kind word or two : he is very nice, certainly,
surely a man very pure of heart.

I am getting on with the reading of Lange better than
I expected, having done between a quarter and a third
of him, not very carefully, but following his sense. I
dare say, for all that is needed to be done to him, I may
do as well as another. I have worked at him very
persistently for these last few days, and very, *very* often
wish that *somebody* was here to do a bit with me. Still
the idea of sermonizing is abhorrent to me, and I don't
know how ever I am to get begun again. To preach
over what I have done in the High will not do, and yet
I very much fear I shall do it.

Tell me fully about your ways, whole walk] and
conversation.

Stewart was up on Sunday, and insists that I shall
write new sermons. I am sure had I nothing to be
thankful for but my friends, I should have the ' abundant '
cause. And to have you—when one comes to think of it
—to be *your* brother—it is enough to turn one's head.

What sermons might be written on this topic, but this is not the paper, so good-bye.

PS.—Your letter just come; it is rather mono-syllabic, for you, *i.e.* it reads in jerks and statements. Next time be what Innes calls ' profluent.'

I give you an easy lesson in Latin :—

Ego amo te.

i love u.

To the Same

11 CASTLE STREET,
15th October 1863.

Your short letter came last night in its deceptive envelope, and I am not quite sure that I should answer it.   If leisure were to be the requisite of a reply, certainly you would not hear from me just now.   I went over to Smeaton's the other morning, and told him what I was doing for Clark, so he had me into his library and showed me piles of books, German and Dutch, that I should read if I am to be at all up to the matter.   He thinks it will be a great pity if I do not make it as com-plete as possible, and does not see how I can do other work at the same time.   So if Dr. Bruce does not get better in a week or two, I think I should give him up. Lange is very pleasant work, and I can make out what the other men mean pretty quick ; but I do regret that some of my idle months were not devoted to German ; it would be a great difference to me now.

I should mention that Smeaton gave me a lecture about my delivery for the 105th time.   Charles and I nearly came to blows, the only time I have seen him lately.   He is a Socialist, you know, and going to all the meetings, and is inspired suddenly with a vehement desire to study political economy.   I hope he won't, for

I 'll get it all second-hand, and disagree with him on every possible point.

This is Friday morning. Yesterday Clark sent me a great bunch of MSS., and the labour is something quite beyond what I expected. The translation is good, but of course needs numberless amendments. Then there are sentences left out, and notes altogether omitted ; so I fear what I looked forward to as a pleasant occupation will prove a frightful drudgery. Then I can get no time for adding anything of my own, which I was hoping to do. So much did the work appal me that about 7 last night I could stand it no longer, and actually ran away from it. I went to the Hogues, took tea, but was dumb and felt out of place, so just came away and went at it again till my head grew useless. In bed it was with me, and I have been waking all through the night with difficult lines of German before my eyes. I never wished for you so much as last night. I would have given mints to have had you beside me—there *is* something in you there is not in other people. However, I suppose I must make up my mind to get through alone, though just now it is awfully on the top of me.

You must excuse me writing much to-day, for every moment is precious till I get fairly started, if ever I do. I have nothing to tell you either—unless it be that I hear I have no chance at Bannockburn.

To the Same

11 CASTLE STREET,
22nd October 1863.

People who do the right thing are at this moment receiving the benediction of their several ministers before coming home to their fast-day dinners, but I thought it best to stay in the house all day and get on

with that German, and so here I am, right or wrong.
You may know how laborious it is when I tell you that
16 pages is all I have got done to-day, though I have
worked myself almost blind. The MS. is scored and
blotted with corrections, and has often to be still further
corrected ; but a little of the same work would be very
nice, and it is an immense relief to see as much well-
defined work before me as will last for months, and not
to have to wonder What shall I do to-day ?

On Saturday I went to Bannockburn, and preached
my best on Sunday, not reading a word, one part of the
day, but it would not do, for on Monday I only got 36
votes, and my opponent 71, the consequence of which
is that he is to be called.   If this had been my first, I
should have been much disappointed, but I have no
distinct feelings on the subject.   It is a very nice place,
but I suppose Mr. Emsley Brown will find it as pleasant
as I should have done.   On Monday I went to Lochwinnoch, and had a most enjoyable day with Cunningham, though I had to carry my work with me there too,
and get him to help me with some difficult bits in Lange.
Also I had some examination papers to prepare for the
New College fellows, one of which we did together.

On Tuesday I saw Miss Johnson, who told me of
Rainy's little girl asking her ' Is Papa the very best man
in the world ? ' and fancy how Miss J. did violence to her
conscience, saying ' Well, he is one of the best '—as if
she did not wholly agree with the girlie !   I told her I
knew what your answer would have been.   He had been
speaking to her as kindly of me as he spoke to myself
in the vestry.

I am going to establish myself here by getting a bookcase, as I find I can't get on without my books now that
I have this new work.

Don't you think I may give up all idea of a country

Y

charge now ? I never had such a sense of the childish position popular election puts one in as this time—going and being pitted against a man like schoolboys wrestling, or who to write the best theme. Surely it is the wrong way to get a minister. I felt like a horse being trotted out to show his paces.

10 P.M.—Stewart has been here, and is really a refreshment, so uniformly affectionate, and wise often for others. Simeon and Whyte have also been up, so Lange is up too, for a day ; but I must try and get a little done before Curfew, so good-night, my dearest.

To the Same

11 CASTLE STREET,
End of *October* [1863].

Work, too, continues quite as abundant. I have to lecture Dr. Bruce's young men on Sunday, and have been vamping up a paper on the characteristics of the gospels, being wholly unable to turn my mind to anything else. Dr. Bruce is not to preach on Sunday yet, but I wish he would be quick and get well. I have finished the MS. of half a vol. of Lange ; it is the smallest but most difficult. I have not put many notes, always feeling insolent in the act and ignorant to the last extreme. I hope Clark won't find out.

The bookcase is to be oak, is to be made by Glen, is to cost £10, 10s., and is to stand where the sideboard now is. It will not hold all my books, but I could not well get a larger one here, and I can get wings on when I need them. Painted wood, deal, would have been only £3 less, so I think I am not extravagant to get oak. I could have got one for £5, but would have had to banish it if ever I got a decent house ; and as this is my one piece of furniture, I think I may be pleasing myself.

The German does not get much easier, though I don't quite so often as at first wish it would all become Greek. There is a little cat about the size of a guinea-pig comes in and keeps me company here, lying mostly among the tongs. She can't make out the wind to-day at all, it being, I suppose, the first she has heard during her pilgrimage.

This is as miscellaneous as the general news column of a paper, but I really have not time to arrange or think, and I know I am omitting two or three things that I stamped during the week as things to be told to you. You miss a great deal, mind, of fine thought, picturesque narrative, and delicate humour by not being here, for of course it is always the best things that are forgotten, and the worst that get your length.

To the Same

11 CASTLE STREET,
5th November 1863.

I think that after all Saturday evening is the best time for your letters to come ; not thereby precluding a second edition on Monday, Wednesday, or any day of the seven, but there is a dowiness about Saturday evening that needs a stimulant, and especially just now. This double work is not the thing at all—for it is not double work, my whole time is given to Lange ; and when I find myself in the pulpit I feel astonished and out of place, and last Sunday might far better have been at home. What to do I do not know. I fear I am stamping myself as a careless, sleepy, insipid preacher, yet I can't give up Clark now ; and if I did, I suspect I should just preach my old sermons still. I am getting more and more interested in Lange, though some of the MS. is most perplexing. On Sunday evening I addressed the young men in Dr. Bruce's, but felt no connection with them whatever.

Wednesday evening.—I have been doing examination papers all day almost, and am about sick of young scholars. Guess, then, my delight on getting (quite unexpectedly) your letter.

Does it ever strike you how entirely those old days are gone, the summer evening walks, and the long winter evenings ? How far away all that seems, and what a blind, unfledged, puppy-like life on my part, and on yours how much there was then, as always, of unthanked generosity.

Mrs. Gregor has been here a long time this morning rebuking me for having a headache on Sunday, and telling me in her own way what I told you above, that I am spoiling a preacher. She brought me also a bottle of raspberry vinegar, and three vols. of Robertson's sermons, which cost me 4s. 6d., smuggled from Leipsic.

To A. Taylor Innes

11 CASTLE STREET,
11*th November* 1863.

This is term day, you see, and I am determined it shall be the term of my silence ; besides, personally considered, this day is a kind of holiday with me, which I have celebrated by having a fang extracted and sitting condoling with my own miserable carcase, the facial extremity of which is at present swollen to an indecent size, so I have not been pretending to work. And really my silence is due only to the hurry I have been in lately. Had I been the Siamese twins, or the India-rubber or Corsican brothers, I could have found work for all my hands. What Clark wants me to do in a few weeks, I have calculated should take about six years. Of course, one has always minutes, and half-hours even, but writing to a friend is a business that demands a large sphere of potential vacancy or available leisure, and should be done peacefully, easily, and deliberately, or not at all.

Your last letter was precisely what I needed at the time, only the worst of it is, I cannot follow out your advice. Clark's work eats up my *whole* time, and asks for more, so that I cannot write anything new, but every Sunday am filled with new shame to see some faces that have been present at the same performance before, looking up at me with a mingled expression of real indignation and pretended interest. Dr. Bruce has not preached yet, but expects to do so soon. His elders are nice men, but I am not sure if they know theology, or even spiritual things in a loose way, so well as some of the High men. But —— and —— are no longer High men, which deducts from the theology of the edifice.

There is a general longing for your presence and society in this poor city ; if it affords you any gratification to know it, you are missed. Miss Johnson mourns in the deepest crape, some younger ladies dare only show a lavender-coloured bow, but a lot of young men are proud to show a black ring on the arm, as those that have lost a comrade and a leader. A little detail, therefore, about your life would be acceptable. Are you *reading* law, or making it as you go ? Are you becoming a Glasgow man, walking fast, and always going somewhere, looking sharp and collected ? Do you really teach the Glasgow young men theology, and do you influence the green room in ecclesiastical plays, as you did of yore ? And above all, do you expect ever to be here again ?

At the opening of the College here Davidson made an Introductory full of pretty fancies, and one might almost say rich in gems of thought, not all his own, but finely wrought together.   He showed, as was expected, a decidedly liberal tendency, and yet was guardedly orthodox, without letting it be seen that he was guarded, or careful to conciliate.   He paid a very fine and most heartily received (by the audience) tribute to Duncan.   I fear some, perhaps many, of the students thought Davidson's introduction a better performance than Rainy's, which of course is utterly misjudging the men.

To his sister Marcia

11 CASTLE STREET,
THURSDAY [? 20*th November* 1863].

If letters were to be bought you would get a good one this week, but as they call for time and not money, I fear you stand a bad chance.   I went out to my dinner at 6.30, and thought I would be in in fine time to get a long screed to you, and here it 's past eleven.

On Friday, after posting your letter, I proceeded to Dave a second time, and he fairly ripped up my gum, and made a hole like a coal shaft, and so I could preach on Sunday ; but if they ask me to many more dinners I 'll be done ; but I suppose it 's part of what I 'm paid for.   Isn't it queer ?

I like all you tell me about your doings and feelings, and I have done your commissions, or to be cautious, I should say I have told —— to send your things, so you are sure at least to be charged for them, at least once, so you will have all the feeling of having made a present.

To-morrow is Annie's birthday, and she in the fulness of her heart asked ' all the Hogues,' her Mamma having never been informed of her intention to ask any of them ;

she then told Mima she had asked me to meet her, so she must come.

Clark's work is frightfully on the top of me ; proof is coming in now daily, and MS. in bundles ; and tearing one's hair does not help on the business. I wish you were here to give me a hand. Every now and then there 's an intricate chronological or doctrinal question which takes me a day to examine, and then at the end I find out Lange is right, so all my work goes for nothing, for I can scarcely put a note saying he is all right.

But, by the bye, let me not forget to say that Weisse introduced himself to me in Bruce's lobby the last Sunday, and said you were so nice, and so kind to his children, and that I was ' *a* severe preacher.' What he meant by that I do not exactly know.

To the Same

11 Castle Street,
Edinburgh, end of *November* [1863].

I am almost afraid to begin a big sheet to-night, for though I thought on Sunday and Monday that I was one of the best conditioned of beings, I have got a thoroughly blackguard eye to-night ; so I fear I am still but a whited sepulchre. Where the rottenness is I don't quite know. However, I have got clear of 100 pages of MS. to-day, and have no more on hand, though Clark threatens me with two vols. in the end of the week, which I think will finish me ; so I should be cheery, but it is very slow work, I can tell you, lying on your back in the dark with a cloth to your eye, and nobody to say you 're ill. I do wish you were here ; it 's so different to have a word to say to *anybody*, but to have you, whose every word is light and strength to a man's marrow, is enough to cure any eye or stomach. I often make a little dove's nest in the sunshine, and think how somebody would suit it, but when it comes in the real practical course of things that I want company, it's never anybody but you I want ; and if I had you, anybody else would be mere intrusion.

By the bye, I must make what they call at College 'honourable mention' of your last letter, and do you know, Monday morning is not Saturday night, but there is a sensation about getting your letter then which is not to be despised.   Dr. Chalmers used to maintain a good breakfast was the best thing to begin a day on, but, poor chap, he did not know what a letter from you was.

No bookcase yet, for poor Glen has been fairly doubled up with rheumatism.   The fever ward is so full at the Infirmary that there are beds on the floor, though that is quite contrary to rule.   So Will Jeffrey says ; he is very full of business, you may be sure.

I met —— on the Mound on Monday.   I thought I knew the step, but her mourning and my blindness made me quite uncertain, when lo ! the kind figure stopped, and you may be sure I was not long in getting across the street.   I don't think she is well, and she looks horribly solitary, and just as if she were a mere spectator and had nothing to do with events generally. She read Renan's *Vie de Jésus*, and I am now going to lend her the antidote—a tippy little bit of criticism by Pressensé.   If Wm. Fordyce is reading Renan, or is going to do it, as he most likely will, let me know, and I 'll send him P.   We used to hear him in Paris, and he may take an interest.

I think about Weisse you may dismiss all fear that he will know me 'as your sister.'   Though he is blind, I should think he so far knows our English habits as to understand that females are not allowed to preach statedly.

Thursday, 5 P.M.—Eye no better—old bit in gum
swelling—barometer threatening for Sunday. I have
spent this day in a very promiscuous manner, trying to
vary the thing as much as possible, now writing a tidy
little note to Lange, and again reposing on the sofa
hanging on by my eye, and then walking up and down
trying to make believe green fields and good atmosphere.
I think I 'll be all right to-morrow ; only a whole day in
one room is bad, and not a soul has had compassion on
me.

To the Same

11 CASTLE STREET,
9th December 1863.

Of course I believe you ever my affectionate, and wish
I could say so in the sweet language of the lips and not
with a horrid, sharp steel pen, one of a present which
Jack gave me in the fulness of his heart and pocket.

I think a five or six days' experience in a hotel will be
good for you ; and then what a hotel, do not the waiters
seem still under a mysterious influence, has not the land-
lord an air of dignity, do not the chambermaids know
themselves ennobled ? for in that hotel Stewart and I
slept, or did our best to sleep—double-bedded room
about No. 457.

I should certainly stop, for I have Hanna's new book
to review, and that interminable German. I am just
now at the most difficult part—the plan or idea which
Christ had of His work, and the means of its fulfilment,
including, of course, the whole question of miracles.

Whyte I do not see often, but we are quite as friendly
as ever. Simeon very often comes in the daytime.
Willie Jeffrey and I often have a walk, and esteem one
another highly, though we are quite conscious of the flaws
of our friend. Stewart is in a wretched state of body,

can't look at anything they give him to his dinner—thinks the mutton is still sheep, walking about and tasting of wool.

My bookcase has come, and I at last see a great part of my books set up before me.   Mrs. Archibald is quite satisfied, and I am more than so.   I did not expect Glen to make so handsome a thing.   I am now very glad I chose oak instead of painted wood.

I heard Mrs. Kemble read *Macbeth* on Monday night, and *entre nous* my eyes filled with tears at ' What, all my pretty chickens ? '   It was dreadful the feeling of cruel bereavement she gave you ; fell forward on the desk for some moments.   But what a man William must have been—as you and Carlyle say, the main thing we English have to be proud of.

I do wish you were here.   When I open my eyes to it, it is often dreary, dreary ; but you must often be worse.

To the Same

11 Castle Street,
17*th December* 1863.

How this has come to be Thursday already, I do not know, but certain it is that I have eaten four dinners since Sunday, and on no day have I eaten two.   But if we go on at this pace, time cannot stand it long.

I called for Miss Johnson this week, and tried to give her a little idea of what you are.   I find Innes had been telling her you were much superior to me, but of course, poor fellow, he is not always right in his judgment, and does not know either you or me so well as I do.   She thinks, I believe, not only that Rainy is the best man she knows and the nicest, but also the best possible. She does not say so, but inwardly that is, no doubt, her belief.

The printers have been keeping me hard at work, and now will do so till the book is out ; but it is much lighter to me now that I have a general knowledge of the work, and am accustomed to work for an hour at vol. i. and next hour at vol. iii.

I get more butter than bread just now, or at least more butter than is good for me.   I cannot deny that I have a very different estimate of myself from what I had five years ago, and know that *when* I do not show this, it is only because I wish to be thought modest and simple. But I am not going to run myself down.

Now I must stop, not only because I have nothing to say to you, but because I must have something to give to the greedy little P. D. that comes punctually as breakfast and demands food for the gluttonous press.

Everybody likes the bookcase.

To the Same

11 CASTLE STREET,
31st December 1863.

Here is the last day of this year, and it does seem an incredibly short time since I was writing to you from Newcastle ; but I suppose we are each of us a year older by the almanac, and how much by real growth I would not undertake to say.   To-morrow I hope to be writing a sermon for the first Sunday of the year, so I shall considerately reserve till then all my moralizing.   I feel scarcely up to the rejoicing and hurrahing stage this year, such a lot of things seem to be going wrong ; Willie Jeffrey and two other of my youthful and generally jubilant friends beginning to find that life must be serious frequently, if not sad always.

Lange goes on as usual ; about one-third of it is now off my hands, except correcting proof and a few odds and ends, which a week will finish ; the remainder will, I hope, be easier.

If you could reconcile Matthew, Mark and Luke in the matter of the blind men at Jericho, you would do me a favour. Only, if you find any way of harmonising them, don't tell James D. Fordyce, for he will knock a hole in it at once.

1st January 1864.—And I wish you a very happy new year—the best yet by far—particulars to be filled in by One who does not err.

Simeon came over early to wish me joy of the daylight, and had himself much need to be cheered up. Then Whyte came, and I have been trying to get at something to put in a sermon for them at Dr. Bruce's, and have not been very successful. And now it is nearly time to go to Anne's goose.

To the Same

11 CASTLE STREET,
EDINBURGH, *7th January* 1864.

To-day I have been visiting a lot of Bruce's people— those who have asked me to their houses. There are some nice people among them, but one can't make much of a friendship, hovering about on the outside as I almost must do. If I were to leave Bruce's, a lot of them would of course know me no more, and I do not wish to put either them or myself into an awkward position. I get on very comfortably among them, and so long as there is none of the responsibility, minister's work is very well. I am to breakfast with the young men on Saturday morning.

Markie has made me a present of, I think, the very funniest kitten that ever ran after its own tail ; the states of alarm it puts itself into at a piece of paper, and the manner in which it dances on its hind legs round

about my foot, or rushes up my leg, are as good as five
pantomimes.

Lange goes on at the usual pace, and I wish there
were a succession of Langes to be edited henceforth.
When this one is done, I hope to be prime for a course of
lectures on the Gospels, only there is such a lot of the
most interesting stuff that you cannot put in pulpit
lectures.   There is a good deal of humbug in the book, as
there is in all Germans, I fear, but there is also a vast
deal of good thinking and admirable exposition ; but
I dare say you will be able to write a review of him before
he is out, so I won't bore you.

I have been out a great deal, and have met a great
variety of young persons, but not, so far as I know, my
fate.   Lange and my kitten do just now.

Friday.—I went to Miss Johnson's last night, and
guess what the woman has done !   She has given me
£10, 10s. for the bookcase, for she says she always meant
to do that.   I do not very well know what to do, for she
says (it was by a note she did it) she will be offended if
I refuse, and that it will grieve her very much, and all
that, and the money is very acceptable to me just now,
for I am very low in funds.   Was I right to take it ?

Again I must make a short letter, for the day is far
spent already, and I have a lot more visiting to do,
besides Lange, Lange, Lange, and two preachments on
Sunday.   But mind I love you now as then, and *know*
that the better I grow the more I will love you, and that
is a perennial joy and a lasting refreshment to . . .

To the Same

11 CASTLE STREET,
EDINBURGH, 20th *January* 1864.

The printers are going on at a terrific rate now, and
I can scarcely get anything done but a bare read of the

MS. and the proofs, so that though my name stands as Editor on the title, there is in the body of the book very little sign of anybody but the author. I should have had five years to it, and might then have made something of it. But I dare say people won't expect much.

My kitten continues still to eat me, and has as voracious an appetite for her own tail as ever. At this moment she is engaged curvetting round my toe in the form of a triple arch, into which she erects herself if I dare to make the slightest movement. Of course she scrambles up the bell-pulls, and walks chiefly on the back of the sofa, and is always in the exact place she is not wanted, like all other kittens ; but that keeps me lively, you know.

Thursday evening, 9.—Just in, very tired, but how set up by your letter. I never think anything of your Saturday ones compared to one that pops in incontinent. On those occasions I think the kitten thinks me slightly deranged ; and you know, I have to set her an example in that respect, so I must subdue my feelings.

I have been intending to call on James [1] every hour this week, but I am fearfully run for time, and had to take Dr. Candlish's meeting to-day, and have to preach for Dykes on Saturday and address the children on Monday, and dine with —— on Tuesday, and through all, Lange. However, before me just now lie about 700 printed pages, which, however, is not a third of the whole. I hope a discerning public will consider the rush in which it has been done, and not measure me by it altogether. I send you a prospectus, and if you go to town next week could you mind to show it to J. C. M. [2] and anybody else you think would buy it. You may tell —— that it 's the very book her brother would like for a welcome-home present.

---

[1] James Dingwall Fordyce.
[2] Rev. James Calder Macphail.

Did you get your Diary ? It was a selfish object I
had in view, because I hope to read you off it when you
come here, and see into all the nice secrets you don't
tell me.

To the Same

11 CASTLE STREET,
28th January 1864.

I am more than ever at a loss to know where in the
world the weeks go to, and only perceive that it must be
a place of huge dimensions and appetite. I seem to be
at the beginning of a new letter before you can have read
the last ; and when I sit down to write and look back
for something to say, there seems to be nothing but
Lange. I find myself, too, getting gradually more and
more silent in company, and will shortly be considered
dumb except one day a week, like an intermittent spring.
Would that when I did speak it were at the stirring of
an angel ! This has been my heaviest week of Lange
yet : the nearer the publication it comes the faster they
go ahead. I see more and more that I shall have no
credit by the work ; and people won't consider that
work done so rapidly must be slip-slop.

A great many thanks for your pencil letter, but is it
not taking from somebody else when you send me two
a week ?—though I know no one can get so much good
from your letters as I do, and I need it all. I feel as if
there were a crust growing over mind and soul, and some
foul substance growing from within outwardly to meet it.

Here is Friday afternoon, and I don't know what to
say for sending you such a miserable scrap, but really
my time flies, and this morning half a volume of MS.
is handed in. What a relief the poor translator must
feel it. I wonder if he thinks of me.

I would send you other people's letters if I had any,

but I have not.   I must get on to the next page somehow, for this will never do.   By spacing out like the printers I may manage it ; but you see I won't condescend even to miss a line.

I know this is mean, nefarious, cruel, abominable, but what can I do but sign myself . . .

To the Same

11 CASTLE STREET,
4th February 1864.

What a jolly letter to send me for my abominable little scrap.   I think I shall try again and see if like causes produce like effects ; and I don't think there is more time this week than last.   I am being gradually submerged.

Innes was in yesterday, and I saw him for an hour. Knight dined with me to-day and stayed an hour also, so I have been sociable so far.

The kitten continues as friendly and ferocious ; but the wee beast has both sense and affection.

Augustine has come.   I found he was *almost* a necessity, and I don't think myself extravagant at all.

Saturday ; and I am very vexed there should be no letter for you the first Saturday in Aberdeen, when likely you will not be hearing from any of us.   But then you would not be reading this just now if you had read it on Saturday.   I *could not* get any written yesterday.

I found a long, silky hair in Miss Taylor's [1] MS. yesterday, which was life in the desert.   I had been thinking of her merely as a pen, somewhat ill-mended, when lo ! she springs before me a woman ; and how could I but

_____
[1] One of the translators of Lange.

think of other hairs that used to be found in books ? Pardon.

It is hard frost, and I am frozen from my skin inwards to my life, wherever that is or is not.   All my blood is ice, except in my eyes and the back of my head, where it is fire, and in the ends of my fingers, where it is lead.

To the Same

11 CASTLE STREET,
EDINBURGH, 10th *February* 1864.

To show you that I have at least no wish nor intention to play you false this week again, I begin to write on Wednesday, though I do not seem to have much more time than before.   I hope now to have the first three volumes of Lange off my hands by the first week of next month ; the others will not take me by any means so long.   It is quite time I was through them, for it is very unpleasant preaching old sermons always, and seeing Mr. Maxwell and Mr. Aitken hearing them for the third time.   I expect to do great things, of course, in the way of sermon-writing, as soon as I get clear.

Dr. Bruce is not much better this week, so I fear I may have the whole again on Sunday, which is not by any means good for me.   He looks very old when he is ill.   I am getting to know a number of his people, and like them well.   Only they dine horribly late.   To-night I am going out at 6.30 ; as if that was the way to treat a guest.

10.15.—Home from dinner ; very thankful that I have you to write to, but not over thankful that I have to write to you.   I think it shabby of these people asking me, and letting me meet only married couples.   I never meet the attractive young females one sees in the streets. Where they live I can't make out, but I suppose it is better I don't meet them.

Z

Now I must have an hour or two at Lange, so good-night, my darling darling (as the girl in *Punch* says), and believe there is nobody in the world so dear as you are to . . .

PS.—My volume [1] has begun to pay Maclaren now, so I intend offering him the copyright for £30. I think that will be fair to us both—or it may be easier for him to give me £10 of books and promise me £20.

To the Same

11 CASTLE STREET,
EDINBURGH, 16*th February* 1864.

I write to you for a few minutes just now, because I am bad and wretched, bad and wretched, but especially bad. Into particulars I shall not enter, but the world is too many for me, and I am thinking of a monastery ; only it 's not easy getting into a mediæval monastery at the present day, and I suppose the Benedictines had their fits too, when they stopped editing that dear old soul Augustine. The world owes a deal to *him*, first and last. To do his work, and be as little elated by it as he, is to be a great man indeed. But is it not more difficult to be a little man ? I mean that it 's more difficult to be a great little man, *i.e.* a good little man, for to be a little little man comes wonderfully natural to some people. If it were not for Lange just now, I think I should be mad, or else I should have committed some crime and gone beyond seas. How particularly easy it seems at times to go to the bad. Do you think a man can from a vain person become humble, from light serious, and how ? All that I seem to be able to do is to keep myself out of the way till all this world be past, that is, to get so immersed in work as not to have time to be bad.

[1] *The Prayer that Teaches to Pray.*

How I have longed for you the last week : it is horrid desolate coming into this lonely room with no voice nor ear. My kitten is real company ; she always wakens up when she hears me at the door, and comes frisking and frolicking about my legs when I come in, and then scrambles up and licks my chin. If she were anything but a cat, I would say she was fond of me.

I tried to rouse myself to-day by going and calling for Mrs. ——. (Peter complained greatly of my taciturnity, and I have felt it most offensive myself. When I go out or meet people on the street, I can just look at them unless they talk theology.) But the recipe did not work ; I could not speak, and hobbled out of the room, and out of the house, as if I had committed an indiscretion, whereas it was only a pastoral visit. When Lange is done, I must take a course of newspapers, novels and flirtation.

Poor Dr. Bruce has lost his sister, who has been his stay all his life—partner in all his sorrows and joys. I don't know how ever he will get on now, poor soul. Her funeral is on Thursday. I had, of course, both services on Sunday, which was too much, only I am finding it easier to preach in Bruce's. A number attend *well*, and seem to want me to improve, as if they took an interest in me.

Wednesday.—It is a day since I wrote these last words, and nothing has transpired. I have called on no one, and no one has called on me. And Lange is still the chorus to everything ; the *burden* of my life at present he certainly is.

Dave has got a house, top of Dundas Street and Abercromby Place. He is in high spirits—not excited by any means, nor even talkative, but just apparently in the belief that some people have been rather hard on the world, and misrepresented it. He continues to go round the terraces every evening, and takes a warm bath on Fridays.

Lo ! here enters a letter, and the very stunningest. I laughed so at it, that the kitten arose from slumber, and looked anxiously into my face, but seeing I was not going to go quite yet, lay down on her other side purring, and that 's quite my sentiments.

To the Same

11 CASTLE STREET,
February 1864.

As I seem to have a great deal to tell you, I begin my letter early. Well, to begin where I left off, viz., at the reception of your letter, I went in the strength of it against the heretics in Lange, and then issued forth to get orders from Dr. Bruce for Sunday. I met sunshine on the road in the shape of Ailie, who surely is about the neatest little woman, especially with her muff. I spoke to her, and got more refreshment. I think some of her ancestors must have been a singing bird, she is so easy and happy ; but she also, I dare say, has her fits and her pits. May she get well out of them all ! If I could get past Ailie, I would be at Bruce's, who was, poor man, very dull ; however, I got my orders to preach all day.

To-day I met ——, and could have kissed her in the Queen's Highway, she looked so like her old self, little, round, and happy. I don't know when the sight of a person so elated me. I wish *we* could have a quiet evening of —— and her here once more. These old days look very nice when one only looks at the good of them. It comes to me over and over again as a most refreshing thought that there are such people in the world, that these are the people one is living alongside of, and will live alongside of. I don't know who was with her— she had one on each side of her—but the honest, happy, laughing face was all I saw, and most decidedly what I took off my hat to.

This week sometime I am to get my preface done, but have nothing to say, really nothing, and Clark wants me to write twenty pages, which is impossible. After that, one or two days will take me clear away from the first three vols., and it's quite time, for this preaching twice is running both my sermons and my strength uncommon low. I am feeling, too, distinctly, as I said before, the effects of living alone, and most painfully—not *at all* now in the way of low spirits, but very much in selfish ways, and a ferocious and altogether intolerable way of thinking of myself and of others.

Thursday evening.—I have been toiling at that preface, and am making about the dullest thing of it I ever wrote, and that's saying a good deal. I am very vexed about this, but cannot make it better, and will have the pleasure of seeing the six pretty volumes always weighed down with a great, stupid clod at the beginning.

I would give a great deal for an hour just now of anybody one could be confidential with and utterly repose in. But I must not open this tap, or I'm done; so let me choke it by telling you I had Candlish's prayer-meeting to-day and was not successful therein; and find so much joy in nothing as in being yours, yours through all folly and emptiness and dullness and selfishness . . .

To the Same

11 CASTLE STREET,
8th March 1864.

Old Anthony might have objections to your manse scheme. All I have to say on it is that some manses are worse furnished. I live in hopes that the inexpressive will yet be thrown in my way, or that some **extra**-ordinary circumstances will show me what I am not

seeing in some nymph of my acquaintance. If desolation
could make any one fall in love, I should be in that
elegant predicament.

Clark has settled up handsome, giving me £100, so
if you want anything, a new riding horse, etc., now is
your time.

Here is Thursday, and I have just received your very,
very, very nice letter. I can't express to you how I feel
towards you when I get your letters. You don't dislike
me telling you how well I like you, do you ? Surely you
can't, for it seems so natural just to say so again and
again, to sit down and tell you in each letter that you are
the best and nicest creature on earth, so far as I know
or can imagine. All these interesting young women we
speak of don't all of them together occupy one-tenth
of the place you do ; they will need to grow immensely
if ever I am to like any of them as well as I like you, and
it 's pleasant to know that even should that happen, it
won't be in the way of rivalry.

What nice letters Mary writes. She is a sister worth
while, isn't she ? Speaking of her makes me think of
a great number of special providences I have noticed in
connection with Lange. Things I would have omitted
noticing have quite accidentally been suggested to me,
and I have heard of books in a quite casual way that have
become most useful. And to-day, most extraordinary
of all, I went to the University to read three quartos
which could not be had anywhere else, and I was sitting
down to them, feeling that I could not read a thirtieth
part of what I ought, when a fellow I have only *once*
spoken to came up and offered to get them out for me,
so that I have got them here by me for weeks. I knew
the fellow so little that I could not name him till after
he was away. But this may not be so interesting to you
as it has been useful to me.

To the Same

11 CASTLE STREET,
25th March 1864.

You are aware that my temper is under no circumstances altogether of the sweetest, but really to-day it has been severely tried. I arose to what I reckoned on being a nice day's work, and a letter to you at the end of it as a reward, when lo ! I was speedily reminded it was a public holiday, which is another name for a private nuisance, by the incursion of two nephews. I was settling down again after them when in came —— ; just as he was going away, ——, who sat an interminable time ; so I have got nothing done.

Your letter came last night, and was supremely restorative. Also Andie came, which, to one looking at things from an Edinburgh point of view, would seem an additional inducement to you to write. Of course, if you send any amount of messages to her, I'll see that they are safely delivered.

The first three vols. of Lange are out, not much to my satisfaction, nor, as I think will soon be seen, much to my credit ; a good deal, however, to my own personal advantage, as if I get any people to let off to, I shall be at no loss for something to say to them, at least for a time.

To-morrow I am to meet Innes at dinner, in Glasgow, where I am going to preach in his church.[1] I think this must and ought to be the last time I shall ever preach as a candidate. It passes in course of time from a humiliating to a mean and childish business.

I *am* in love, but it is not dangerous, severely wounded, but doing well—and you are the party.

Now I must be done, though this is scandalous, but really it is not my fault, but my very great misfortune.

[1] Renfield.

To the Same

11 CASTLE STREET,
EDINBURGH [*29th March* 1864].

This note [1] is all I can tell you about the result of the Glasgow business. I went unwell, and on Saturday night woke to the consciousness of an inflamed eye and a stomach most wretched, and toothache, and rottenness in all my bones ; so that when I entered the pulpit I felt as if I were not there, but in that dismal wilderness and solitude that a bad cold sends you to. I *could* not get up the least animation, and had a very heavy sermon.

Mr. Lawson, with whom I stayed, was very kind—so Mrs., who is sister to Hogg of Coldstream, and Miss M'Intyre was staying there, and Innes and his sister were at dinner, so I was quite at home.

Innes was very kind, and would like me to come, only it 's a great big church, and might kill me off quick. However, I must not be writing now, or there will be nothing to say on Saturday.

To the Same

11 CASTLE STREET,
Æt. 30 years and 4 days.
[*15th April* 1864.]

What the Renfield matter may come to I don't know ; but for Innes and Lawson's sake I hope the people may at least be made to understand that their candidate was in some measure worthy of them. For myself, of course, I am so very comfortable here that any removal would have much of the nature of trial in it, and I am such a brute—such a vile piece—that I don't know how in the world I could stand ordination. Sometimes I fear some

[1] The letter begins on the back of one from the Clerk of the Renfield Session.

awful thing would happen, at least that I would take very ill, or lose my voice, or something that would incapacitate me from speaking.

I do not know a more lovely album than the one you have given me ; it is perfect. Stewart at once approved, as also of Andie's photographs. I like Mima and him both better for their kind way with Andie ; they treat her better than I myself do. The book I gave her was *Illustrations of the Ancient Mariner*, by Noel Paton, very beautiful, price £1, 1s., but don't tell anybody ; it is quite worth it to her—would be so indeed to me. I wish I could have got one for you and another for ——, who would appreciate.

Andie did not go till Wednesday morning. I don't know that she enjoyed her visit much. I was horrid to her, and am generally to everybody something unutterably abominable. But I dare say she would not see it ; you women seem to like people so blindly, and so unselfishly.

Mrs. Fordyce's present, of course, was intended to signify that I should read more new books, and so I have been obliged, alas ! to be a little extravagant in providing food for the pretty knife. It *is* very pretty, but will never be so dear as the album.

To the Same

11 CASTLE STREET,
EDINBURGH, 18*th April* [1864].

I have somewhat to tell you, for Peter has been here, the genuine, identical Peter, and so I spent Friday evening with him and alas ! fifty others at 9 So. Gray Street. However, we walked about till two in the morning. He says he has been very dull this winter—I suppose with being alone.

On Saturday I had a call from Rainy about the Glasgow

business; I almost wish they would give me up, for yesterday I preached twice and my chest was very sore all evening, and their church is certainly twice as hard to preach in as Bruce's. I am sorry for them, specially Innes and Lawson; for myself I can't say I care at all about it. At least, I only get up some anxiety by considering that it is my duty to be very much interested. I wrote the Committee a *stern* letter.

I hear your fellow-townsman, Dr. David Brown, has been uttering *Good Words* about my share in Lange, so kiss your hand to him if you see him.

I finish Lange to-day, and go away to Glencairn to-morrow, and on Monday think of returning by Anick, staying a day there, which will set me up again. And now it is Friday, so I must stop.

To the Same

11 CASTLE STREET,
EDINBURGH, *2nd May* [1864].

I have had kind notes from a lot of people congratulating me, and I do wish they would stop, for each makes me feel duller than the last, and sometimes I am very miserable. I should never have lived alone. I think that is at the bottom of it, and if I had any one now that I really loved, I would marry next week. I think I will ask Andie to come and be with me in Glasgow, though I am not sure about this, for it might injure her health again, and besides she seems to be taking pretty good root at Hexham, so I suppose I must just fight away alone yet and endure all the nervousness and selfishness of it. No one can conceive how insidiously and certainly solitude wears one down, till they have experienced it. Two nights last week I had just to go and sit at Torphichen Street; but don't you be telling this of me, for perhaps I shall be better if I was healthy in body.

I don't know how long the Presbytery may take to conclude the Renfield business, but I believe the congregation are very anxious to have it over speedily. I do hope they won't make any humbugging soirée or dinner, but let me begin quietly and decently.

PS.—Oh for a rural district—a sensible wife—and a sane mind in a sane body—and enough work to give me a headache once a year !

To the Same

11 CASTLE STREET,
EDINBURGH, 13th May [1864].

This letter must be about as short as yours for three good reasons : (1) It is Friday, the day of preparation ; (2) it is a day following a barren week ; and (3) I am in a frightful state of E. wind.

I seem to have nothing at all to say to you, only that the harmony committee has met the congregation, and several have expressed their concurrence with the majority, so that it is supposed that on Monday the Presbytery will appoint a day for moderating in the call, which, however, will not, I fancy, be done till after the Assembly ; then about a month will elapse, I presume, before they ordain. Isn't it a pity things can't be done quietly, and without fuss and a public ?

Innes has promised to spend Sunday with me, and I do wish you were here to help me to entertain him and say how good he has been.

But the wind continues steady in the N.E., so goodbye ; and when you write a book on human sadness send for a chapter on East winds to one who knows something about them, and who would like to have a smash at them, to wit . . .

To the Same

11 CASTLE STREET,
EDINBURGH, WEDNESDAY [18*th May* 1864].

Of Innes' visit—it was quite as nice as I expected. Both Saturday and Sunday evenings we had great talks of all things and persons under heaven, and some above. I wish you had been here, very much. I could not help saying so to him, and I think he thought this was a considerably duller habitation than it used to be. We got nearer one another than ever before, mainly, I think, because he had been at Sandeman's marriage, and opened the subject of matrimony ; in regard to which both of us are found in the same predicament, angry at ourselves that we cannot fall in love, but believing as part of our Providence theory that there is our woman somewhere, and that if we wait, we may yet fall in love ; certainly, that whatever else is an antecedent to matrimony love ought to be, and that we being little over thirty have no right to jump into matrimony hastily, and without nature's invitation *in full* being forwarded to us. It was very fine to hear the grim lawyer talking sentiment, and he did it with wonderful good grace.

Of my preaching, and how it might be mended, he had much to say, which I need not record : a good deal of philosophy was tacked on to this part of the evening. Then of Renfield prospects he is sanguine, though the Presbytery's meeting on Monday last has not been altogether so favourable as he seemed to be expecting. One or two members are determined to keep the Presbytery to the strict law of the Church, which is that the call shall not be sustained except it be signed by a majority of those on the communicants' roll. This I doubt they may not get, as only 124 have declared for me and 402 are on the roll. Howsomedever——

To the Same

ANICK GRANGE,
HEXHAM, *25th May* [1864].

I never felt so little set up by this place, and fear that it also has lost its influence upon me ; but another week may work wonders. If I am to be no better than this all my days, it is useless my thinking of anything but some pottering little charge in a very remote and rural district.

Since coming here I have done nothing worth mentioning—indeed nothing I can remember except reading *Esmond* and dipping here and there into *Pendennis* ; and I admire Thackeray more. I find that is the case with most of my reading ; I am slow to take up or take in at the first reading, and need to come back and reflect before I see what other people seem to see at first sight.

I intend going down to Peter on this day (Wednesday) week, staying over Thursday with him, and going back to Edinburgh on Friday to my books, which I find make home to me ; so see and have a comfortable letter on Saturday, or Friday if you like.

I am heartily glad I am away from that Assembly. How abhorrent it is to my soul, and how stupid, stupid, mean, affected, and altogether an ass I was to be a minister at all. I don't know one part of the business I care for except writing sermons, which I can't do, and the nearer I get to a settlement the more, of course, do I long for something else to turn up—some honourable back-door by which I could escape to congenial labour in which I would not need to put on and pretend until I don't know what in me is real and what not.

I have had no letters but yours since I came here, and have scarcely had one idea either original or contributed, and am as if I were dead and everything else dead, or at least as if I were deaf and dumb, not only in outward sense but in soul.   But what possible use it can be writing you a letter like this I don't know.

To the Same

11 C<small>ASTLE</small> S<small>TREET</small>,
E<small>DINBURGH</small>, *5th June* 1864.

This is not my weekly missive, but only an interjection of thanks for your very delicious letter, which was company to me when I came home on Friday evening to a cleaned and frightfully tidy room.   My holiday has not done me the good I expected.   I am still very uncomfortable in body, and never was so unfit for work.   I can't find anything interesting, nor, I may say, any person.   I have often been disinclined to work, but was never so disinclined at once to work and to play. It is all one whether I sit here and mope, or go along to Torphichen Street and make myself disagreeable; and I seem to be years away from 65 and everything else that used to revive me.   I am sure people were never kinder to me, but I think it is just the effect of living alone with no one to think of but self, and no one to share joys and sorrows with.

The St. Andrew's people have made me a most undeserved and handsome gift—£55—which oppresses me as if it were laid in coppers on the top of my head.   I do respect and like the people very much, but am too much in fear of them to work altogether well for them. Dr. Bruce is very well, and says that though he will always be a minim (he hopes not a crotchet), he is becoming a man of weight.   I think I never heard a more thoroughly satisfactory service than his yesterday morning's.   I have heard abler sermons often, but the whole thing was so much what a diet of Christian worship ought to be.

You see I am staving off saying anything about Peter ;
he is certainly the person who sets me on my mental legs
with greatest readiness ; his presence makes me a different kind of being, and while he does not infuse so much
good into me as you do, the strength he gives is almost
as much.   He fits me.   I had two days with him, during
which he photographed me twenty-four times, most of
them very successful, but when the prints may be published I know not.   We had a great deal of discussion and
talk, and friendly interchange of ideas, so that I wished
myself a tea-dealer, and the ' Co.' of P. M. & Co., and
sharing his house ; only that, too, would no doubt have
its bane.   He is reforming his wicked practice of sitting
up at night, and now goes to bed about two or three.
There is something very genuine about him, and unselfish,
reasonable and generous.

To the Same

11 CASTLE STREET,
EDINBURGH, *9th June* 1864.

I am just home from Glasgow, very tired and somewhat
wet, and it is 10.30, but I want before going to bed to let
you know that the Renfield matter is settled at last.
The Presbytery have sustained, and I have accepted, the
call.   It was signed by 240 members, there being only
about 400 on the roll.   They are to give me £400 a year,
and I wish they could give me a new inside and a new
spirit.   Surely I shall learn to pray now ; and yet what
can one trust about the future ?

I am filled with all manner of dubitations about the
work, and find the only way to get peace of mind is to
shut my eyes to the whole affair.

Concerning the less important matter of housekeeping,
do you think I should take a small house and furnish a

sitting-room and two bedrooms, or go into lodgings ?
And when are you to have your holidays ?   Because to
have you with me when I begin (first week of August)
would make it all quite another thing to me.   And what
should I do with myself for the month of July ?   If you
have your holidays then, and go to Anick or Glenluce,
I would, of course, go too.   I would very much like to
go some new place, but to go alone is useless.

By the bye, I have great news about Stewart.   He has
got a great step in the Bank, but not to be confirmed for
six months.   You are not to speak of it just now, but he
thinks it pretty certain it will end in his being manager
of the Glasgow office, which is nearly equal to being
manager here—not in salary, but in importance.   He
is to go to Glasgow now, so that we may still have one
another to growl to ; but is not it rum and rare ?

To the Same

11 Castle Street,
Edinburgh, 16th June [1864].

I think, my dearest Marsh, that the world is being
turned upside down, or going through some other equally
precarious process.   Every arrangement I make is
knocked on the head, and all my forenoons are spent in
writing letters countermanding what I had the day before
besought.   No sooner do I secure a man to preach for me,
than I get a letter from Glasgow telling me that day is
already supplied, etc., etc.   Your letters breathe a
temporary peace on these troubles, and I wish I could
communicate to you half the pleasure you give to me
by each of your epistles.

I enclose for inspection and *immediate* return Peter
and Innes, whose initials, A I, do record in shipping
terminology his true character.   Isn't he handsome ?

Simeon and Whyte have given me a very valuable book—Howe's Works, which is about the finest I have. Also Miss Wright, the lady who gave me £5, has given me six pairs of *bands* and twelve cambric handkerchiefs, which is very nice of her.

I am not distressing myself with sermons. Last Sunday I preached my last in Bruce's, and next Sunday I preach in Tasker's, which is *Finis* here. I don't know yet when the ordination is to be, but I wish it and the succeeding month were over. I am rather afraid of going to begin there living alone, and do not know what to do about it. Only it may perhaps not be so bad when I am hard worked.

I hope to spend a fortnight at Glenluce, which will be very jolly ; but I 'll need to preach, and also to get up my first sermon for Renfield. Is there no word of your holidays yet ? It would be sublime if I could get you at Glenluce or Anick. You must, at any rate, make up your mind to spend part of them in Glasgow.

To the Same

11 CASTLE STREET,
EDINBURGH, 21*st June* [1864].

I write you to-day because I see no prospect of having a place to rest my paper on for some days to come. To-morrow I have to be at the funeral of Prof. Miller, a duty which is every way very painful. He makes a very perceptible hole here—only 52. He might have been of use and available for all good for thirty years more, and in thirty years his own children will only at times have him in their thoughts. In Dr. Bruce's congregation he makes a sad blank : the two elders who died in the beginning of the year were men of almost equal worth, and poor Dr. Bruce is very much cut up about it.

To-morrow I have, besides, a lot of odds and ends to

2 A

clear off before leaving on Thursday morning, as I intend doing, to compear before the Glasgow Presbytery and be tried for ordination. Then I expect to stay in Glasgow till Saturday to see about lodgings or a house, and on Sunday preach for Cunningham, and proceed to Glenluce next day. So please write to me there.

To the Same

GLENLUCE,
28th June 1864.

I wanted to write to you at Lochwinnoch on Sunday, where I was all alone in the evening, after preaching twice and taking Mrs. Cunningham's class ; but I was aware of a disposition to read Greek Test., and I have a kind of rule (which I follow once in a dozen times) to follow an inclination of the kind when it comes, so I did. It was rather a slow evening, though it was country, and Sunday after work, and Greek Test. I could not take it in, somehow.

I got here yesterday at four, and found nobody in, but a host outside, as it was Sarah's birthday (7), and she had a lot of small friends. I knew the two nieces at once, and very nice little girls they are, I think ; Sarah a good deal like you, surely, and Mary a very winning little thing ; but you know all about them. Mary senior is looking lovely, and I think I'd be game for Glasgow had I a body like hers. And what a life surely she is leading ; good seems to run out from her perpetually. Surely the small people should be much the better of it, and be able to do good abundantly to others.

But I have all about Glasgow to tell you, by the bye. First, I went to the Presbytery and got tried. If you ever become a Presbyter, don't ask a fellow the difference between Justification and Sanctification. Fancy such a question to ask a Scotch youth ! A *nice* question in

Church History which every Presbytery seems to ask every man that appears for licence or ordination, is 'When was the Council of Nice ? ' However, I was passed, and then went with Innes and heard Candlish open a church. I thought the sermon dry, and said so. Innes slept, and said he liked the sermon. We both liked the dinner that Howie gave after it. Dr. Henderson and Dr. Candlish were both there. The former is a very delightful person, one of those people that keep an atmosphere of health and brightness all round them. I sat looking at his face, and it is one of the nicest things in Glasgow.

At night I went home with Innes, feeling very fondly to him. At ten I went out with him to seek for my abode, and lo ! I had the wrong number, so we had to go back to his place for a directory, where also they were not, and finally, after a long search we found them, not too late for Miss Maclagan to spring to me as if she were three generations younger and I her lover, nor too dark, though it was dark, for her to see a strong resemblance to Papa ; so you see she has originality. She was *very* kind, and again I say there is nothing like hereditary friendships. She is also of good mental gift, so that I think she will be a very useful and pleasant friend. They could break the windows of Renfield Church from their dining-room, but are not members of it.

On Friday I went house-hunting with indifferent success, but I see that I can get one, which is always so far good. Every one seems to think it better to set up house at once, and I don't see how I could do in lodgings.

To the Same

11 Castle Street,
Friday Night [22nd July 1864].

I am much vexed that I can only send you a line the very week I should have wished to write most fully, but I am sitting here in the midst of packing-boxes and matting, and am wearied with a very hard day's work. On Tuesday I got to Glasgow from Glenluce, parting with much reluctance from them all, and Wednesday I employed hunting for a house, which resulted in my taking No. 6 Clifton Place, a flat two stairs up with large attics. I hope it will do, but of course house agents do not tell you whether their houses smoke or are given to any other vice. Also I have gone into furnishings at a great rate, and will almost be stocked before Mary arrives. Last night late I got here, and to-day have got everything under nail and rope, and am now fit only for bed.

Innes and I dined with Stewart on Wednesday, who entertained us regally in swell lodgings he has taken. He thinks of taking a house, but has not made up his mind. The more I thought of the thing, the more I saw it would not do for me to go into lodgings ; and I hope I may not have done something very stupid, for people have left me very much to my own devices. Buying a kitchen range I felt very much in need of Mary. Choosing a study carpet I felt much in want of you. Miss Maclagan has been very kind and helped me much.

APPENDIX

THE DIARY

[EDITOR'S NOTE.—One small volume of less than 150 pages sufficed to contain the journal of this writer for a period of fifteen years, and of these pages only about a third were used for daily entries in the manner contemplated by the designer of the diary. Begun in August 1857 it was kept only intermittently from the first, though occasionally a number of past weeks or months were collected and summarised in an entry of a reflective kind. The Newcastle periods are both characterised by notes as to pastoral visits and particulars as to his 'patients,' and jottings about books read and writing done. After the call to Renfield there is little but lists of books read or reviewed, many of them with brief comments attached. The Diary has an appendix designed to receive notes on books and general reflections, and this has been to some extent filled in the manner intended. These latter entries are of course undated, but the apparent age of the handwriting, together with various items of internal evidence, make it safe to ascribe almost, if not quite, all of those quoted to the period with which this volume deals.

The title-page of the 'Journal' is reproduced in facsimile. The first extract is printed as a specimen page of the daily entries of the New College student at a time when his private reading was in full swing. It shows the occupation of the four days 17th to 20th August 1857.

But as those days are in the depths of the summer vacation, a more normal day is added (in its chronological place) from the following autumn, 10th November, in which he gives a statement of his College classes and the teaching work by which he supported himself. The other complete page, 12th to 15th March 1860, is reproduced in order to illustrate in like manner the employments of the probationer. The remaining entries are those which have been deemed illustrative of his manner of life and thought, and include, in fact, nearly all the longer passages which occur throughout the volume.]

Work ye manful while ye may
work for God in this your day
Night must stop you rich or poor
Godly deeds alone endure

THE JOURNAL.

Nulla dies sine lineâ.

If one could take note of the real mental
progress made it wd be more to the purpose

Fast life's sands are going
  Sparkling as they run
And for ever shewing
  That ere setting sun
Much we have to do
  And much to be undone

Cogita si esse velis.

4   17th *Day of* August [1857]

MONDAY.	6.30-7.30 Hebrew. Deut. xi.
	9-10 Murray began History of Rome (Chepmell).
	10.30-12.30 Finished the reading of Wiggers, and read Turretin
	        viii. 1.
	        [N.B. Read to-morrow Tur. vi. 6, ix. 7, and x. 2.]
	    -3 Sophocles, Grammar of—Gibbon cap. vi. (Gallienus-
	        Carinus).
	    — Shakspere's *Rich. III.*
	    -10.30 With J. C. S. Cemetery — Trinity — Graham's
	        verses.

TUESDAY.	-9.30 Hebrew. Deut. xii. with LXX.
	-10 Hagenbach, Pelagian points.
	10-1 Murray—Portobello.
	1-2.30 Turretin vi. 6, ix. 7, x. 2. De concursu Dei. A1.
	        De causa lapsus, not so satisfactory, & De necessitate
	        libertati repugnante, A1.
	After dinner. Gibbon cap. vii. (Diocletian, Maximian and colleagues).
	-6 Grammar of N.T. in Winer and Stuart.
	6-6.30 Shakspere's *Rich. III.*
	— At the Robertson's met 2 Sardinians—my French lame.

WEDNESDAY.	SLEPT IN. A few verses of Deut.
	9-11 Wrote some remarks on the primitive State. Reading
	        Burnet. For Burnet's own sentiments v. preface
	        to XXXIX Articles.
	11-1 Murray Portobello—1st Punic War.
	1-2 Sophocles O.C. for Grammar—ll. 130-230.
	After dinner. Gibbon cap. viii. (Constantine), looked over former caps.
	        Finished *Rich. III.*
	4-6 Exeg. Titling Matt. and Mark. Stuart's Grammar.
	        Out—wrote to M. and M.
	9-11 Reuss 2 §.

THURSDAY.	7-8 Hebrew and LXX. Deut. xiii. 9-11 Tried to write something on the Fall and failed. 11-1 Murray. 1-2 Sophocles 230-340 with Gram.—Wunder's notes. After dinner. Gibbon cap. ix., & Turretin on the Fall, but am no further on. -7 Reuss 2 §. At 65. 10.30- N.T. Mk.

[The references to Gibbon are to Dr. Smith's *The Student's Gibbon.*]

November 1857.

During October prepared for the Presbytery Calvin iv. i. ii. (and for my own behoof read iii. viii. ix.) Hebrew Psalms 1-6, etc., etc. Gaussen's *Inspiration*—Owen on Spiritual Mindedness—Ezra—Neh.—Haggai—Zechariah—Malachi—Romans—1 and 2 Tim.—Titus—Galatians—*Life of Burke*—a little of Reuss—Locke on Toleration—Pope—Finished Lowth's Lectures.

10th November 1857.

TUESDAY.	Invariable employ^t 8.45-11.45. P. Murray, for India.
	   12-1 Smeaton's Class.
	   1-2 Bannerman's Class.
	   4-5 Dundas. 7-8 Fordyce.
	
	7.30-8.30 Proverbs and breakfast.
	2.30-4 Augustin—very little.
	   5-6 Reuss on Paul. 6-7 Hebrew Gen. vii.
	   8-9 at 65.
	   10-1 Fairbairn—and wrote to John.

12th November 1857.

It is humiliating to feel that the mind is relieved by discovering that many of those predictions which it has been accustomed to dread as pain to the flesh are *only* to be spiritual punishments.

14 October 1858.   Edinr., 2 Alva Street.

During June and July I was occupied chiefly in writing discourses for the Presbytery. (Latin Ex.—Homily—Lecture—Sermon and Exegesis.)

During August and September I was away from home preaching at Flisk (4 Sabbaths), Hexham, Mordington—and for Mr. Martin.   Wrote 2 Sermons at Flisk and read some German (Schleiermacher), also Spencer's *Pastor's Sketches*, some of South's *Sermons*, etc.   At Hexham I read more German—*Vicar of Wakefield—Alton Locke—Life of Howard* with intense admiration.

Since coming home I have written a lecture on the martyrdom of Stephen, and hope to finish to-day a sermon on Job xlii. 5 and 6 (was licensed on the 7th by Dr. Clason), read Arthur's *Tongue of Fire*, which might be more calm (and perhaps more discriminating ?), some of Traill's *Sermons*, which deserve all the praise they have got, some Gibbon and Neander (also a good deal for me of Hebrew, Psalms).

As books from which I have derived the most conscious benefit during this summer remember Witherspoon on Regeneration—Calvin's *Inst.*—Edwards on the Affections—Neander's *Ch. History*—and always Owen and Bengel, Pearson and Burnet.

I observe a change in my reading which I hope is for the better—I rather go back to my old friends than take up with new ones, so that most of my books are becoming books of reference. This is probably owing to my being now obliged to write more and therefore to draw upon what I have already (though only partially) acquired. There are books which we can never exhaust, and which yield the more the more we draw : such are Milton, Bacon, Foster, Calvin, Augustine, and many more.

28th November 1858.   Newcastle.

Visited Deans (crushed by a boiler, and has lain for 13 weeks unable to move) and to-day found him dead. His widow has great hope, but is herself very ignorant.

Read Calv. *Inst.*, De Crucis Tolerantia.

Require to be more serious—where is the time for frivolity when men are dying around me without the knowledge of God ?—more conscious of the presence of God and more continually in communion with Christ, more devoted, *i.e.* habitually to feel that I am not my own—to deny myself. Would I be my own at any price ? Then let me definitely consider myself another's. God is desirous of accomplishing a great work, and asks me to be an instrument—marvel of condescending grace—yet how do I respond—by working with my own aims for myself, or refusing to work at all.

6th December 1858.

Attend more to words—here is a word I have never used—is the idea expressed one that I have never entertained ?

Good—is that which satisfies. God pronounced His works good— they satisfied Him—His intention and contemplation.

11th December 1858.

Step 1st at Newcastle—Self-surrender.

Step 2nd, Be objective—(Mr. M. said of sermons—I would have it in everything).

? Early in 1860.

Things that ought to be done—
  Visit 4 hours in an active aggressive way.
  Hebrew and Greek Exegesis.
  Church history with theol.
  Reading the fathers, classics and moderns.
  Writing sermons.
How much of this can be done ?

9th February 1860.

Last night heard that I am not to go to Dalkeith ; so here I am, dissatisfied with my present work and yet without prospects of anything else. Yet I am not in grief at this disappointment, for though Dalkeith is the only place I ever felt any strong desire to settle in, my prayer has been that if unfit for it I should not be chosen. My hope of getting a congregation in the ordinary way is small ; I have learnt that whatever qualities I have they are not those that at once secure the esteem of a number of people, and so far as I know there is a want of sustained life and vigour in me that disables me from doing much good to men by personal contact with them. But then what am I good for, must I not be content to do the work in a way very very far from perfect because I have not the ability to stand in the first or second rank?

This hanging off and on, frittering away one's life in week-lengths, teaches this very forcibly, that I am in this world not to be a professional man, but a man—so that I am to remember that success in one line is not the standard of success in life.

8th March 1860.

This morning the Revd. Mr. Davidson of Lady Glenorchy's called and told me that his people are desirous (*though not enthusiastically*) to have my services as assistant. Their fault with me is my cold manner. Every one advises me to give up reading—and I dare say it is pride that keeps me from doing so—fear of delivering a worse sermon than I had prepared. However, here I am with work before me for at least a few months, I hope, and I bid farewell to my old work not without compunctions, and in order that I may not have the same compunctions at the end of this new work, or most terrible of all, at the end of my whole earthly work, let me not be afraid to look my sins in the face.

(1) I have not depended as I ought on the guidance, help, and blessing of God—I have not been *instant* in prayer; let me then set apart some definite time to bring in detail before God the work He has given me, and to lay the burden of it on Him. Why is time given us in distinct portions if not to help us through calling us to remembrance?

(2) I have not considered myself so entirely the servant of the people as I ought, δοῦλος αὐτῶν διὰ Ἰησοῦν. And to bring me to a right mind in this, nothing but the Spirit's direct influence is sufficient. May I have tender and wise and constant love for those among whom I am now to labour. May I seek not my own things but the things of Christ.

(3) I have not been aggressive enough, have feared to offend people and so lose their love, and so have let slip good opportunities—*opportunities that may have been given me for the saving of souls.*

Besides these things I have been *physically and mentally indolent*—lazy to go to bed at the proper time, lazy to leave it at the proper hour, and so things have got out of joint. I have studied, but not with that power that system gives, and much has been lost by being broken up into little bits separated by long intervals of time. The moral effects of this desultory laziness have been visible also. Let me note this with shame, and such a shame may God grant me as shall keep this sin and its vile accompaniments odious to my soul. I find a growing indisposition for work I don't like.

At the root of all shortcomings throughout the past nine months lies selfishness, the worst foundation for the life of a δοῦλος. With how different a zest have I sat down to study and gone to the closes;[1] grace has not yet become a second nature to me; only at times have I felt at all willing to be nothing; my prevailing feeling has been one of earnest desire to live a comfortable life, earning respect by pleasant labour. How have I absorbed the least drops of praise that have fallen to me,

[1] [The 'closes' are the narrow stone passages which are a familiar feature of the High Street, Edinburgh.—ED.

and if ever I have not been moved by it, it was not that I was beneath, but felt myself above it. This has cut me off from praise I would otherwise have won.

But let me not refuse to acknowledge the goodness of God in directing me to some few to whom He gave me a message. Let me be grateful for Mrs. Bolyan, for Margaret Holton, even for Mrs. Macpherson, and Mrs. MacLeod, for old Ross ; (remember for other uses Buchanan, who died in the Infirmary ; Ross the shoemaker, who died in Advocates' Close ; Mrs. Smith, Sergeant Graham, the 4 children in his stair, and the 3 in Adv. Close.)

A Probationer's Probation.

No day passes without strong temptation to give up this work—this temptation appeals to me on the ground that I am not fitted for pastoral work ; writing sermons is often the hardest labour to me, visiting is terrible. I often stand before a door unable to ring or knock—sometimes I have gone away without entering. A lowness of spirit that it costs me a great deal to throw off is the consequence of this, and a real doubt whether it would not be better for myself and all whom it may concern that I should at once look for some work that I could overtake. However, the one thing that has kept me going hitherto is this, that when I am in the best state of spirit these disinclinations to work go from me, and I fear I have hitherto had so little comfort in the work only because my habitual state is unspiritual.

Unbelief in the importance of men's spirits and all that concerns them, carelessness about the prosperity of Christ's cause, give power to the temptation that rises continually from the lust of the world and the pride of life. It is rarely I can believe that I am doing anything in visiting a poor sick old woman, or in holding a prayer-meeting. I could more easily believe 1 was doing something were I teaching, or forging anchors, or building houses, or in any way keeping the social system a-going. This takes out of me all vigour for the work ; I don't believe in it, and I don't succeed in it ; I see the labour of others valued—for it men willingly part with money, but I am paid more from old-established usage than anything else. The labour of others is anxiously looked for, the completion of it hailed with real joy, but how many would care if the weekly prayer-meeting were missed, or what change would it make were the service omitted ? The morning does not call me to work that must be done ; I may or I may not do it.

It is a shameful thing to pray for God's Spirit to help me in a work I don't believe in ; but I must pray also for this belief, I must be taught to prize the saving and edifying of Christ's people more than all, more than comfortable and respectable and reputable and remunerative labour. In this teaching there must be included a humbling of my pride ; I must learn to be thought nothing of by men, possibly I may have to learn to be thought nothing even by the people of Christ, but 'Seekest thou great things for thyself, seek them not,' saith the Lord. I am in an advantageous position for working for Him now, and will He who has put me in the outward circumstance leave me destitute of the inward grace ? If so, I of all men am the most miserable.

MONDAY.	Up at 7.30 Till eleven with Will. Jeffrey, and seeing blind Mackenzie—bought Long's Plutarch, Lives of the men in the Civil Wars—wrote to Mr. Macphail and Mr. Logan. Then read Hodge, *Idea of the Church.* 2.30-8 Dinner—called on Macgregor, taught John Forbes at Morningside—Tea—Bob's lessons. 8- Was to go with Will. J. to see Willie Addison, but Stewart called and stayed till 10.10, went out with him, came home & read a little of Bunyan's *Grace Abounding,* then bed.
TUESDAY.	7.20 Began work at 9.20. Rewriting sermon on Rev. iii. 12, $6\frac{1}{2}$ columns to 1.20 (only about $1\frac{1}{2}$ columns new). 1.20-6.30 Visited in the High St., leaving S.S. cards with Mrs. Campbell—Macpherson—Taylor—Beattie—Calder—Berry—then home to dinner—then a little bit of the *Jus divinum region. Eccl.*—then Morningside and home and a bit of *Grace Abounding* and tea—and Bob's lessons. 7- Down for Marsh to Mr. G.'s Prayer-Meetg. Wrote 3 columns more.
WEDNESDAY.	Up at 7.10 Began work at 9.20 (having to look for keys of book box). 9.20-1.10 Wrote Rev. iii. 12, 6 columns, which finishes the Sermon. -2.30 At Glen's ferreting in my book box, find it almost filled with *Xn. Instructors*—a few school-books and a polyglott Lex. 2.30 After dinner took a few useless books and for them and 2/9 got Andrewes' *Preces Priv.,* a gem—Called on Rev. H. Martin— to Morningside — Tea — (Murrays and Innes) along to Mr. Davidson—large party—pleasant—young people affected, but a few out of their tubs—home at 11.30. Innes thinks Thackeray the most artistic of writers, and studies every scratch of his pen. *Vanity Fair* powerful, *Esmond* beautiful, *Pendennis* pleasing and healthy.
THURSDAY.	Up at 7.35 Read over sermon on Rev. iii. 12 and some of Andrewes. Anderson of Falstone called—went with him to Thin's then called on Mrs. Hill—M'Millan—M'Lagan and Reid in Gowinloch's Land—Home and prepared for meeting—John xvi. 7-11. 2.30-7 Dinner—Plutarch's *Gracchus*—Morningside — Tea (Mima)—B.'s lessons. 7-8 Meeting. 8 Writing what I said—Willie Jeffrey came.

Good Friday, 6th April 1860.

I do not feel quite comfortable in the consciousness that so many have this day been very devoutly remembering the death of our common Redeemer. Is it a sufficient reason for my separation from these that this is not the true anniversary of His death? There was one day that is the true one, and few enlightened men maintain more than this. Let me in spirit at least connect myself with them.

22nd April 1860.

To-day was such a day as I never pass a week without; a day when I felt utterly out of my element in my work, when I envied the men who had employments they can enter into without anything beyond their hands and brains, their natural gifts. I begin to see more clearly that pride is at the bottom of my uneasiness and my discontent. In this work of mine I cannot go on without prayer; I find I cannot go on without prayer *from day to day*, for I do not get the Spirit in retention for *one* asking, but must be ever back and back to *the* Giver. Now it is not very humbling to acknowledge that my natural gifts are from God, because while I do so, I yet believe they are my own; what is my own if not these, are they not me? So while I say to God, These are Thine, it is with no real depth of meaning; but to be daily *obliged* to God for a gift I cannot do without, and can get only from Him, and from Him only by humble entreaty, this cuts deep into my pride, this teaches me that I am nothing. And therefore every natural feeling rises against this; no more comfortable jogging on, no more living by myself and on myself, but dependence on and nearness to this Holy God.

14th June 1860.

A thought that has been pretty frequently present to me lately is that life is passing; I begin to see now the end of life. I suppose this is a sentiment that matures to manhood, while it indicates its approach.

The practical outgoing of the thought is I must work to-day at whatever I can, if I am to have anything done at the end.

Is there not a tendency in this present time to a very subtle form of self-righteousness, that which makes fellowship with Christ in His sufferings the way to Glory, sharing His cross not only in the true sense, but something more?

25th June 1860.

Within these last weeks (six) I have not worked very steadily.

I have written—a sermon on (1 Kings, 18th) 'How long halt ye?'—one on 'Be sure your sin will find you out,'—notes weekly on the Parables for the class—short lecture on Phil. iv. 1-8—a paper for *Good Words*. Read some Plato, some Plutarch, some Horace, Delitzsch on the Psalms—(Cairns's *Life of Brown*—Farrar's *Eric*—Arnold's *Sermons*).

25th November 1860.

I. Taylor in his *Spiritual Christianity* takes to prophesying with somewhat better success than usual—p. 124.

'Much has been done within the compass of forty years, having the aspect of a preparatory work, and the full effect of which may be expected to appear, like the sudden verdure and fertility of a northern summer, at the moment when a new promulgation of great truths, an uncontradicted expansion of evangelic doctrine, shall throw fresh life into the Christian body. . . . (Describing care taken of the masses, etc.) May we assume that the preparation foreshows such an awakening to be at hand?'

Is this not pretty accurately corresponding with this present revival, though written in 1841?

20th June 1861.

Books for sermons on the Lord's Prayer :—Witsen—Tholuck—Calvin —Trench's *Augustine*—Origen—Gregory Nyss.—Maurice—Stier—Cyprian —Tertullian—Olshausen—Neander.

26th November 1861.

Mr. Davidson back from the Continent and a good deal the better of his holiday—has preached once for the two last Sundays. Don't know whether I am to stay or go, and don't know which to desire. Have lectured through the Lord's Prayer and the Epistles to the Seven Churches, and written some sermons, visited two or three districts, but not a great deal.

James Macphail has just been here, and wants me north, and as usual can't make up my mind what to do. Clark wants me to write for the *North British*, but I have no subject and no time and no spirit.

Feel the same as I did last winter—the old thing inside and the same head—have the same reasonings with myself as to what I should do, all ending the same in doing nothing. Think as of old of giving up—but then I have got through these six months—(but scrambling—and who is the better?) It should be put to every one intending the ministry : Is it yourselves or others you want to serve? I don't hide from myself that it was from self-interest I first thought of studying, and therefore am not surprised that now self-interest should seem all on the other side. Whatever the ministry may be for others, it is terrible for me ; no part of the work do I like but the writing of sermons and the visiting of sick ; all else is dreary in the extreme, and is only done under the pressure of necessity.

March, April and May 1863.

Shakspere.—Benvenuto Cellini—Sophocles.

Fairbairn's *Typology*.	Worsley's *Odyssey*, Al.
Hopkins—Goodwin.	Saisset's *Mod. Pantheism*.
Clement.	A. K. H. B., *Graver Thoughts*.
Matter's *École d'Alexandrie*.	De Quincey.
M. *Guyon's Life*.	Trench's *Sermons*.
	Robertson's *Sermons*.
	Wheat and Tares.

Colenso's vols. (The second shows much greater aptitude for criticism than the first, and is a popular exposition of the ordinary signs of later date in the Pentateuch.)

I read *Shirley* and Thackeray's *Humorists* a good deal just now (16th March 1863), also Westcott's *Introd.*, Cunningham's vols., Macaulay and Thucydides.

Westcott has abundance of material and is an excellent book for its good spirit and diligent research. There is, however, a want of logic—a frequent mistiness.

6th and 7th April 1863. Müller (Max), *Lectures on the Science of Language*—an admirable book—full of instruction, both direct and indirect, the work of a thoroughly scientific man—shows that there is a Science of language and explains it—traces its history—the influence of Sanskrit upon it—shows the different stages of language, the origin of language, etc.

(In the *Oxford Essays* for 1856 an Essay of his upon Comp. Mythology.)

A. K. H. Boyd's *Graver Thoughts of a Country Parson* is very easy and pleasant reading—things are well put, striking without being original or profound—perhaps there is a tendency to sentimentalism in it, not because it is namby-pamby, which it is not, but because it says too little or nothing at all of the justice of God—and hides the terror of this world while he speaks feelingly of its weakness—hides the guilt while he shows the misery and folly of sin.

Fielding's *Tom Jones* contains more humour and minute observation of the motives of men, and wisdom, than any novel I have read. It is not for a lady's boudoir certainly, but there is nothing adhesive in his filth—and he is to be commended for his little essays throughout his vols.

Began 9th April —finished 16th April. Pressensé, *L'Histoire de l'Église* — 2nd vol. of 2nd series — pleasantly and eloquently written like the most of French books that come over here—is based on an original and fresh study of the ancient writers, and contains a scholarly and philosophical account of the position of Christ as against Paganism. His account of Neoplatonism is especially good.

Goulburn's *Thoughts on Personal Religion* (398)—an attempt to guide the Christian in his daily life and tone—very practical—English—a considerable insight into the heart—true and real—not very striking but useful—evangelical but not over warm—calm but encouraging—he is not always careful—nor always in perfect taste (literary).

Tauler's *Sermons*.

Trench's *Sermons*—In these there is nothing out of taste—nor senseless—nor contrary to the precise meaning of S.S. There is much clearness, earnestness, and thought of that kind which has the human spirit for its object and which prefers rather to set old truth in new light and to give it fresh application than to discover new truth.

Thackeray's *Four Georges*—a lively, entertaining account of the personal character of the 4 G.s and a good exhibition of the manners of the time.

Macaulay's 3rd vol.—finished 17th April.

Plutarch's *Isis and Osiris.*

Stevenson's *Praying and Working*—worth telling and well told.

Westcott on the Miracles—some hints in it.

Johnson—Extracts from writings—all good.

Trench on the Miracles—has been and will be much used, not because there is much or any original matter in it, but because there are the best results of other men's thinking very well put—but he rarely does much himself except in the way of judgment and taste.

Buchanan's *Ten Years' Conflict*—Began 6th May. Finished 18th.

Madame Guyon's Life—used in comparing the French Pietists with the 2nd century Alexandrian Gnostics, of Clement—a very rich and well-written book, interesting, instructive, and edifying.

Boswell's *Life of Johnson.*

Hugh Miller's *Headship of Christ.*

Cunningham's *Discussions on Church Principles.*

19th April, 1863.

Began article on Clement for *B. & F. Review*—wrote on Monday, Tuesday and Wednesday (Thursday Fast Day), Friday (Saturday frightfully cut up with running about looking for supply); have made out 13 sheets (*i.e.* 15 pages of *B. & F.*), but not good. I wonder if I should write this kind of thing—if it would not come much easier and better to some other man. [The thought here occurs to me that if any one should ever happen to take up this book and read this, they might think me a modest individual—and here again, that if they read this they might say what a candid person—and again, what a penetrating person.] But it is time I knew what I should work at regularly and not be so much ruled by accidental fancies. Might I not make more of Exegesis? I used to think so—yet somehow, without any intention, I am drifting into Ecclesiastical History of the light and fragmentary order. [Especially might not my studies bear more upon others and not be so selfish—rising from my own taste, aiming at my own glorification?]

I might have had as accurate (though of course not so living) an idea of Clement by reading Pressensé as by spending so much time in reading Clement. P. is decidedly the most helpful book I have seen on him.

September 1863.

I have now been licensed five years and have preached at the following vacancies : Dalkeith (twice) — Irvine — Kennethmont — Old Aberdeen — Kirkcaldy—John Knox, Glasgow—Garvald—Birdhopecraig—Laygate and St. John's, South Shields—St. George's, Liverpool—Cheltenham—Helensburgh—Roxburgh Place and Greyfriars, Edinburgh—Bannockburn — Trinity, Aberdeen —South Leith—Dudhope, Dundee — Portobello—have also had to consider the propriety of going to Singapore, Sydney, Naples, and Bombay, so that if I have been considerably unsettled I have had some excuse, though had I known I should be five years knocking about I would have begun some study which would have

employed me well. However, I have been gradually brought to see that
throughout I have been aiming at getting a position for myself, and
have very rarely had any strong desire to win men to Christ and do
good—living for others ; and in this case it is probably better I have
not been settled. I believe, however, that I should work better in a
permanent sphere than I can do shifting from place to place preaching
to people I know very little about, and consequently having little
stimulus to write at all, and no means of putting a point on what I say.
But this kind of life needs constant watching ; how many weeks have I
let past without one trace of work done—except the semi-mechanical
Sunday performance.

APPENDIX.

In looking back upon my student life I see one very great defect—
inaccuracy. The ideas I have of things are general and confused, so
that when I begin to write I feel very much at sea. It would be surely
of great benefit to those who have not sense or experience sufficient to
enable them to lay down a course and rules for themselves, that others
who know more should aid them. To direct them to those particular
points they should most attend to, and to tell them what questions
should be settled definitely—for no doubt, as the ancient said, we should
while young learn principally what we will most require as men.

A student should not only keep a daily record of what work he does,
he should also at the end of every week or month ask what he has
gained by the work—what he knows better, etc., etc., and whether that
gain he has made is likely to be of any use to himself or others.

Cornewall Lewis laid down this sagacious rule: '*Read* when you have
plenty of time at command ; *write* in the shorter spaces, when your
time is broken up : this is the way to employ yourself to the best advantage ; you will forget what you read in fragments of time, what you
write then will not be lost.'

From Baxter's *Reformed Pastor.*

'Content not yourselves with being in a state of grace, but be careful
that your graces are kept in vigorous and lively exercise, and that you
preach to yourselves the sermons which you study before you preach
them to others.
  ' He that means as he speaks will surely do as he speaks. One proud,
lordly word, one needless contention, one covetous action, may cut the
throat of many a sermon and blast the fruit of all that you have been
doing. Tell me, brethren in the fear of God, do you regard the success
of your labours or do you not ? Do you long to see it upon the souls of
your hearers ? If you do not, what do you preach for ; what do you
study for ; and what do you call yourselves the ministers of Christ for ?
But if you do, then surely you cannot find in your heart to mar your

work for a thing of nought. What! do you regard the success of your labours and yet will not part with a little to the poor, nor put up with an injury or foul word, nor stoop to the meanest, nor forbear your passionate or lordly carriage—no, not for the winning of souls and attaining the end of all your labours?

'If the salvation of souls be your end, you will certainly intend it out of the pulpit as well as in it. If it be your end, you will live for it, and contribute all your endeavours to attain it. You will ask concerning the money in your purse as well as concerning other means, "In what way shall I lay it out for the greatest good, especially to men's souls?"'

That I may be enabled to devote myself to the service of Christ. That I may be enabled to bear more constantly in mind that I owe all to Him.

That I may be brought to a more spiritual mind.

That I may resolve to crucify the flesh with itself.

That I may feel more poignantly contrition for sin, and be enabled to see what sin really is, and to feel towards it as God does.

That I may increase steadily in love to Christ.

O Lord, Thou knowest my nature, its defects and infirmities, and Thou knowest the sins by which it has become further weakened and incapacitated for Thy service, and Thou seest where I can be of most use, where my sin shall least hinder me and my nature find its most suitable employment, and thither I pray that Thou wilt bring me, causing me to enter heartily upon the work that is set before me. Thou knowest what is now offered me, and I desire that I may be enlightened by Thee, so that I may not choose or refuse it contrary to Thy will, but may be effectually guided by Thyself and animated by Thy Spirit to make and abide by a right and godly choice. And as Thou orderest all things aright, I ask that such circumstances may arise as may compel me to Thy way.

πάντοτε ἀγωνιζόμενος περὶ   ἐν ταῖς προσευχαῖς.

Be objective—think of God and things above more than of your relation to them. Live for others—for the sake of Christ.

Consider what God would say by me to the people rather than what the people would like to hear, or what I would like to say.

Be in harmony with the audience, understand their tone, discover what the subject teaches, and write about it easily—do not strain.

Considerations to promote better delivery:—

    (1) I may preach this again, but these people will not hear it again—they are hearing these words but once—let them be so said as to fix and not need to be heard again.

    (2) They may possibly never hear any preaching again—*I may possibly never preach again.*

(3) I prayed for help in writing this, I must therefore deliver it to the best of my ability—otherwise I disbelieve the Spirit's willingness or slight his ability to help.

(4) Why am I preaching, what am I hoping to effect, am I listless or flippant in the utterance of what I hope will save men from eternal death ?

'I have learned from the Holy Scriptures, that it is a perilous and a fearful thing to speak in the House of God ; to address those who will appear in judgment against us, when at the last day we shall be found in His presence ; when the gaze of the angels shall be directed to us, when every creature shall behold the Divine Word, and shall listen till He speaks.'—Luther.

Printed by T. and A. Constable, Printers to His Majesty
at the Edinburgh University Press